F YOU CAN FIND A BETTER CAR, BUY IT!"

This brash challenge to the car-buying public on onal TV made Lee Iacocca's name and face iliar to millions of Americans. From Iacocca's nnings as the ambitious but dutiful son of Italian igrants to his masterminding of the astonishing naround at Chrysler, David Abodaher reveals the spiring story of a remarkable business leader who efused to accept defeat.

"A stimulating biography . . . An excellent history of ord and Chrysler, big business, and the auto indus- ry . . . Enjoyable."

—*Library Journal*

"Lee Iacocca . . . America's hottest folk hero. He tells it like it is, and others are telling him what ought to be: Iacocca for President. His dealers adore him, the unions respect him, and many ordinary Ameri- cans see him as a symbol of the never-say-die spirit."

—*Time Magazine*

IACOCCA

BY DAVID ABODAHER

ZEBRA BOOKS
KENSINGTON PUBLISHING CORP.

Cover photo courtesy of Wally McNamee © 1984

ZEBRA BOOKS

are published by

Kensington Publishing Corp.
475 Park Avenue South
New York, NY 10016

Copyright © 1982 by David Abodaher. This edition is reprinted by arrangement with Macmillan Publishing Company.

Fifteenth printing: October, 1989
REVISED EDITION

Printed in the United States of America

For David and Jane Gillespie,
my world's most beautiful people

ACKNOWLEDGMENTS

First I must thank John J. Morrissey, chairman of the board of Kenyon & Eckhardt Advertising. As a member of his staff, it was incumbent on me to clear through the agency any outside work related to an agency account. Mr. Morrissey's enthusiasm during the writing calls for this special expression of thanks. Without him the book never would have been written.

I also feel indebted to Lee Iacocca, who while not directly supplying any material used in the writing, did allow me to interview members of his family, including his wife, mother, and sister.

I am grateful to Bill Winn and Frank Zimmerman for much of the material delineating Iacocca's early times at Ford. Others involved with Lee Iacocca at Ford or Chrysler to whom I am obliged include Harold Sperlick, Gar Laux, Walter Murphy, L. H. McCormick-Goodheart, and Wes Small. I owe particular thanks to Jay Dugan and gratitude to Bill

Fugazy.

I am obliged to my colleagues at Kenyon & Eckhardt. Leo-Arthur Kelmenson of the New York office, president of K & E, provided me with important background on Lee Iacocca and on his arrival at Chrysler. Don Grant of the New York office was also quite helpful.

Among my colleagues in the Detroit K & E office I thank Paul Stevens, Linda Kuzawinski, Wayne Saylor, and Michelle Nosco for their encouragement and Bill O'Neill (now heading the Minneapolis office) for providing valuable information.

For help in proofreading, thanks are owed to Carol Yavruian. For typing and retyping through six tedious months my love and appreciation go to my daughter, Lynda. I am grateful to her husband, Bob Henderson, for sparking me into action when spirits sagged.

Lastly I wish to express my gratitude to a number of men at Ford Motor Company who wish to remain anonymous.

INTRODUCTION

As the calendar flips ahead into the early months of 1986 nearly five years have passed since this biography of Lee Anthony Iacocca was sent to the publishers. In that span of time much has happened in the increasingly eventful life of this man who has in the past decade become a folk hero to a broad segment of the American public. One of the most significant is Iacocca's emergence as a probable political candidate.

Lee Iacocca, President of the United States? That is a question now being pondered by political commentators in the nation's capital and in all fifty states, as well as by millions of American voters. Even five years ago when this book was written, the last chapter weighed the probability of whether Iacocca might indeed make a run for the Presidency. Time, and a rising tide of Iacocca-sculpted events, have made it even more a probability and less an impossible dream—especially in view of today's political climate.

The Iacocca-for-President groundswell has been almost totally at a grass-roots level and not the result of the machinations of any movers and shakers within the ranks of either major political party. The escalation of interest in Iacocca has been generated strictly by a public perception of him as a man who has achieved the near impossible, a man who could, hopefully, put America on a sound financial basis.

Over the past few years as Iacocca has become the darling of the American media, his very name has come to symbolize for many Americans the hope for a better tomorrow. From Boston to Hawaii, from the Great Lakes to the Gulf, the men and women of low and middle-income America hail him as a phenomenon the likes of which this nation has rarely seen.

In fact, Iacocca's fame as the father of the Mustang and the savior of Chrysler Corporation has spread world wide. Somewhat ironically, growing interest in Iacocca brought about in 1984 the publication of this book in Japanese. More recently, publishers in Germany, Great Britain, and Spanish-speaking countries including Mexico have purchased rights to publish this biography in their countries. It is, however, the American image of Lee Iacocca, and how it came about, that is most fascinating.

Under normal circumstances Iacocca would be no more important than the chairman or president of any large industrial complex. At best he would rate no better than second to Roger Smith, chairman of General Motors, for three-quarters of a century the giant among the automobile manufacturers. Iacocca's image as a folk hero to most Americans is a strange phenomenon in itself.

No one outside the fields of sports and entertainment, has enjoyed acclaim for so long a period as Lee Iacocca. A Babe Ruth, yes. A Frank Sinatra, Ted Williams, or Pete Rose. But never any other industrialist, no-scientist, educator, political figure or American winner of a Nobel prize. Any who did achieve measures of fame were given but fleeting moments in the spotlight.

But along comes Lee Iacocca, automobile executive, to put a dent in the long-time American obsession with sports idols. Some critics have said that his climb began with a carefully planned and orchestrated scenario initiated long before his first move into prominence in 1964. It was that year that Iacocca burst on the American scene as a miracle man who accomplishes everything he sets out to do.

The great American populace takes such men to its heart, particularly if they perceive him as having started his climb with nothing. It was so with Babe Ruth who came out of a Maryland orphanage to hit home runs almost at will, with Stan Musial from the Pennsylvania coal mine area, and Pete Rose, a most unlikely baseball prospect playing on Cincinnati playgrounds, who through sheer determination and a never-give-up spirit transformed himself into one of the greatest ball players in history.

It was natural, then, that Americans would quickly relate to the Iacocca they saw on television day and night. Here was the son of an Italian immigrant who came to the United States with about thirteen dollars in his pocket, fighting the establishment and selling cars like any pitchman.

Day by day and month by month Iacocca drew more followers. He was one of them, the public claimed. The working class, especially seemed to take him to their hearts while the upper middle class was somewhat more cynical.

The Iacocca mystique, fed by daily media reports of his activities and accomplishments, thrived and flourished. Many of us saw him as a David conquering Goliath, a latter-day Moses leading hundreds of thousands out of the wilderness of unemployment.

Iacocca had done what so many of us could only dream of doing. He had received a masters degree from so prestigious an Ivy League University as Princeton. We may not have been able to do what he did but we can live his life vicariously. We put ourselves in his shoes and see ourselves boasting to our university classmates that we'll be a top executive at Ford before we're thirty-five—and missing it by only a few months. We relish the fencing with Henry Ford II, the fight with Congress for a billion dollar loan, and the astonishing turnaround of Chrysler.

Before Iacocca, many other innovators and achievers laid some claim to fame. These included such greats as the Wright Brothers, Carnegie, Kelvin, Pullman, Chrysler and Henry Ford I, who had aspirations, ill-fated as they were, for the Presidency of the United States. But not one had the diversity of interests and knowledge of Lee Iacocca, and not one captured the public imagination as much as the son of Nicola Iacocca.

Lee is very much like his father, a man loved and admired by those closest to him but hated by the many over whom he ran roughshod when they stood in his way. Nicola, like his son, was a first-class entrepreneur. He made a million after coming to America empty-handed, lost it in the crash of 1929, then made another through sheer grit and determination.

Until the day Nicola Iacocca died in 1973 a close rapport and an abiding love existed between father and son. In fact this closeness between Nicola and Lee almost cost Lee the wife he so dearly loved. As she told me during a taped interview at the Iacocca home in Bloomfield Hills, Michigan, their courtship was an interminably lengthy one because Lee insisted on going home to Allentown every weekend. Time and again she had decided to break up their relationship.

Lee Iacocca was carefully groomed and shaped by his father. He has the same never-say-die spirit, whatever the odds. And, peculiarly, there is a strong parallel between the rise, fall, and rise again of Lee Iacocca and his father's loss of one fortune, only to recover and make another.

Lee Iacocca came to national—and international—prominence in 1964 as the father of the Mustang, the sensational little sporty car that took America by storm and became a favorite in a dozen countries overseas. Father of the basic idea, that is. Naturally, the creation of the final design and the engineering was done by others with Iacocca's approval. As head of the Ford Division at the time, Iacocca had dozens of other responsibilities.

There is no denying the fact, however, that the Mustang was Iacocca's own concept. He had the foresight to realize that American drivers were ready for a small sporty car. The great acclaim given Mustang at its introduction proved him right. General Motors, which had Camaro on the drawing board as Mustang made its public appearance, did not hit the market until two more years had passed.

It had been a long, hard, eight-year climb for Iacocca when the Mustang made his name a household word. He had come to the Ford headquarters in Dearborn in 1956. Ten years earlier, in 1946, he had gone there as an engineering trainee fresh out of Princeton University. The ups and downs of this twenty-year period, as well as other factors influencing the years through early 1981, are narrated in detail in this book. But let me review for a moment the most significant events leading to the final chapter in this biography.

On November 11, 1960 Lee Iacocca was named vice president of the Ford Motor Company by Henry Ford II. He had failed by a mere one month and one day to make good the boast to his college classmates.

In early 1965, with everyone at Ford from Henry II on down euphoric over the Mustang, Iacocca received another promotion. This brought him a higher level vice-presidency as head man over everything having to do with Ford-made cars and trucks. For Iacocca it meant something even more important. He would now move his office from the Ford Division building to Ford's World Headquarters, the long rectangle known as the Glass House and jokingly called God's House because Henry II's office was on the top (12th) floor.

Iacocca was now in Ford's center arena, an ideal spot from which to campaign for his longed-for presidency of Ford. Unfortunately for him it also placed him close to Henry II, who soon would begin to have second thoughts about Iacocca's rise. As a result, the next five years were to become both years of glory and years of despair and frustration for Lee.

Time and again during those five years the office of president opened up. Each time Iacocca waited for the appointment and each time was disappointed, by-passed by Henry. Iacocca never hid his displeasure and disappointment, but Henry continued his little game.

Iacocca continued doing his job. In 1967 he unveiled two low-priced cars he expected would rival the Mustang and Cougar in the marketplace. Bearing the Ford name was Pinto. Carrying the Mercury trademark was Bobcat. Pinto did better than expected in sales, but it was not long before the roof fell in. To cut costs in building each Pinto and Bobcat the gas tank was placed too far back on the car chassis, according to claims made in lawsuits later on. The result, allegedly, was a series of rear-end collisions in which the cars from Ford exploded, killing occupants, and costing the Ford Motor Company many millions of dollars.

The problems with the Pinto notwithstanding, Iacocca seemed to pay little attention to the storm brewing inside the Glass House. At least outwardly. Inwardly it must have been traumatic. Through the next few years he must often have gritted his teeth while seething inside as he was made aware that Henry II was searching for ways to force his resignation.

Iacocca's pride would not permit him to resign. That would be quitting under fire. Papa Nicola had done his work well. Besides, Iacocca must have felt a sense of security. Since the Mustang he had been the darling of the Ford Board of Directors and more than a few times the Board had refused Henry's request for a vote that would have separated Iacocca from the Ford Motor Company.

The end, however, was inevitable. When Henry put it to the Board on a "him or me" basis, he got what he wanted. After all, Henry II's last name was the company name. The afternoon of July 13, 1978 Henry called him and gave him the bad news.

It was a crushing blow for a man as talented, ambitious, and proud as Iacocca. And it was an act that stunned the entire automobile industry, although many in the know had been expecting it. And more than a few of those licked their chops, relishing the summary firing.

Even less regret was felt by Iacocca's contemporaries in the automobile industry when they learned the terms of settlement between Iacocca and Ford. Iacocca was to receive one million dollars a year for five years so long as he did not join another automobile maker during that time. He was, it seemed, sitting pretty.

Lee Iacocca apparently did not agree. The million dollars meant little since he was already a millionaire several times over in his own right. Retirement did not appeal to him. He was only fifty-four, an active doer through most of those years, and the prospect of playing golf or tending flowers the rest of his life was unthinkable.

Within months of his inglorious firing at the hands of Henry Ford II, opportunity came knocking. To accept meant giving up the million-dollar-a-year settlement from Ford, but Iacocca hardly hesitated. In a bold, gutsy move, he said yes to the invitation to help save Chrysler Corporation. Once again the automobile industry, perhaps the entire business community, was flabbergasted. Some critics called him a fool for giving up a million a year to take on an impossible job. Chrysler was in such bad financial straits that only an act of God could save it.

Iacocca claimed he could do nothing else. His principal reason was to save the hundreds of thousands of jobs that would go down the drain if Chrysler failed—jobs at Chrysler plants and at businesses that supplied Chrysler with parts and other necessities. It would have been a critical blow to the American economy, he said, and in that he was right.

Detractors persisted. Iacocca had nothing to lose, they claimed. The settlement money was inconsequential considering Iacocca's personal wealth and the high percentage he would lose due to personal income taxes at the federal and state levels. No, taking the Chrysler challenge could be only a sop to his ego. If he failed, no one would blame him, the situation at Chrysler was so bad. If he succeeded, he would be a hero.

Iacocca was undaunted, and had the last laugh. As is now common knowledge he confounded his severest critics by restoring Chrysler to a competitive level with General Motors and Ford, and making himself a giant among giants in the eyes of the American people.

Iacocca's phenomenal success in rescuing the Chrysler Corporation from bankruptcy did not still his critics. Many still point to the fact that it took a $1.5 billion dollar bail-out from the United States government plus concessions from his union workers, suppliers, banks, and the sale of Chrysler's most profitable subsidiary—its tank plant—to get the job done. A Roger Smith, GM Chairman, a Philip Caldwell, then Chairman at Ford, or the president of any of the car companies could have succeeded in doing the same with all that help. The fact remains, however, that Lee Anthony Iacocca actually did do it and deserves credit for accomplishing a Herculean task.

In the five years since this book was written Iacocca's accomplishments have become even more legendary. He repaid the $1.5 billion government loan long before its due date. But even this raised eyebrows among America's financial community. Common sense, the financial pundits said, called for Iacocca to keep a tight fist on cash flow as long as possible. Emergencies do arise, they said and money on hand for plant improvements and expansions and other needs was far more important than saving interest or basking in the spotlight the announcement of an early repayment brought him.

In Iacocca's defense it could be said that his action was a brilliant public relations ploy. His primary job was to keep his company afloat and to do that he had to sell cars. Paying back the loan was the best possible way to publicize Chrysler's health. As he expected, the general public reacted favorably and sales of Chrysler and Dodge cars and trucks increased substantially.

Iacocca did build new plants and closed down outmoded ones. He did renovate other facilities and beat both GM and Ford in the introduction of high-tech equipment into assembly plants. He introduced robotic welding for his assembly lines, assuring more precise welds on vehicles, eliminating leaks and rattles that have always been the bane of motorists.

Knowing full well that only dependable high quality in cars could keep his company profitable and hold public confidence in Chrysler products, he left nothing to chance. And to assure the buying public of his own confidence he initiated a five-year or fifty-thousand-mile protection plan that, on paper at least, offered twice what either GM or Ford had to offer.

Then to get his quality story over to the public he presented himself as a prime spokesman for Chrysler on television and in the printed media. As a backup he approved use of nationally known stars for certain car lines, with Ricardo Montalban successfully handling one or two.

In days long past, Imperial was a famous name in the Chrysler line of cars. Iacocca brought it back from the ashes as a truly fine automobile equipped with the latest in computerized driving assistance. To launch Imperial he chose Frank Sinatra. Imperial, a car with class to rival Cadillac and Lincoln, never did take hold. By the end of 1983 it was relegated to the scrap heap.

One truly revolutionary move Iacocca made since 1981 was the naming of Douglas Frazer to the Board of Directors of Chrysler Corporation. It was a giant step toward building rapport between union and corporate structure. Frazer, then president of the United Auto Workers, had helped greatly in bringing about the concessions that aided Chrysler in the early days of the struggle toward solvency. His presence on the Board helped keep union workers patient in their demands for a restoration of the concessions and a return to pay parity with both GM and Ford.

As Chrysler began to rack up profitable quarter after profitable quarter the union workers began to clamor for a piece of the pie. They had given up money to help the recovery and now that Chrysler was building profits and paying its bills the laborers wanted their share.

Iacocca had been a poker player from way back. In fact, during all his days at Ford his one night of relaxation was Friday when he and his closest friends would gather around a table in the den of his Bloomfield Hills home for an all-night session. To him, handling union problems was little more than a poker game.

Someone had described Iacocca as a poker player with a sphinx-like inscrutable face, who holds nothing in his hands and thus everything in his hands—because he has nothing to lose.

In the initial bargaining sessions that won him the pay cuts that helped Chrysler survive it had been comparatively easy to get his way. For one thing, he had the president of the union on his side. For another, the workers felt that with the American unemployment situation so bleak better to have a lower pay check than no pay check at all. But with Chrysler making money it was no more than fair that their pay scale be at least equal to that earned by their union brothers in other big automobile plants.

Another factor had also raised havoc within the union ranks. Iacocca was no longer on the $1 a year salary he had so dramatically announced during his early years with the company. Now he was back in the high six-figure pay category and he and other top executives were also earning huge bonuses.

Through most of '83 and all of '84, union demands to re-open the contract were voiced by the union's Chrysler representative, Marc Stepp and Owen Bieber, who had replaced Douglas Frazer as president of the UAW. All fell on deaf ears. An expressionless and unyielding Iacocca claimed the time was not right.

Iacocca, in conscience, must have realized the union demands were legitimate. But obviously he was thinking in terms of dollars saved. The existing contract would expire in mid-1985 and waiting and holding back action until a renewed contract could be negotiated would save Chrysler millions of dollars. Came 1985 and negotiations for a new contract got under way.

Weeks passed with no agreement. Finally a strike was called. It was a costly one, lasting weeks. Chrysler's labor negotiators were getting nowhere as they faced their union opposites at the bargaining table. Suddenly the suspense was broken. Lee Iacocca himself took over the bartering. A settlement was quickly reached and labor got most of what it wanted.

The cynics again had their say. Was this sudden and dramatic appearance of Iacocca on the scene, with its sudden and even more dramatic ending, a planned ploy to make Iacocca look good?

The general public cared little. It mattered only that Lee Iacocca had saved Chrysler. They had seen and heard Iacocca on television telling the world that Chrysler profits had topped the billion dollar mark, that in the third quarter of 1985 profits were more than $315 million. This while General Motors profits were down and Ford suffered a loss.

And, to further excite the American public, Lee Iacocca was increasingly heralded by both the broadcast and print media as each month of 1985 passed. Some three years earlier Iacocca had accepted President Ronald Reagan's invitation to head a group charged with restoring the fabled Statue of Liberty. Day after day, week after week, Iacocca could be seen and read about pleading for funds for the Statue of Liberty project. He was now perceived as a dedicated public servant. Giving him even more appeal as a public servant, Iacocca proceeded to take on the renovation of Ellis Island.

For Iacocca, this latter assignment was a labor of love. Ellis Island had been the port through which thousands of immigrants had once passed to enjoy the freedom of life in America. Among those immigrants had been Nicola and Antoinette Iacocca, his father and mother. To transform the deteriorating and decaying Ellis Island facility into a beautiful park and shrine dedicated to the millions who had come through that gateway to freedom was, for Iacocca, a personal tribute to his parents.

The two public service projects, especially the restoration of the Statue of Liberty, stirred up more patriotism and flag waving than had been seen in years. Millions of dollars were raised and Americans began to anxiously await the rededication of Lady Liberty in mid-1986.

Promotional genius that Iacocca is, the commercial value of this mushrooming Americanism could not have been overlooked. In late 1985 Chrysler Corporation launched a new advertising strategy. Television screens revealed Lee Iacocca against fluttering stars and stripes and "Born in America" or "Made in America" slogans.

Using patriotism as a sales tool was no new concept. Iacocca himself and other advertisers had used a "Buy American" theme many times earlier. But the Doubting Thomases had now found something new to carp about.

The "Born in America" line didn't bother them too much. After all, the Chrysler and Plymouth and Dodge nameplates were American and had been in existence for more than a half century. "Made in America," however, was a joke. Were not the majority of parts in Chrysler and Dodge cars bought from foreign suppliers? Assembled in America, said the purists, was a more legitimate approach. A matter of semantics, no doubt, but folk heroes have to watch their words and deeds.

Lee Iacocca, ever the opportunist, was not to allow 1985 to pass into history without once again hitting the headlines. In mid-November he announced a surprising and startling reorganization of Chrysler's corporate structure, one that would further promote Chrysler as a leader in the automobile industry, bringing it more fully into high-tech business. Earlier in the year Chrysler had purchased one high-technology company and was looking for more.

Under the new plan Chrysler Corporation would be split into four divisions—automobile, technology, aerospace, and finance. This reorganization, he claimed, would bring about a more flexible operation of the company and make future expanion easier to implement.

Almost simultaneously Iacocca announced that he would move his own headquarters from Highland Park, Michigan to New York City. He believed that from his new location, he could better oversee the total operation of the reorganized Chrysler Corporation, now to be considered a holding company with him as the Chief Operating Officer. The present vice-chairman of Chrysler, Gerald Greenwald, seen by most insiders as heir apparent to Iacocca's throne, would be in charge of automobile and financial matters out of the Highland Park, Michigan office.

These announcements, particularly the move of Iacocca to the Big Apple, sparked speculation in the media. Reporters, as they are wont to do, wondered why such a move—and why at that particular time? Could it be a prelude to a soon-to-be-made declaration of Iacocca's run for the presidency? After all, New York was certainly a far better launching point for such a candidacy than Michigan. Or, some mused, was it to be closer to Peggy Johnson, the young lady Iacocca expects to marry in 1986?

However one looks at it, the years between 1981 and 1986 were busy and productive ones for Lee Iacocca. Everything, it seems, had come up roses. He had Chrysler giving General Motors and Ford a good run for their money. He was being perceived as a candidate for the White House. And he had had his own autobiography published. Only one tragic note had marred five years of glory. That was the death of his beloved wife, Mary.

Iacocca's own life story, *Iacocca; An Autobiography* by Lee Iacocca with William Novak hit the bookstores in 1984, two years after this biography. I would be remiss if I failed to acknowledge Mr. Iacocca's own book and offer my personal views.

William Novak has woven the information given him by Iacocca into a fine, readable book. He did an excellent job of capturing the brash, supreme self-confidence and terse, tell-it-like-it-is image of a great industrialist. Using Iacocca's own words Novak makes it abundantly clear that Iacocca visualizes himself as a self-made celebrity "responsible for my own fate."

The autobiography, as a whole, has a mystical heart-warming quality thanks to Novak's own sensitivity with words. At the very beginning Iacocca is portrayed as speaking directly to his deceased wife, whom I found during interviews to be a charming, witty and very compassionate lady. Iacocca's great devotion to her and his two daughters, Kathy and Lia, is made evident in chapter after chapter.

Even more compelling is the evidence of Iacocca's love for his father and his father's for him. We are treated to a consistent picture of this mutual affection beginning with Iacocca's youth and continuing until the father's death and beyond. The inference made earlier in this introduction that Nicola Iacocca created his son in his own image comes through clearly. Further indication of Lee's devotion to his father is the use of his father's name in the first sentence of Chapter One and in the last sentence of the last chapter.

When I had finished reading Iacocca's own story I found myself surprised and disappointed on two counts. The fact that much pertinent information had been left out and that the book as a whole was quite self-serving did not bother me unduly. Most autobiographies contain only what the author wants to include. Nothing that might mar the image he or she wants to leave with the reader is part of the narrative.

The first of my regrets was that Iacocca never even speculates on what he believed was the reason he was fired by Henry Ford II, although at various points in the book he seems to promise the revelation will come. Though he bemoans his own firing, as one would expect, he makes no mention of the many men he himself separated from their jobs for one flimsy reason or another, men he believed were in his way up the corporate ladder. And, perhaps, he over-reacts over the trauma of the discharge. Anyone in any echelon below the top in any organization is a prospect for severance from his job. It is the hazard of employment.

Secondly, I was more than a little disturbed by the excessively harsh picture Iacocca paints of Henry Ford II. During my months of research for this book, and the countless interviews I had with men who worked for Ford or knew him as a contemporary, not once did I hear a single derogatory remark about him. Certainly not such words as frivolous, confused or stupid.

True, Henry did not pursue his university education with the dedication and determination of Lee Iacocca. True also that he enjoys life to its fullest. But such characteristics and his happy-go-lucky life-style hardly justify the caricature Iacocca left of Henry. In the one meeting I had with Mr. Ford some years ago, he went far out of his way to be most courteous and considerate. And, in a radio interview I recorded with him at the time, he came off as a sharp, intelligent, and knowledgeable individual.

Despite these few criticisms, I confess that I found Lee Iacocca's autobiography to be an interesting and informative book. And I again salute William Novak for having written an excellent portrayal of a man who might be President of the United States.

In two years time the 1988 campaign will already be well under way, with the important New Hampshire and Iowa primaries coming about within weeks. At the moment of this writing, Lee Iacocca has made no formal announcement of his intentions. The questions persist. Will he or won't he declare himself for the 1988 election? Will he prefer to wait until 1992? Or will he just decide to let the politicians fight it out among themselves?

Cagey man that he is, Iacocca no doubt realizes that tipping his hand too soon might take the bloom off the Iacocca-for-President bandwagon. Often in the past a too-early announcement proved a Waterloo for the candidate.

One example was George Romney, former Governor of Michigan, and—like Iacocca—once head man of a large car maker, American Motors. Iacocca, much like Romney, is inclined to talk without thinking, putting his foot in his mouth. And the longer you have before the nomination process is concluded the more opportunities there are to make some ludicrous statement, as Romney unfortunately did, that takes you right out of the race.

Iacocca has one problem Romney did not have, and one not facing most of his adversaries in a 1988 campaign. He has no political base. And he has no organization already in place working for a possible candidacy. Without a working group, holding off making his intention known could be the kiss of death for a candidacy. Iacocca, however, does have one advantage over any other potential rival. He is well fixed financially and has the money for any campaign, however expensive.

There seems little doubt that he would relish capping this meteoric career in so prestigious and historic a manner. And his ego no doubt tells him that he would finish eight years in the White House beside Washington, Jefferson and Lincoln as one of the greatest presidents in history.

Let's assume that he will run. Certainly if one analyzes his strictly non-business public appearances—his speeches before men's and women's clubs, political and fraternal organizations—he comes off as a candidate running hard. His subjects are the same as those being fought in Congress—the trade and budget deficits; the disastrous impact of the imbalance in exports versus imports; the present and future conditions of the economy.

Having made the assumption, let's take another step and consider the likelihood of winning a nomination. First, will it be as a Republican or Democrat? He has not openly declared himself one or the other, and based on his public utterances one must conclude he is either a Liberal Republican or a Conservative Democrat.

The political realities being what they are, Iacocca cannot expect either party to welcome him into the fold on their own. He will have to identify his party affiliation and do it soon, or he will have to run as an independent or third-party candidate, a course that would substantially minimize his chances for election. John Anderson tried it recently and failed miserably. As a matter of fact, never has a third party candidate run successfully.

Getting the nomination as either Republican or Democrat has its own pitfalls. Each of the parties must be considered a closed corporation, not exactly thrilled with any johnny-come-lately. Each has a plethora of hopefuls eagerly awaiting the call. On the Republican side there is George Bush, Robert Dole, Howard Baker, and Jack Kemp, among others. On the Democratic side, with Ted Kennedy having removed himself from the race, it may be a wide-open battle. At the moment Gary Hart, who announced he will not seek re-election to the Senate from Colorado, is a formidable front runner. He has an organization already in place plus the experience of one previous candidacy for the nomination. And Hart himself will have to contend with three or four governors and senators for the Democratic crown.

Carrying speculation a step further, what if Iacocca overcomes every obstacle and does win the Presidency of the United States: What kind of a President would he be? We can only judge by what we know the office calls for and what we know of the man and his abilities thus far.

So far as internal affairs go—the economy, the budget, tax reform, the farm problem and other problems today facing the nation—Iacocca might do quite well. On most of these issues his business acumen and foresight, already proven, will stand him in good stead. And, if he does receive a substantial mandate from the American people, he is strong enough and tough enough to deal successfully with Congress. If he had any trouble with Congress it might be due to his inflexibility.

Iacocca's most glaring deficiency could well be his ability to handle foreign affairs. He is not known for diplomacy and tact. Add to that an impatience and a quickness to anger and you begin to wonder.

We are now in the sixth year of a Ronald Reagan presidency. During that time Mr. Reagan has stubbed his toe any number of times. Yet we have admired his ability to quickly right himself with a ready smile and a witty word or two. We have heard Reagan upset heads of state with his hard rhetoric, and soon after calm the troubled waters with a statement or two that take him off the hook. Such attributes are not normally associated with Lee Iacocca. A rarely smiling man, he does not have the easy charm or personality usually required of someone bargaining with the king, president or premier of an adversary state.

How effective can he be dealing with our allies? And how will he fare coming up against the clever, strong, and personable Gorbachev? What would result from an Iacocca confrontation with the madman Qaddafi, given Iacocca's shoot-from-the-hip style.

Iacocca, given the chance, could prove these suppositions all wrong. And, as I wrote in the final chapter of this book, Reagan himself had little or no experience in foreign affairs before he became president, but did quite well.

There are some parallels between running a huge corporation like Chrysler and operating a complex national government. For one thing, there is the need for selecting capable staff. Iacocca, in that regard, did excellently at both Ford and Chrysler. He does have the intuition and know-how to surround himself with loyal personnel with the expertise to do their jobs. There is little doubt that he could choose a cabinet and other officials as well as Reagan or any preceding president.

Then there is the matter of fiscal responsibility. In a business corporation, as we well know, the reins are held much tighter than in a government as loosely run and as complex as ours. As to money, Iacocca has proven himself a master at making it stretch.

All of which brings us back to Iacocca's vulnerability in foreign affairs. In this nuclear age when the push of a button could mean worldwide devastation, would he be the man to have at the helm?

The American public will have to decide that if a Lee Iacocca candidacy comes to pass.

Meanwhile, all we can do is relish the suspense.

PROLOGUE

The tinted windows of Ford Motor Company's world headquarters reflected the glare from a blazing, early-morning midsummer sun as Lido Anthony Iacocca wheeled his Continental Mark down the southbound Southfield Freeway. Mildly aware of the cars whizzing past at more than the fifty-five-mile-an-hour speed limit, he turned into the Ford Road exit in Dearborn. That morning, Thursday, July 13, 1978, Lee, who preferred the Americanization of his given name, expected to arrive at his office in the northeast corner of the building's twelfth floor at his usual time. Someone privy to the circumstances, but unfamiliar with Lee Iacocca, might have been amazed that the president of the Ford Motor Company was following his normal routine on this day of all days.

A lesser man might not have bothered to show up at all, much less endure what had to be an anxious, even bewildering, twenty-five-mile drive from his home in Bloomfield Hills, a posh suburb north of Detroit. Most would have found it far less agonizing to chuck it, to walk away from the emotional roller coaster that the day promised. But to Lee Iacocca it was, at the least, an uncomfortable situation, at the most a crisis to meet head-on.

His bland, almost tranquil expression belied the inner fire that might be expected from his Italian heritage, nor did it betray the resentful bitterness fueled by the painful prospect that awaited him. But from his youth Lee Iacocca had never dodged a bad situation. This unhappy Thursday would be no different.

Despite the inescapable hornet's nest toward which he was heading, here he was—as he had been daily through twenty-two years—in the very heart of "Ford Country." And no one could mistake the fact that in this sector of Dearborn, Michigan, everything in sight—north, south, east, and west—bore the Ford brand.

On the right, south of the Ford Road exit, even such non-Ford enterprises as the Hyatt Regency Hotel and the sprawling Fairlane Shopping Center stood on Ford land, as did the low-rise building to the left of the freeway, which housed the J. Walter Thompson Company, the advertising agency for the corporation's Ford Division. Beyond the Thompson facility, also on the left, were the Ford-built, Ford-owned, and Ford-leased Parklane Towers, twin high-rises that were dubbed the Washer and Dryer by some, the Salt-

and-Pepper Shakers by others, because of their architectural conformation.

In one of the twin towers were the offices of Kenyon & Eckhardt, the ad agency that served various other Ford Motor Company activities, including the Parts and Service, Glass, and Lincoln-Mercury divisions. Locating offices in the heart of Fordland was, of course, a convenience and time-saver for the executives and account representatives of the agencies who shuttled back and forth daily, visiting clients for program approvals.

While their physical closeness is a practical and generally accepted business setup in doing business with a giant, even in spheres other than advertising, it is more than just political expediency. The rental and lease revenues that accrue to Ford Land Development, in this instance from J. Walter Thompson and Kenyon & Eckhardt, substantially influence the bottom line in corporate profits.

Directly south of the Parklane Towers, also on the east side of the freeway, stood the building to which Lee Iacocca was headed, the centerpiece of Ford Country, a long, rectangular structure with exterior walls that appeared to be unbroken expanses of reflective glass. It is appropriately known as the Glass House.

The top floor of the Glass House is the twelfth, although there is a penthouse-type structure above that houses executive dining rooms and sleeping quarters for busy executives or visiting dignitaries. Ford employees called the suite in the southeast corner of

11

the twelfth floor, the one next to Iacocca's own, the place "where God lives." From this suite Henry Ford II ruled the Ford empire like an autocrat, more in the mold of his legendary grandfather than his father.

No other automobile executive ruled his fiefdom with the absolute power of Chairman of the Board Henry Ford II. Not Thomas Murphy, chairman of General Motors, not John Riccardo of Chrysler Corporation, not Gerald Meyers of American Motors. These men held their posts by the grace of directors' votes and shareholder acquiescence.

Of course, Ford Motor Company also had its stockholders and board of directors. Thanks, however, to the establishment of the Ford Foundation in January, 1956, the Ford family had firm control of voting shares in the company. Henry II, as a result, wielded unchallenged authority by virtue of the prepotent Ford name, one that checkmated directors and stockholders alike. If any dared question Henry's right to make a final decision, his irrefutable answer was quick in coming.

"Look whose name is on the building!"

Henry meant this often-made pronouncement literally. At the top right of the wide exterior of the Glass House is the familiar Ford trademark, a royal-blue oval bearing the Ford name in white script, a symbol instantly recognizable anywhere in the free world.

This Thursday morning the traditional emblem looked down on Lee Iacocca as he guided his car around the building and down into the executive parking area. With an unchanging expression he parked and walked briskly to the executive elevator. He was ready for whatever Henry Ford II had wrought the night before.

As was his custom when business didn't have him in some faroff hamlet talking to dealers or overseas checking on operations at one of Ford's worldwide facilities, Lee had spent the previous evening quietly at home with his wife and younger daughter, Lia. Kathy, the fourth member of the family, was away at school.

Late that evening, when the telephone rang, Mary Iacocca answered and heard a voice she recognized as that of Keith Crain, publisher of the Detroit-based *Automotive News*, the automobile industry's leading weekly. The caller asked to speak to Mr. Iacocca.

Lee took the receiver and, after a few pleasantries, heard Crain say he had just received a puzzling phone call from Henry Ford II.

"What the hell's going on?" was the gist of the publisher's message. "Henry told me he's going to fire you tomorrow."

Lee was visibly shocked as he recradled the phone, but not totally surprised. He was shocked to hear such news from a third party, and a company outsider to boot. But not really surprised because he had been aware for some time that Henry, for no legitimate reason he could fathom, had been maneuvering to force him out of the company presidency.

Lee had first sensed the maneuvers to oust him when he had heard repetitions of what he had originally passed off as idle rumors. All started from sources he was unable to identify. Most were inconsequential, possibly intended to encourage him to resign or take early retirement.

Too busy to consider them any more than irritations, Lee ignored them and went about his work. Ultimately he had to acknowledge, to himself at least, that something odious was indeed in the wind.

Lee could discount the stories no longer when he discovered that Henry Ford actually had begun his oust-Iacocca campaign as early as three years after he had named Iacocca president. He had ordered an audit of Iacocca's expenses and dealings with certain suppliers, hoping to find evidence of kickbacks.

In any large organization such actions could not be kept secret for long. When Lee first learned of Henry's demeaning tactics, he was embittered and furious enough to consider resigning, but only momentarily. A resignation might be construed as an admission of guilt, and he knew he had done nothing to degrade himself. He also knew that he had made far-ranging contributions to the company, that he had fought and worked too hard to make his boyhood dream a reality to just give up and walk away. As far back as his sophomore year in college he had said he would get a vice-presidency at Ford before he was thirty-five. He would not taint his achievement with a resignation.

No naive neophyte in corporate life, he was now past the age of fifty. More than thirty of those years had been spent in the service of the Ford Motor Company. The automobile industry was little different from other big businesses—the climb to the top had been hazardous, an everyday battle for survival. Each successive rung up the ladder added pressure from below as well as from above.

One's immediate superior controlled a man's future, demanding action and accomplishment. And those below on the stairway to the executive suite waited for the slip that might enable them to leapfrog ahead.

Lee Iacocca had made it as far as he could go in the Ford Motor Company. He knew it, and was fully content. He was president and had no illusions about the next highest position, that of chairman of the board. That post, by virtue of the Ford stockholdings, would remain in the Ford family. He had known that when he came in. He was even more aware of it now.

As Lee had turned from the phone that Wednesday evening, the questions he couldn't answer—all things considered—were "Why this?" and "Why now?"

Despite knowing of Henry's tactics over the past few years, the message from Keith Crain still had come as a thunderbolt. It made no sense. Less than a month earlier Iacocca had taken part in planning for ceremonies celebrating the Ford Motor Company's diamond jubilee. He had felt a surge of pride in the contributions he had made during thirty-two of the company's seventy-five years of building automobiles for the world.

The gratification he had felt made this news from an outsider harder to take. It was possible, of course, that Henry's harassment had gone underground only because of the extensive preparations for the big anniversary ceremonial. Then, too, it was possible—even probable—that Crain was merely fishing, as newspeople

15

so often do to get a scoop.

Crain simply could have mistaken something Henry had told him, or, having heard revivals of the earlier rumors, he might have been trying to weasel a confirmation out of Iacocca himself. Knowing Keith Crain, however, that was hardly likely. The man had a reputation for being a straight shooter.

Whatever the answer, Henry's lengthy campaign had never made much sense. Even those at Ford who were aware of Henry's not-too-subtle plotting were hard put to understand why he wanted to dump his second in command. Next to Ford himself, Lee Iacocca was the best-known individual in the entire industry. And he alone brought the company more favorable publicity than the heads of all the other auto manufacturers combined.

Auto-industry executives respected Iacocca for his abilities, his driving force, and his accomplishments. If a reporter had approached any of them on this July night in 1978 and said that Lee Iacocca was to be fired, he would have found his sanity questioned.

The very thought of firing Mr. Mustang was laughable. How could Henry Ford II afford to give up the man who had stood automobiledom on its ears in 1964 with his marketing of the pony car? Such a dismissal would send shock waves through the business and financial worlds.

Then, too, with his stock options and contract that reputedly would not expire for another four years or so, Lee Iacocca seemed as rock-steady at Ford as Henry himself.

Even before he took over the presidency, Iacocca had put his brand on Ford profitability. As vice-president and general manager at Ford Division he had given General Motors and its Chevrolet Division plenty to worry about. His Mustang had clobbered its come-after Chevy counterpart, the Camaro. His Maverick had multiplied Chevrolet concerns as well as helped stem the early-1960s trend toward the small imports from Germany and Japan. Later, after his promotion to president of Ford, Iacocca had breathed new life into its Lincoln-Mercury Division.

Lee Iacocca had given the Ford Motor Company what it needed most at a time when it was most needed, a healthy bottom line in profits. While 1974 and 1975 were not good years, a period of slight recession, under Iacocca the company had achieved a record $938 million profit in 1976. That mark was shattered the following year as Ford racked up sales totaling $37.8 billion and profits of $1.7 billion. And the projected figures for 1978, as of July 1, clearly indicated that profits for 1978 might set a new record were it not for the lengthy and costly strike at Ford's English subsidiary. Such numbers made Henry's itch for Iacocca's scalp incomprehensible.

The burning question was "Why?" One possible answer lay in the natures of the two men. While they are similar in many ways, in essence they are as different as chalk from cheese. Both are strong, hard-nosed, and blunt-speaking, but poles apart in background and character.

Henry Ford II is the gregarious, curt, often caustic

aristocrat, a charmer and a community-minded citizen who put his talents and money to work to help revitalize Detroit, even though his home, offices, and factories were located outside the city. Although silver-spooned from birth, he has never projected the picture of a pampered son of opulence.

Conversely, Lee Iacocca was not born to inherited wealth. But he did not come from what is generally termed a "poor" family from the other side of the tracks. At the time of his birth in 1924 his father, Nicola, was considered well to do.

Incongruities in the temperaments of Henry Ford II and Lee Iacocca are made more evident by their intra-family relationships. Henry loved his father, Edsel, but it was his uneducated, acerbic, and provocative grandfather, the very antithesis of Edsel, on whom Henry doted and who more surely shaped his mind and personality. The entire Ford family, except for the till-death-do-us-part devotion of the first Henry and Edsel for their wives, has been loosely knit. Months may pass with no contact between the Ford brothers and sisters other than in business.

On the other hand, the Iacoccas' background is that of their motherland, where family is paramount, whatever the circumstance. Lee more than loved his father; he revered him. Some claim he was dominated by Nicola. If so, the dominance was born of Lee's respect and reverence. From his earliest teens Lee strove hard to be like his father, a hard-charging doer.

Phlegmatic though he seems at times, Henry Ford II is not callous and insensitive, but often a kind and thoughtful man who takes the time to stop and chat with the grubbiest worker on an assembly line. He is the unabashed extrovert, a man who projects an image of the glad-handing traveling salesman.

Iacocca is no less kind, but he is not so outgoing. He is a warm, impassioned, and zealous individual who is extremely protective of his privacy and that of his family and who is fiercely loyal to his friends. Always maintaining a sense of quiet dignity in public, he is nonetheless a witty and charming man.

Gar Laux, who came to Ford about the same time as Iacocca and climbed the corporate ladder a step behind him, says that, contrary to press caricatures of him as a tough, salty-tongued enigma, Lee is easy to understand and like. He is, says Laux, what he has to be, a demanding man at the office and a loving husband and father at home.

In every aspect the Lee Iacocca lifestyle is far more conservative than that of Henry Ford II. Henry has always been the sociable, fun-loving cosmopolite, a man who loves a practical joke and could not care less about dignity. Once, in his early adult years, Henry stood outside a fine restaurant in Grosse Pointe, the elegant Detroit suburb in which he lived, and blew a loud, shrill blast on a police whistle to shake up the diners inside. On another occasion, at a party overseas, he dueled with an Italian count, riposting the nobleman's tosses of ice cream with a soda siphon.

While Lee Iacocca was happily married to his first sweetheart, Henry is twice divorced and three times married. He is a dedicated girl-watcher who has not lost his zest for a pretty face and trim figure. Unruffled, however embarrassing the situation, he lives and plays by his own rules, offering no excuses.

In February, 1975, while his second wife, Cristina, was in Katmandu attending the coronation of the king of Nepal, Henry was arrested in Goleta, California, and charged with drunk driving. His companion in the car was Kathy DuRoss, a redhaired model who had worked for the Ford Motor Company and later would become his third wife.

Henry was given a blood test and offered release on a $375 cash bond. After stubbornly refusing to post bail, he was jailed for four hours. Finally he paid. As he left the jail, he found reporters waiting for a juicy tidbit or, at least, a roasting of the police. Henry gave them neither. He merely waved and went his way.

The next day Henry was scheduled to address the Society of Automotive Engineers at Detroit's Cobo Hall Convention Center, and he flew back to meet his speech commitment. During his talk someone in the hall shouted out a question referring to the previous night's happening in California.

"Never complain, never explain," Henry answered with a laugh. He received a standing ovation from the hundreds of engineers gathered at dinner.

Henry Ford II is a newsmaker whatever he does, but a man little concerned whether the attendant publicity is embarrassing or complimentary. Invariably he is insulated from any lasting harm by his name, position, and nonchalance.

Lee Iacocca entered his twelfth-floor office that

Thursday morning still mystified and bewildered by the turn of events. Had Henry, the night before, really initiated another bit of headline news, one that would startle and galvanize the entire business world? Keith Crain had told him that a board of directors meeting had been called hastily by Henry and that Lee was finished as president of the Ford Motor Company.

Whether any or all of Crain's report was valid hardly mattered now. Lee would soon know. And he was ready for the phone call that would come if Crain was right, ready also for the walk to the suite next door.

He sat at his desk waiting, realizing he could do nothing, that he had no way to exorcise the specter that hovered over his shoulder. Only Henry could do that.

He took care of routine business. The phone rang often, but every call was from an associate with a report or a question. Obviously, the word had not been spread around the Glass House. The hours passed, and though he wondered, Lee was not overly surprised at the delay in hearing from the chairman. Henry was not one to worry about hours.

"I don't like to get up early if I don't have to," Henry once said. "It gets you into crazy habits. If I've got a meeting at nine, I'll get there at nine o'clock. But if I don't, what's the use of sitting behind my desk waiting for somebody to ask a question he ought to answer himself?"

Obviously Henry had set no definite time for giving Lee Iacocca the news. It was possible, too, that contrary to Henry's avowed statement that he would never pass the buck and would do what had to be done himself, he hoped that Iacocca, alerted by Keith Crain, might not show up. But certainly, after so many years Henry should have known Lee Iacocca well enough to know that that was highly unlikely.

At noon Iacocca was still waiting. He had lunch in the penthouse dining room. Henry was not to be seen. Lee finished his light meal and returned to his office.

Lee's secretary had placed an afternoon newspaper on his desk. Its headline story seemed a most fitting one. Andrew Young was being edged out as the U.S. ambassador to the United Nations.

Iacocca sat back in his chair to wait. Many things crossed his mind as the minutes ticked by. In any such situation there are always bits and pieces that might suggest a reprieve.

The phone call of the night before might not have been what it was purported to be. It might not have been hard fact. Also, considering Henry's past vacillations, he might have had a change of heart. The three years or so that Henry had done much to encourage Iacocca's resignation lent credence to a possible change of mind.

In midafternoon the phone rang.

"Mr. Ford wants to see you in his office," his secretary reported.

CHAPTER 1

Lido Anthony Iacocca was born in Allentown, Pennsylvania, on October 12, 1924. An astrological enthusiast might see astral influences at work, for 1924 was a year of coincidental significance to the adult life of the newborn infant.

That year the Ford Motor Company set a record in building its ten millionth car, and while the first Henry Ford's beloved "tin lizzie" would live for another three years, the death knell had already sounded for the legendary Model T. And not long after baby Lido was first placed in his crib, another automobile company was being established.

Walter P. Chrysler had taken over the dying Maxwell—the very Maxwell later made famous by Jack Benny's humor and the driving of Benny's chauffeur, Rochester—and brought it to profitability. Chrysler, one of the foremost engineers in automobile history, bought out the Maxwell company and made it the

23

foundation of his own Chrysler Corporation.

Lido was the second child born to Nicola and Antoinette Iacocca. Nicola Iacocca—the correct Italian pronunciation of the last name is Ee-a-ko-ka—most influenced his son's life, encouraging the determination, persistence, and ambition that would make the name Lee Iacocca a household word.

Nicola first came to the United States from San Marco, a village in Italy's Campania province, as a restless, energetic youth of thirteen. The town, in the foothills of the Apennine Mountains about 100 kilometers northeast of Naples, had nothing to offer a boy of ambition.

Life in Campania at the turn of the century was more barbarous than civilized. Naples was a hellhole of tuberculosis, where too many lived a hopeless existence underground in caves. In Benevento, a few kilometers from San Marco and the nearest town of any size, a young person might find himself auctioned off as a farm laborer. And wild, overcrowded Rome, far too dangerous for a lone thirteen-year-old, was a world away.

There was one answer to Nicola's itch for adventure agreeable to his mother. A prosperous half-brother of Nicola lived in the United States. So Nicola Iacocca, a credulous adolescent, came to Garrett, a Pennsylvania mining town southeast of Pittsburgh and a short distance from the Maryland border.

Nicola found Garrett a dirty town on the way to oblivion. No more populous than San Marco, it was also in a mountainous area, enough to make him feel at home, but Nicola soon hated the coal-dust-polluted atmosphere of the northern Appalachians. And he had problems.

Nicola's half-brother owned the mining camp's supply store. About twice Nicola's age and married, he was impatient with the hyperactive, impetuous youngster, Nicola's sister-in-law, irritated by his ebullience and ever-present ear-to-ear grin, made him feel uncomfortable and unwelcome.

It was too much for the happy-go-lucky young Italian immigrant. He ran away, not caring where, and was caught. He disappeared again and again, but was always found and brought back. Warnings had no effect.

"If you keep on doing this," the half-brother threatened, "I don't want the responsibility. You'll have to go back home to your mother."

Nicola returned to Italy. Within two years he was back in America, this time accompanied by his two older brothers and sponsored by an uncle in Allentown. This, Nicola found, was a city of love. Here, he could learn, work, enjoy life, be somebody.

Allentown, a historic city on the Lehigh River in eastern Pennsylvania, then had a population of about 70,000. Its hilly terrain and fresh air reminded him of the Apennine foothills where he once roamed. He loved crossing the bridge over the Lehigh and walking into the country where an occasional deer might be seen. He enjoyed Allentown's clean, neat streets that took him up hillsides covered with brick and frame row houses, so different from the little houses in

San Marco.

Nicola listened in awe to stories of the American Revolution, of how the famous Liberty Bell was smuggled into Allentown from Philadelphia in 1777, when the British threatened the headquarters of the Continental Congress. He visited the church in which the Liberty Bell had been hidden and the Liberty Bell Shrine, where he saw a replica of the symbol of America's fight for freedom.

To the uneducated but ambitious Nicola Allentown was just this side of heaven, a place where he quickly made himself self-supporting. Working in his uncle's hot dog restaurant he began to save money. His charisma, infectious grin, and jolly nature—destined to be the hallmarks of his future success—made him a customer favorite.

The Nicola who had been a problem in Garrett two years earlier had matured into a serious young man of sixteen. Allentown, with its beautiful hills, its metal and textile industries, and its many people, unlike Garrett or San Marco, was exciting, a place where money could be made. Like so many immigrants to America in the early years of the twentieth century, young Nicola was determined to be somebody the American way.

Like so many of those immigrants, he soon realized that the way to achievement in America was to work hard, save money, and make that money make more money. He was also determined to be American, act American. It would be all right for his brothers and uncle and the other Italians to call him Nicola, but

26

around Allentown calling himself Nick would better show his mushrooming love for his new country.

When Nick had saved enough money working for his uncle, he opened a hot dog restaurant of his own, his first of many steps he would take toward becoming Allentown's premier entrepreneur, a thinking, speculative, and innovative businessman with a Midas touch. An early decision, a portent of the future, was his purchase of an automobile, a Ford Model T.

One of the few in Allentown to own a car, Nick Iacocca was making himself visible, while rushing along the road to success. His restaurant was doing so well that profits built quickly. He began looking for new ventures for investment.

New ventures, however, had to wait. Calamitous events had taken place overseas. On June 28, 1914, Archduke Francis Ferdinand, heir apparent to the Austrian throne, was assassinated, and World War I erupted. America became directly involved on March 18, 1917, when three United States merchant ships were sunk by German submarines. President Woodrow Wilson immediately called for a declaration of war against Germany.

Nick was not yet an American citizen. But seeing the Uncle Sam "I Want You!" posters, he quickly made up his mind. He would not wait for the draft process. He volunteered.

Because he was one of the few able to drive an automobile, his army service was spent at Camp Crane in Allentown, a training center for the United States Ambulance Corps. Located on the fairgrounds, the camp had been named for Dr. Charles Henry Crane, U.S. Army Surgeon General in 1882.

Nick did double duty at Camp Crane. He helped train ambulance drivers and used his Model T to drive doctors and surgeons to duty during training maneuvers. As a resident of Allentown he could have slept at home, but he refused. He insisted on sharing quarters with other soldiers, tents hastily constructed in front of the fairgrounds bleachers.

Another occupant of the huge bleacher tent was Adolphe Menjou, the motion picture character actor who later starred in such films as *The Front Page* with Pat O'Brien, *Little Miss Marker* with Shirley Temple, and, among many others, *A Star Is Born* with Fredric March and Janet Gaynor. Evenings, the tent was a hotbed of hilarity when the jolly, uninhibited Italian immigrant and the suave, debonair French-American exchanged quips.

After the war Nick returned to his hot dog restaurant. His older brother had maintained the business and its level of profit so well that Nick opened a second restaurant.

Having done so well, Nick decided that his mother, alone in San Marco, should come to the United States. As an American citizen now he could have arranged for her entry. In his early thirties at the time, a touch of nostalgia and a desire to surprise his mother convinced him he should bring her back himself. He left his brothers to manage his enterprises and sailed for Italy.

When Nick arrived in San Marco, his intention

was to spend no more than two weeks visiting relatives and friends. He was impatient to get back to business. His first visit to the family of a shoemaker he had known as a boy erased all thoughts of a quick return. The moment he saw sixteen-year-old Antoinette Perotto, the shoemaker's eldest daughter, he became determined not to return to America without her.

Courtship in the Italy of the day was no simple boy-meets-girl-boy-gets-girl procedure. It was a lengthy, involved process where one did not go to call on the girl of his dreams, but rather made courtesy calls ostensibly to honor the parents. One visit led to another, with Nick in a trance as Antoinette entered and reentered the room setting the table and serving the meal, seldom glancing in his direction.

As the reason for his many visits became obvious, young Antoinette would suddenly disappear, running across the street to the village church. She felt she was too young to marry. She feared leaving her home and going to a strange country. Always when she returned home, Nick was still there, enchanted by the grace with which this tiny girl with the angelic face moved about and by the sparkle in her dark eyes the few times they met his squarely.

At the proper time he talked to Antoinette's father, who told Nick that if Antoinette agreed, he had his permission. Antoinette could not deny her own feelings. There was something about this happy man with the laughing eyes she could not resist.

Nick had arrived at San Marco in April. In July he

and Antoinette were married in the San Marco church across the street from the Perotto home.

Preparing to leave for the United States, Nick Iacocca took his new bride on a honeymoon to Rome and Capri. Nick's mother joined them in Naples for the trip across the Atlantic.

Just as Nick, Antoinette, and Mamma were ready to board the ship, Antoinette became ill. It may have been the blistering heat of a southern Italian July or the trepidation of leaving home for a strange land, or a combination of both, but she came down with typhoid fever, which was not diagnosed until the ship had left the harbor.

The frail newlywed, just turned seventeen, was placed in quarantine on the ship for twenty-two days, transforming the jolly, lively Nick into a frantic bridegroom. Not until two weeks passed could he see his bride, and then only through a tiny window.

Nick's brothers came to New York to bring the three travelers back to Allentown. Antoinette recovered fully after a three-month convalescence. Nick remained at her bedside every possible moment until she was well.

Nick then found a new home for them, a brick row house on a quiet Allentown street. It was in this house that their first child, a daughter they named Delma, was born. She was followed less than two years later by the boy they christened Lido Anthony Iacocca.

Newspaper reporters and magazine writers have romanticized Nick's and Antoinette's naming of their son Lido, writing that he was so named because of his father's memories of a glamorous honeymoon spent on the Lido at Venice. Actually Nick and Antoinette's brother had taken a trip to Venice and the Lido before the wedding, and Nick had not forgotten the beauty of the spot.

Nick's business ventures mushroomed. He opened a new hot dog restaurant in Allentown after his return. Located on Sixth Street, a few blocks from his new home, he called it the Orpheum House. When Antoinette was well enough, she came to help, even though she was still learning English.

Lido was a handsome two-year-old when his father, whose brain was always awhirl with new business ideas, came upon a moneymaking idea that would later blossom into one of the world's great enterprises. He was driving his Model T through Allentown one day when the thought struck him that many people could use temporary transportation.

Never one to let a potentially profitable idea lay dormant, Nick established a business he called U-Drive-It, very likely the first rent-a-car business in America, perhaps the world. This new enterprise may have provided the spark that influenced his son's future. From the time Lido was four years old he was taken often to his father's U-Drive-It. Certainly, as youngsters beg to do, young Iacocca often sat behind the wheel of Model T's, and later Model A's, for Nick's rental cars were almost exclusively Ford. Lee Iacocca figuratively teethed on Fords.

The U-Drive-It business was no less a success than his Orpheum Wiener House, so the enterprising Nick was able to move into real estate development, a dream he had been nurturing for some time. By the late 1920s Nick Iacocca had grown wealthy.

Nick Iacocca was not so much all business that he neglected his family to build a fortune. On the contrary, he loved his family, and togetherness was the rule when the business day ended. On Sundays at the Iacoccas it was open house, with friends and relatives overflowing the small rooms from midmorning until late in the evening. Everybody was welcome for Sunday dinner, with the pasta ready at all hours for Antoinette's own spicy tomato sauce.

The environment was ideal for a growing Lido, shy and reserved. On the one hand was the spirited character of his father, garrulous, warm, and hospitable. On the other was a family intimacy and love that would last his lifetime, an atmosphere underscored by Nick's personal philosophy that when it's time to work, give the job your all, and when it's time to play, relish it.

Nick Iacocca felt strongly that no place was better for his maturing son than Allentown. An Italian, born to the thrills of soccer, he found that Italian and other immigrants who had come to work in Allentown's mills, had brought Europe's favorite sport with them. So Lido could play soccer. And softball. Even though Nick was vague about any form of baseball, softball was an American game and something his all-American boy should enjoy.

Then, too, not far from Allentown were hiking trails, camping sites, and boating and fishing to be enjoyed at Leaser Lake. And, less than an hour and a half drive in his Model T, were the beautiful Poconos, mountains that rivaled the Apennines back home.

Few father-son relationships are more steadfast than that between Nick and Lido, a closeness Nick initiated from Lido's early years. Lee rarely went anywhere without his father, for whom he had an abiding respect and love. Through his school years and later in the business world, whenever Lee received an award or promotion, he made sure his dad could be there to share in the joy of his achievement.

Nick—tough, hard-nosed and proud—even ruthless—in business was a caring, loving father who impressed his son at every turn with the importance of standing by your guns when you know you are right. It was the sure path to accomplishment, Nick emphasized. This resoluteness in Nick's character saved the Iacocca family from disaster in 1929.

The Great Depression brought the American economy crashing, and Nick Iacocca's hard-won fortune was washed away with those of thousands of other Americans. Nick, never one to curse bad luck, didn't despair, nor did he permit his family to lose hope, even though his situation became more desperate each day.

A building he had constructed on Sixth Street and three apartment houses were lost. Tenants who had operated restaurants in two buildings Nick owned lost their business and moved out. Nick took over the restaurants in the hope of recouping some of his losses, but it was not to be. Losing money day by day, he ultimately lost ownership of the buildings.

Lido, only five years of age at the time of the Crash, was hardly aware of the family misfortune. Nick, meanwhile, took a long look at what seemed a hopeless situation. There had to be some way to start back up. Real estate was out of the question. He had no money to invest. There was another possibility.

"People have got to eat," he told Antoinette, and finding a promising location, he opened the State Restaurant. He was right back where he had started.

Nick Iacocca had been a food expert, and the people of Allentown remembered. With Antoinette at his side, he worked hard. He saved every cent possible without depriving his family of their needs. Nick still had his touch. The restaurant did so well that he was able to buy two motion picture theaters, one of which—the Franklin—still stands in Allentown.

Profits from the restaurant and the theaters sent Nick Iacocca back to his great love, real estate. He purchased 200 acres of land in East Allentown and developed a fine residential area he called Midway Manor. He began by building one home at a time, then two. As profits permitted, he increased construction. (Midway Manor is today one of the finest residential districts in the Allentown area. Nick had kept one prime corner lot on which he built, in 1950, a castlelike architectural gem of brick for himself and Antoinette, a beautiful home in which Nick's cordial, genteel, and active widow still lives.)

Lido was in the third grade at Allentown's Stephens School when his father began his climb back to prosperity. Throughout his school years he made fine grades, which pleased his father. Having accomplished what he had without a formal education, Nicola believed there was no limit to what his son could become with good schooling.

Lido was a bookworm, but not in the accepted sense. He had his moments for play and recreation. He liked sports. He was no hell-raiser, but he did get into the minor scrapes typical of a growing youngster, though Nick's shadow over his shoulder was a deterrent. Anything his father said was law.

Nick had told Lido that whenever he was in any trouble, got involved in any fight, or fell or got hurt, he should come to him immediately. One day when Lido was about eight years old he was jostling with a friend when the other boy accidentally pushed him through a basement window. The window broke, and Lido cut his hand.

Lido did not go home. He ran to his father's restaurant, his hand bleeding. When his father asked him why he had come there instead of home, Lido answered: "You always told me when I get hurt I should come to you." What Nick said Lido invariably took as gospel.

So when Nick Iacocca said Lido must study, Lido studied and let nothing interfere. Often his friends would stand outside his window and call, "Lido! Lido! Come on out!" Lido ignored the voices, and when they would continue calling, he finally would get up and shout from the window: "Go away! I've got to study."

For Lido there was always a time for play and a time for work. It was his father's dictum, and that was enough.

Lido sailed through grade school, a model student. And in junior high, where he earned an overall average of 95, his two lowest grades were 88, one in music, the other in physical education.

"Lido was a rare student," says Carroll Parks, his eighth-grade English and Latin teacher. "Not a hell-raiser. Not colorful. He was all business, with a lot of initiative, a boy who knew what he had to do, and did it. Maybe a little shy, too much reserved for his young age."

Lido took after his hard-driving father, and this probably contributed to his diffidence, since he respected his dad too much to get into the usual rough-and-tumble antics typical of a youngster in his early teens. He may well have been in awe of Nick, an industrious human dynamo who elbowed his way past obstacles.

Gar Laux, who worked with and for Lee many years, knew Nick intimately and had great affection for him. He tells of an incident that graphically portrays Nick's intensity, his ethic for making it in a tough world.

Laux and Iacocca were attending a meeting of Ford dealers in Palm Springs, California, one summer, and Nick Iacocca was invited by his son to join him there for a vacation. Neither Laux nor Iacocca were avid golfers, but during a business break they went out for the exercise, taking Nick with them.

"I'll never forget," Laux says, "that after we got Nick to hit the ball, he took off in a speedy run. And we yelled at him, 'No! No! You don't run after the ball, you walk! Walk!' But that's the kind of man Nick was. He just had to go, go one hundred percent."

This spirit Nick Iacocca hoped to instill in his son. Lido had to learn that the soul of success was vigorous action. It was the way in which his son could become the renowned and powerful man he wanted him to be.

When Lido entered Allentown High School he began to lose his shyness. He began to take part in sports, enjoyed baseball and football, but found swimming and ice-skating gave him the greatest pleasure. In both he was far better than average.

Unfortunately, when he was a sophomore the thrills of swimming, skating—any kind of sports activity— were taken away. He came down with a severe case of rheumatic fever and was bedridden for three months. Unable to move his legs and in pain most of the time, he was as worried about losing time in school as his parents and sister were concerned about his recovery.

Pain wasn't going to stop Lido. If he couldn't get to school, he devised a plan to have school—so to speak—come to him. He had his sister, Delma, then a senior at Allentown High, bring him his assignments day after day. Despite the discomfort he did the required work, and each morning Delma delivered it to Lido's teacher.

Three months in bed did not lower his scholastic

average. He was placed on the honor roll that sophomore year.

But he was finished as far as participation in sports was concerned. He had recovered, but he had lost so much weight he resembled a toothpick. Even more distressing, his passions for swimming and skating were now restricted to those of a spectator. It was not enough. He channeled his love for sports into managing the school swimming team.

Lido graduated from Allentown High School in June, 1942, second highest on the class honor roll. *Comus*, the Yearbook, lists Lido Iacocca as a member of the National Honor Society, president of the senior class, member of the Oratan Debating Society and of the Latin Club, and manager of the swimming team.

His picture in *Comus* shows a good-looking, thin young man with dark hair and penetrating dark eyes. Under the name Lido Anthony Iacocca a caption indicates his interest in life to be engineering and science, beneath which is Lido's quote: "When you aim at anything you are sure to hit it," a fitting preamble to his future. The brief analysis of Lido's character that follows is also, oddly enough considering his age at the time, a prognostic of the Iacocca to be.

"Lee is a raconteur extraordinary," it reads, "and not only can he quip with the best, but he can pun with the worst. If knowledge really is power, he is omnipotent. This, together with the ability he has developed in managing and directing school affairs, will prove a great asset in his career of engineering."

It was the first time that Lido Anthony Iacocca had been openly referred to in print as "Lee," for like his father before him, though he was proud of and would never deny his Italian background, he preferred the more American version of his name. Whether Lee to his friends or Lido to his parents, graduation day was Nick's to relish, though his heart was bursting and his eyes were tear-filled. The boy he had nurtured was now a young man much in his own image.

And it was a somewhat more capricious young man who emerged as Lee Iacocca, high school graduate. He became more outgoing, like his father, enjoying parties and dances. One evening, when Nick and Antoinette went visiting, Lee invited some friends to the house. There was music, dancing, a little beer, but overall it was just a good time.

"They made such a mess," Antoinette Iacocca says, "I'll never forget it. When we got home, and it was pretty late, the house was upside-down. Nick really said plenty to Lee."

Nick, she points out, never laid a hand on either of his children, but there was punishment. When they were young, it was usually the "go to your room" or "no outside play today" type. On this occasion Nick had his say and sent Lee to his room, depriving him of the family car for a few days.

Nick being Nick, it was taken for granted that when Lee graduated from high school the next step would be college. The matter of where he should go was one Nick believed deserved serious thought.

It had to be the finest engineering college in the country, Nick insisted, and Lee should pick the one he liked best. Lee was partial to the Massachusetts Institute of Technology but really preferred Lehigh, which was practically next door in Bethlehem, Pennsylvania.

Lee, though he wanted it, resisted a decision for Lehigh because it was known as a rich man's engineering university and thus would be too expensive. That was no argument as far as Nick was concerned. In his eyes the best was none too good for his son. Besides, Lehigh's location meant he could see his son more often.

Once Lehigh was decided on, another determination had to be made. Lee, conscious of the great expense his father would undertake in sending him to such a college, felt that with Lehigh so near, he should live at home.

Nick would have none of it. The added expense of living in a dormitory on campus was little compared to Lee's need to get out into the world. Much as he would have liked to have his son home every night, he insisted that Lee live on campus. Lee finally deferred to his father's wish with the proviso that he would come home on weekends and holidays.

During his first year at Lehigh the budding engineer, who was banned from taking part in any sport by his bout with rheumatic fever, buried himself in his studies. Monday through Thursday the hours away from classrooms were spent in his dormitory room with his books. When classes were finished on

Friday, Nick would be waiting in his Ford to take him the ten miles back to Allentown. Early Monday morning the trip was reversed.

Lee's dedication to his books earned him relentless teasing from his dormitory mates, but he shrugged it off. He knew what he was aiming for. Ever since his high school days he had been in love with Fords. Now, at Lehigh, he became all but obsessed with becoming an engineer at the Ford Motor Company, and—as the quote in his high school yearbook said— he was going to hit his target.

When the dormitory joshing continued, Lee stopped the jokers with the remark that became his challenge. "You wait," he declared. "I'm going to be a vice-president at Ford before I'm thirty-five!" The statement was made with such seriousness it stopped his friends in their tracks.

Having lost much of his early reticence, Lee was now a more outgoing person, although his classmates at Lehigh still thought him restrained and reserved.

But Lee had a reason for his standoffishness. He was determined to finish his course in industrial engineering in three years, not the usual four. That meant piling up credits, which in turn called for extra hours of hard work. In his sophomore year, by then almost assured of receiving his degree after his third year, he grew more involved in university affairs and became an active member of the Lehigh student government.

One morning in the late spring of 1945, Lee's graduation year from Lehigh, a long, shiny black

1942 Lincoln Continental came to a stop in front of the university's administration building. Out from behind the steering wheel stepped a short, smartly dressed, dignified gentleman with the unlikely name of Leander Hamilton McCormick-Goodheart. His objective was the office of the Dean of Engineering. "If possible I would like to talk to engineering graduates you consider have the most potential," McCormick-Goodheart said after introducing himself as supervisor of the Ford Motor Company's personnel planning department. "Perhaps those at the top in their respective engineering courses."

Lee Anthony Iacocca was the first Lehigh student to be interviewed by McCormick-Goodheart. Since his early teens Lee, who had idolized Henry Ford as the maker of the Model T that Nick featured at the U-Drive-It, could hardly contain himself. He knew little or nothing of Henry Ford II, who had just been made executive vice-president of Ford, but it had been his dream to work for the Ford Motor Company. And this man with the longest name he had ever heard was offering him the possibility of a job as a Ford trainee.

McCormick-Goodheart explained the great opportunity at Ford for bright young engineers, and though he might have saved his breath, he enthusiastically sold the virtues of the Ford Motor Company. Lee listened intently. However much he had hoped to have Ford in his future, the picture painted by this nattily dressed man with the singular, almost musical name reinforced his determination to go Ford.

McCormick-Goodheart offered Lee a position as an engineering trainee at the hardly munificent salary of $185 a month. The small salary didn't matter, but Lee had a problem. He had already been granted a fellowship at Princeton to get his master's degree, an honor he wanted to accept. Yet his desire to join Ford was equally, if not more, resolute.

He quickly made up his mind. If he had to, it would be Ford, not Princeton. He explained his dilemma and his decision to McCormick-Goodheart.

"One of the remarkable things about Lee Iacocca," McCormick-Goodheart reported to Henry Ford II, "is his tremendous, driving sincerity. He didn't 'yes' me along or anything. He said 'I want very much to work for Ford, but if it doesn't affect me adversely, I want to go on to Princeton for my master's in mechanical engineering.' "

"Go to Princeton and get your master's," Lee was notified. "A year from now your job will be waiting for you."

Lee could not have been happier at this turn of events, as was his father. For one thing Nick was glad to have his son home for the summer. It provided an opportunity to further strengthen the unbreakable bond that already existed between them.

The first order of business after Lee's arrival in Allentown after receiving his degree from Lehigh was a graduation party. Nick went all out. The Iacocca home was jammed through the evening. Nick had invited everyone who knew him or Lee, young or old.

Near the end of the evening Nick presented his son

with his graduation present, a prewar used Ford. The gift was as much a benefit for Nick as for Lee. Princeton was more than fifty miles away, and if Lee had no car to drive home on weekends, there would have been lengthy separations that both were happy to avoid.

Lee's year at Princeton passed quickly. Typically, he kept his head buried in studies. Months went by without a word from McCormick-Goodheart or anyone at Ford, giving Lee cause for some worry. But early in the spring of 1946 a man named Olen Peters came to see Lee at Princeton. Peters, assistant to McCormick-Goodheart, had been sent to confirm Lee's job as well as check on his progress in mechanical engineering.

Peters had taken the entire file on Lee Iacocca, including a photograph, with him to Princeton. Though shocked by the long, lean, almost anemic-looking young man, he was impressed especially when he heard Lee reaffirm his great desire to work for Ford. Peters suggested that Lee come to Dearborn as soon after graduation as possible.

When Peters reported back to Ford's personnel planning office in Dearborn, McCormick-Goodheart asked him, "What did you think of this Lee Iacocca?"

"He's super," Peters replied. "We should get him going right away."

McCormick-Goodheart agreed. "When I first saw him, I noticed a tremendous directivity in the young man, a tremendous awareness of where he was going.

He had a goal, and it stuck out, as much as saying 'I know what I'm going to do with myself.' At his age I found that unusual."

"He made no bones about the fact that he really wants to become a part of Ford," Peters remarked. "I learned that he'd told classmates that he was going to be a vice-president here by the time he was thirty-five. And he meant it according to some of his classmates!"

"He seemed to me the type of guy who'd say a thing like that," McCormick-Goodheart said. "But you know, I think he's also the kind of guy to go ahead and do it. He's got a very strong, serious personality, unusually serious for a kid of twenty-one."

McCormick-Goodheart had been riffling through the Iacocca file and stopped for a moment to look at Lee's picture. He looked up at Peters.

"You know, Olen," he said, "there's only one thing that bothers me about him, especially about his entering the executive world. Look at this picture of him with its head-on look and piercing eyes. Doesn't the expression on his face tell you something? And consider how skinny he is!"

"What do you mean?" asked the puzzled Peters.

McCormick-Goodheart laughed. "Why, he looks like the American bald eagle that found some other bird's egg in his nest." After a moment he added: "Ach, it's stupid of me to say that. He's a good-looking kid with ability, and it's the ability that counts. And he'll put some weight on his bones, I'm sure."

"But not before he takes more off in the open hearth," Peters added. "And that'll make him all bones before he's hardly started. Can he hold up, I wonder?"

Lee Iacocca was awarded his master's degree in mechanical engineering at Princeton in the early summer of 1946. He was not yet twenty-two. Typically, he had chosen as the subject of his graduation thesis the function and use of torque converters.

After a few weeks at home in Allentown Lee reported to the Ford River Rouge plant in August to begin his role as an engineering trainee. He was the last to report of the fifty-man group recruited by McCormick-Goodheart.

The routine for an engineering trainee began with a ten-day indoctrination designed to make the potential executives familiar with the basic phases of car manufacture. Each ten-day phase was under the tutelage of a different safety engineer, each with responsibility for one area in the sprawling Rouge plant.

In order for the trainees to get to know and understand the work done in each area, as well as to acquaint them with the layout of the far-reaching Rouge, they spent a full day with each of the ten safety engineers. This not only oriented them to the plant but also gave them a physical taste of the various jobs being done.

On his first day Lee Iacocca was taken through the Rouge plant by a safety engineer named Malakas, who explained the different phases of the program as they walked along. As they went through the open hearth of the steel mill, they passed huge blast furnaces, which were kept scorching hot, their heat bouncing back in searing blasts at anyone within five feet.

Iacocca's escort stopped him. Pointing at one of the furnaces he said: "You'll be starting here in the morning."

They then proceeded up to a balcony overhang that provided a good view of the open hearth and also shielded them, to some degree, from the incredible heat.

"Do you know any of the guys in the program?" Malakas asked. When the new trainee shook his head, the engineer indicated the young man below, no older than Iacocca himself, and added: "That's Frank Zimmerman."

Zimmerman, a graduate of the University of Connecticut, was the first man signed for Ford by McCormick-Goodheart. He had already spent ten months in the program.

Iacocca looked down at the young man, hardly believing his eyes. This smallish youth, who looked like he weighed no more than 105 pounds, was stripped to the waist.

"What's he doing?" Iacocca asked the engineer.

"He's a number-three melter's helper," Malakas answered, "and he feeds coke breeze into the furnace."

Malakas explained that coke breeze was coke ground to a granular consistency, and that the fur-

47

nace at which Zimmerman was working had been "tapped-out"—drained of the melted steel. Shoveling coke breeze onto the still-red-hot inner surface of the furnace prevented leakage when smelting was resumed.

Iacocca was awestruck. The furnace door was about four feet off the floor, and Zimmerman, short in stature and so lean one could see the outline of his ribs, could hardly get the shovel up to the furnace opening.

"My God!" exclaimed Iacocca, who hardly weighed more than Zimmerman, "what did he look like when he first got here?" He then turned to Malakas. "Tell me, how long does it take to get from number-three to number-two helper?"

Zimmerman, hearing from below, looked up and laughed. The only difference between him and this long, lean Italian Ichabod Crane, as he described Iacocca, was height. It was the beginning of an unending friendship born of mutual respect.

The two had contrasting natures: Lee was quiet, burning with ambition, impatient to get his career moving forward and to a great degree an introvert with a wry sense of humor; Zimmerman was loquacious, a dedicated, innovative practical joker with a sense of the dramatic.

When Lee first arrived in Dearborn, he had taken a room at ten dollars a night in East Dearborn's Fordson Hotel. When Zimmerman had first arrived, unable to find a room, he reputedly slept on the city hall steps. Both later moved to Ann Arbor, some thirty miles west of the Ford headquarters, Lee sharing an apartment with three other trainees, Zimmerman taking a furnished room.

Zimmerman visited the Iacocca apartment almost every evening, playing cards with the three trainees. Lee, who had not learned to relax at a game of cards, made coffee for the group.

Lee had Iacocca cousins studying at Notre Dame, but it was Zimmie—as Lee began to call Frank—who suggested drives to South Bend to see Lee's cousins and not incidentally watch the fighting Irish play football. Zimmie, aware of Lee's passion for sports he could not play, knew such suggestions were certain to get him out of his shell.

Zimmie also twisted Lee's arm into double-dating. Lee was the one with a car, a not-so-new Ford convertible. The pair began taking out two girls from the YWCA. Lee's date, according to Zimmie, was a knockout. Zimmie's girl, however, was described by Lee as a girl already down for the count of ten.

So it went for the remaining year of Zimmerman's training period. Fun-provoking Zimmie slowly transformed the serious-minded Lee into a relaxed young man who appreciated a zany outing now and then. He also interlaced pleasure periods with the engineering talk Lee enjoyed.

Zimmerman had already joined the Society of Automotive Engineers and had SAE friends in Ann Arbor, professors and instructors at the University of Michigan. With these friends he and Lee would spend many hours in shoptalk. Of course Zimmie often spiced up the discussions by suggesting a night on the town.

"As a matter of fact," Zimmerman recalls, "we spent Lee's twenty-second birthday at the Pretzel Bell in Ann Arbor throwing hard-boiled eggs at the ceiling."

The trainee period at Ford was eighteen months, during which each recruit worked in every conceivable area of the Rouge plant. They stoked the coke ovens in the steel mill, forged metal in the blacksmith shop, tightened screws on the assembly line, even worked on the Ford-owned lake boats that brought iron ore from Michigan's Upper Peninsula. They also did duty on the test track and in the Rouge hospital.

It was the most phenomenal education in automobile knowhow imaginable, one especially advantageous to both Iacocca and Zimmerman, by a few years the youngest among the fifty then going through the system. Both had been unusually young as college graduates, Lee with a master's degree at twenty-one, and Zimmerman with his bachelor's at twenty.

"We had it made," Zimmerman says. "For young kids who had a lot of book learning but didn't know beans about automobiles, it was a tremendous opportunity. A superb education in the practical side of building automobiles, why cars are what they are, and what they should be. And Lee was running away from the rest of us."

With Zimmie planning to leave when his training time was exhausted, Lee met a man destined to be another close friend, one who would take over where

Zimmerman left off in keeping Lee alive and vibrant in what is normally a dull, unexciting routine.

Al Henderson, a Ford man who knew Lee, was making a trip to Chicago for the 1947 All Star baseball game with Bill Winn, a young promotion man who did not work for Ford. Knowing Lee's love of sports, Henderson decided to stop in Ann Arbor and invite him to join them. Lee needed no second invitation.

The threesome drove to the Windy City and saw the American League trounce the National, 2-1. After the game Henderson had some personal business to take care of. Lee and Bill Winn took off together to look over America's second-largest city.

They did the Chicago scene, laughing, joking, getting acquainted. They passed Soldier Field, visited the Field Museum of Natural History and the Shedd Aquarium. The more they walked and talked, the more impressed Lee became with Bill Winn, who was in sales promotion. Winn was a gentle individual, soft-spoken, and with a puckish charm. He was nowhere near as tall, a young man of quiet reserve like Lee, but with a roguish wit.

On Michigan Avenue they suddenly decided to go shopping, to find hats as gifts for their girlfriends. They went from store to store, looking, comparing, kidding. Finally each made a purchase.

"We made quite a picture," Bill Winn says, "with people staring at us, two guys walking by carrying two pink hatboxes."

The weekend in Chicago was the beginning of a

lasting friendship. With two of his apartment mates moving on at Ford, Lee was looking for a new apartment, as was Bill, so they joined forces. Remaining together through the balance of Lee's training period helped complete what Zimmerman had begun, the emergence of Lee Iacocca as a resolute, self-reliant young man.

Frank Zimmerman, who had started his trainee period ten months before Lee's arrival, completed his eighteen-month course in November, 1946. He wanted to be nearer his Connecticut home and headed east, applying for a job in Ford's New York district. Short and trim, even younger looking than his twenty-one years, he had to talk the district manager into assigning him to truck sales.

Lee, whose training period would not end before January, 1948, itched to get his career in high gear. He had seen the group called the "Quiz Kids" come into the training center, punch the same time clock he had punched—while making much more money than his $185 a month—and move out of training in a matter of weeks. They were out of the army and few, if any, had a better education than he.

He had an advantage over them in the time he already had spent learning the reality of making automobiles, something the Quiz Kids really could not have absorbed in their short training periods. To remain until August and cover every single facet of the manufacturing business seemed a waste of time.

Lee talked the matter over with his superiors and was able to convince them that with a master's degree he hardly needed the full eighteen-month indoctrination. They agreed and cut his training period to one year. In August, 1947, his trainee days were over.

He was now face to face with his future in the Ford Motor Company. But what turn should it take? In what area could he make the most meaningful contributions to the company and, at the same time, help himself achieve his goal at Ford?

One possibility was engineering, which had been his major, but as far as he could see, few engineers made it to the top of the industry. Styling was another course, but it had its limitations, too. There also were finance, product development and planning, sales and marketing, and a half-dozen or so other areas for which he felt himself suited.

The question was: "Where do I go from here?"

CHAPTER 2

Iacocca decided that his best prospects for progress at the Ford Motor Company lay in sales and marketing. The number of motor vehicles registered in the United States was nearing the 47-million mark in 1947, a leap of 15 million since 1940. More than 10 million of this increase was in passenger cars.

Phenomenal changes were also taking place in American highways. Fast, smooth freeways and toll roads had begun to crisscross the continent. It was being said that one could drive from New York to Los Angeles someday soon in three days or less. A "See America First" spirit, already taking hold, indicated that automobile sales would skyrocket year by year.

In addition the potential for corporate profits in the automobile industry had been increased substantially when a Republican-dominated Congress passed, over President Truman's veto, the Taft-Hartley bill, which abolished some of the restrictions on management imposed by the Democratic administration of Franklin Roosevelt and added several restraints on labor unions. Business in general, and the automobile industry in particular, should enjoy a productive shot in the arm.

Frank Zimmerman was already settled in the truck sales department in Ford's New York district office at Edgewater, New Jersey, on the Hudson River just north of Manhattan. Zimmerman suggested that Lee follow the same course. Anxious to get back east and closer to home, Iacocca headed for Edgewater to see the district manager.

When he arrived, he found the manager away, and was interviewed by two assistants. One assistant manager, as Lee tells it, "never put down the *Wall Street Journal*, he never saw me," and the other said "If you're a college graduate, number one, and from the home office, number two, get the hell out and go back to Detroit."

Lee was taken aback somewhat by such cavalier treatment, but waited and finally was interviewed by the district manager. Lee was with him for some while, answered the questions asked, and waited for the verdict.

"Well, Iacocca," the manager said, "I'm impressed with what I hear, but my advice to you is that you'll never make it in sales. I think you ought to try to get into engineering."

The irony of the situation is that the manager told Iacocca, who would be one of the greatest marketing geniuses since Phineas T. Barnum, that he couldn't cut the mustard.

Whether or not the assistants were merely playing a joke on a rookie or the manager did not know what he was talking about, Lee was crushed momentarily. The reaction was anything but what he expected, but it was enough to make him consider—if only for a moment—resigning from the Ford Motor Company. Imbued from his earliest days by his father's often-repeated "You never give up. You *never* quit!" Lee decided to try again.

This time he approached Charles Beacham, sales manager of the Ford Eastern regional office at Chester, Pennsylvania, a small city near Philadelphia. Beacham, who was very likely the most astute sales manager in the Ford empire, and who was to achieve a vice-presidency in the near future, saw in young Iacocca a latent driving force and a determination to make it whatever the cost in physical energy—qualities he demanded in the men who worked for him.

Lee was able to go home to Allentown for a two-week visit with his family before he started at Chester. Nick Iacocca was overjoyed at having his son to himself for fourteen days, proudly showing him off to friends, relatives, and any strangers they happened to meet.

When Lee reported at Chester, his assignment was that of field manager, a job considered by those who held it "the lowest form of life in sales," despite the title. It involved visiting different dealers in a particular zone—for Lee it was southeastern Pennsylvania—and doing everything possible to stimulate sales by influencing dealers to promote and advertise.

"Low-life" assignment or not, Chester was the ideal starting point for Lee Iacocca's first job. It not only was near enough to Allentown to permit spending every weekend at home, it also put him in the hands of a mentor who was tailor-made to develop his innate talents.

The rebuff and discourtesy he had suffered at the New York office were the best bad luck of his life. Beacham, a hard-driving, ply-the-hammer man in the mold of Nick Iacocca, was just what Lee needed. Beacham was tough and demanding as well as understanding and fair.

Gar Laux, who also worked for him, paints a clear picture of the man in action. "One day Mr. Beacham called me into his office and took me apart," he recalled. "It got to the point where I said 'Mr. Beacham, I don't have to take this from you or anybody else.' I turned and walked to the door, and just as I got to the door, Beacham said, 'Come back here. Damn it, if I didn't think you had anything worthwhile, I wouldn't waste my damn time with you. Now get the hell out of here and do your job.' Beacham was the kind of man who was always on your tail to make you do better, *if* you can do better. If you can't, you don't belong."

Exposed as he was day-in and day-out to a Charley Beacham, and determined to do the best he could as soon as he could, Lee not only came out of his shell but also absorbed what Ford people have called "Beachamism"—an intuitive knowledge that "you've got to move fast to catch the weasel asleep."

Gar Laux carries Charley's influence on Iacocca a step further. "Between them Lee's dad and Mr. Beacham did a helluva job with Lee. But I'll tell you, they had a helluva lot of guy to do something with."

Lee's exposure to the many dealers, sales managers, and other dealership personnel in his assigned territory, with their divergent personalities and educational levels, sparked his inherent talent for communication. That valuable experience, coupled with the tough but reasonable prodding of Charley Beacham, early on proved Iacocca to be a comer who bore watching—a "remarkable young man," in Beacham's words.

One of Lee's coworkers at Chester was a former newspaper editor named Jay Dugan. Dugan, who left Ford soon after Iacocca's arrival to open his own ad agency in the Philadelphia area, helped implement many of Iacocca's future promotions. He, too, was thoroughly impressed with the newcomer to Chester.

"In the few months I was at Chester after Lee's appointment," Dugan says, "I found him to be very forthright, candid, and straight-on in his approach to dealers. He was disarming in his candor when talking to his dealers, or anybody. He could tell you something you might not want to hear, but he could tell it in such a way that you accepted it as something constructive, which it was, he was that sharp."

In two months Beacham promoted Iacocca into the truck sales department, with a territory spreading into southern New Jersey and Delaware. After a few meetings with truck salesmen Lee saw a need for putting into print the important do's and don't's for successful truck merchandising and selling. He took it upon himself, with some editing help from Jay Dugan, to write *Hiring and Training Truck Salesmen*, a handbook for use by dealers and their sales managers.

Each discussion he had with dealership executives, each meeting he conducted for truck salesmen and sales managers, further sharpened his speaking skills. At training meetings he was a spellbinder, with a sharp, sometimes caustic wit. His sphere of action broadened to include the South Atlantic states.

Typical of his ability to take advantage of any situation was his opening gambit at a truck sales meeting he conducted in Atlanta, Georgia. He called the meeting to order and wrote his name LEE IACOCCA in large letters on a blackboard. As if a light had been turned on in his brain, he turned suddenly and erased his last name.

"Now that's better," he said, pointing at the blackboard where only the word LEE remained. "That's a name that really means something down in this country."

It was Iacocca at his best. Throughout that meeting, and in all meetings he conducted in the South, this little touch held attention and produced results.

Whether in the Chester office or on the road, Iacocca took few breaks. He worked long hours, studied the automobile business, particularly sales and marketing techniques, nonstop. Now and again he and his friend Jay Dugan, whose ad agency was now established in nearby Jenkintown, would sit late into the night devising gimmicks that would increase automobile sales.

One afternoon in late spring of 1948, about three months after he started working for Charley Beacham, Lee Iacocca was in a hallway at the Chester office talking to a coworker in truck leasing, when an extraordinarily pretty redhead was passing through a corridor straight ahead.

"Now there's somebody you should check on," Iacocca's companion said.

The young lady was Mary McCleary, a receptionist at the Ford assembly plant in Chester. She was heading for the medical dispensary located in the same building as Lee's office, a victim of too much exposure to a sun lamp. She did not see Lee, but he was immediately impressed.

About a month later, on June 9, the Ford Motor Company introduced its new 1949 models to the Philadelphia district in a gala reception at the elegant Bellevue Stratford Hotel. All Ford employees in the area were invited to attend the company party marking the new car introduction.

After a motion picture preview of the new cars, everyone converged on the Bellevue Stratford cocktail lounge. On entering, Mary McCleary was intercepted by a married man with a reputation bordering on the lecherous. One of the Chester secretaries, who was seated at a table that included Lee Iacocca, saw the man take Mary's arm. She quickly had her rescued, brought to the table, and introduced to Lee.

As he stood to acknowledge the introduction, one he had hoped for since she was pointed out in the Chester office hallway, Mary's first impression was "Oh, my! He's as skinny as a beanpole!" Iacocca was so tall and so thin, weighing, she says, "maybe a hundred and eighteen pounds soaking wet. And very shy."

But Lee was not too shy to show his interest by asking to take Mary McCleary home that evening. They began to date, but irregularly. Lee was tied up with his work most of the week, and on weekends he drove back to Allentown to see his father, mother, and sister. The weekend trips began with his first week at Chester, months before he met Mary, and it was a routine he did not break.

"Must you go to Allentown?" became a regular Friday-afternoon plea.

Mary wanted to visit friends with Lee, have dinner occasionally, go to the theater or even sports events in Philadelphia, since Lee was such an avid sports fan. Finally, eager to spend time with the man she had come to love, she agreed to accompany him on a few trips home.

Mary got on well with the Iacocca family. She quickly grew to love Nick, Antoinette, and Delma, and they her, but even so the weekends at Allentown were often depressing. It seemed that the only time she had alone with Lee was on the drive there and back. So when the question of marriage came up, as it often did, Mary was uneasy. She would not say yes even though she wanted to. Lee, completely taken by Mary's good sense and waiflike charm, continued to ask.

He also continued to work hard, making himself more valuable by the day to Charley Beacham and to the Ford Motor Company. Suddenly, in the early 1950s a slowdown in sales hit the Ford Division. In 1950 total Ford new-car registrations in the United States numbered 1.5 million, but they dropped to under 1.25 in 1951 and plummeted below the million mark in 1952.

The trauma in these numbers, so far as Ford headquarters in Dearborn was concerned, was not so much in the loss of sales. The economy had been sluggish, and Chevrolet, the Ford Division's most formidable competition, had suffered proportionately. The real agony lay in the fact that when sales for both leaped back over the million mark in 1953, the Ford Division, which had gained on Chevy to the tune of 134,000 between 1950 and 1952, fell back some 106,000 in registered sales.

For the executives at Ford Division headquarters in Dearborn losing ground after coming within a hair of topping Chevy was the real cause for alarm. They ordered an austerity program across the board. The Chester office was forced to cut back on personnel. Lee did not lose his job, but he was dropped a notch in grade.

Taking that one step back on the promotion ladder just as he began moving ahead fast was a crushing blow. For a short time he began to have doubts about his future at Ford, but the realist in Iacocca prevailed.

After all he was still with the company he had longed to work for since his teens, and a setback wasn't the end, but something that could be turned into a plus if he applied himself. This was Nick Iacocca's philosophy filtering through Lee's brain. As his father did after the Crash of '29, Lee went after his job with intensified effort.

The success of his talks to dealer groups had instilled an intrepid and spirited self-confidence and had given him the on-the-stump charisma of a spell-binding preacher. What he said made sense and stimulated sales managers and salesmen to increase closings on car deals. His hard work paid off. Within six months he was restored to the grade he held before the rollback. Beacham's faith in the marketing neophyte he had hired had been more than justified. In another six months Lee Iacocca was named assistant sales manager of the Philadelphia district.

Meanwhile the romance between Lee and Mary McCleary had run hot and cold into its seventh year. Things had not changed for Mary as Lee continued his weekend drives to Allentown, failing to do so only once in about six months.

When the winter winds ease up and the grass begins to green, the automobile industry traditionally begins planting the seeds of promotion for the oncoming model year. On the national level corporate sales and marketing executives work in concert with their major advertising agencies. Their aim is a broad-scale concept to position the virtues of their four-wheel offerings more dramatically than the competition.

On more local levels, particularly district offices, the emphasis is on support for the national effort, based on observations that stress sales in tune with the buyers of the immediate area. At the Chester office Lee Iacocca buried himself in finding the sales stimulus that would best serve the Philadelphia district in moving the upcoming 1956 models. Mary saw even less of Lee than usual as he thought of and discarded idea after idea.

He spent days patiently searching for the surest way to thaw public resistance to the purchase of new cars. He was born in the area, knew its people—the German, Italian, and Irish immigrants and their first-generation offspring. He talked the matter over with his friend, Jay Dugan.

What, he wondered, could influence car buyers whose paychecks had to cover rent, food, and clothing, in addition to car payments? Lee took pencil in hand and began doodling figures. He analyzed the buyers in his area and their reticence in saddling themselves with car payments.

The base for the ideal sales stimulus was right there. The car payment. People who needed or wanted a new car were less likely to worry about the sticker price—the total they had to pay—as long as they knew they could afford the monthly installments.

"That is the genius of Iacocca," Jay Dugan insists. "The capacity to visualize a need, to prepare a plan and implement that plan to meet the need long before anybody else sees there is a need for it."

The idea proposed by Iacocca, commonplace today, had marketing men throughout the industry shaking their heads. It was so simple, so obvious—why hadn't they thought of it?

The heart and guts of the Iacocca promotion was its theme: "56 for 56." People could buy a brand-new 1956 Ford for $56 a month after a moderate down payment. Only $56 a month? It was peanuts for the average working man.

The idea, revolutionary in its day, took hold in the Philadelphia district like a brushfire. Dealers loved it. The "56 for 56" really sold cars. But Lee was not content to rest with the concept alone. To milk every possible sale it had to be merchandised and given maximum impact and visibility. Just as visibility makes a man better known by selling him to his superiors, putting a good idea squarely in the public's eye would generate interest and, in turn, generate sales.

He talked over merchandising ideas with Jay Dugan, and they came up with a gimmick they called "wujatak"—a play on the phrase "would-you-take." On streets and on parking lots throughout the district cards attractively designed by the Jay Dugan Agency were placed on automobiles by Ford salesmen. The card asked the car owner "wujatak" a specified number of dollars, based on the value of the particular automobile, "for your car on a new 1956 Ford."

Attached to the wujatak was a small bag of potato chips bearing the words "The chips are down. We're selling cars for $56 a month" and the name and address of the Ford dealer in the specific sector.

Potato chips were hard to come by in the Philadelphia area for some time. Jay Dugan had cornered the market as he bought trailerload after trailerload to give Lee's promotion a rousing and stimulating sendoff.

"You should have seen us," Dugan laughs, "me, my wife and sons, sitting in our kitchen night after night stapling wujataks to potato chip bags."

The slogan "56 for 56" proved to be a blockbuster, one of the most innovative and successful promotions in the history of automobile sales. The 139 dealers in the Ford Philadelphia district could not keep up with demand. Chester led the nation in Ford sales. Lee Iacocca's name was heralded at Ford's Dearborn headquarters as well as at Chester.

Robert S. McNamara, then vice-president in charge of the Ford Division, took Lee's program and made it a nationwide campaign for 1956 Ford cars. It produced extra sales approaching 75,000.

The gratification and pleasure Lee enjoyed as his "56 for 56" swept the country was not without pain, partly caused by his inability to get Mary McCleary's consent to marry him. His courtship took a turn for the worse in the spring of 1956.

On one of the rare weekends he did not drive back to Allentown, he and Mary joined a group of married couples on a trip to the Poconos. Mary, perhaps envious of the way the marrieds enjoyed the outing, was distressed by the thought that such wished-for happiness was denied her. Lee, whom she could not stop loving, was wedded to his parents and his job. When Lee dropped her at her home after the minivacation, they decided they would not see each other again.

The morning after their return Mary came down with a high fever. She called her office to report being sick. Throughout the day she had an insatiable thirst. She drank water, Pepsi, Seven-Up, any liquid available. Nothing helped. She became weaker as the day went on. When her brother came home, Mary's mother insisted he take the girl to the hospital immediately.

Lee himself had spent an apprehensive day in his Chester office, boggled in mind, saddened by the decision made the night before. He did not want to lose the one girl in his world. At five o'clock he phoned Mary's home and learned from her father that she was in the hospital. Lee wasted no time in getting there.

Mary's illness had been diagnosed as a severe case of pneumonia. Throughout her stay in the hospital Lee was there every possible moment. The hours he spent at her bedside made him more determined. For him there was no one but Mary McCleary. And Mary, seeing his concern, loved him more dearly. Yet . . .

After Mary came home from the hospital, her mother sat and talked to her at length. The mental anguish her daughter was suffering had to end. While she had vowed earlier not to interfere, she believed now was the time to say what she felt.

She told Mary how much she loved and respected Lee Iacocca, that the love Lee had for his father was a good thing, not parental dominance, because Lee had proved himself a strong man in his own right. Besides, she pointed out, a man who had such high regard for his parents made the best kind of husband.

Lee and Mary were engaged on Mother's Day and began their plans for a September wedding.

Lee arrived at his office the next day, buoyed up and exultant. After calling Nick to give him the news, he went at his job with a vengeance. The demotion that had dashed his hopes a couple of years back had taught him that one should nave no illusions about instant progress, that perseverance could turn a seeming failure into a conquest. Getting Mary back was proof enough.

In July came a sweet yet saddening surprise. Charley Beacham, who was now at Ford Division headquarters, notified Lee to pack his bags and move from the banks of the Delaware River to the shores of the Potomac. He had been promoted to manage the Washington district office.

It was the development he needed to get back on track toward his goal, a giant step toward that vice-presidency he aimed for. Yet, with the wedding almost two and a half months in the offing, it also meant seeing less of Mary. Their only chance to be together would be on weekends or at such times as Mary could come to Washington or his work take him back to Chester.

Hard work provided the healing balm for Lee's

temporary separations from Mary. There were problems in Washington, and thinking about possible solutions kept his mind occupied. It was his first full-charge management position, and Lee made the most of it, putting the Washington office on a crash status for improved productivity. His growing reputation as a marketing expert was not overlooked.

On the Wednesday before his wedding day he began a short leave of absence, arriving in Chester that evening. Thursday morning he and Mary went to the courthouse for their marriage license, after which Lee took Mary home and then paid a visit to the Chester office. He was surprised to find Charley Beacham waiting for him.

"Pick up your paycheck and forget about Washington," Beacham told Lee. "When you come back after your wedding, you'll be coming to Dearborn. You're my new truck marketing manager."

Lee was speechless. Too much was happening too fast. Or was it? In less than four weeks he would be thirty-two, which left him a bare three years to hit the target he had predicted while at Lehigh.

"But don't tell Mary until after the wedding," Beacham added. "She's got enough on her mind right now."

Lee kept the good news secret from Mary, but, as he had with every promotion and award he had ever received, he could not wait to tell his father. It was a lengthy phone call of repeated congratulations. Nick, naturally, was overjoyed. His unequivocal pride in his son's future, boasted of for years as a sure thing, was now substantiated. Certainly almost everyone in Allentown became aware of Lee's good fortune before Mary.

September 29, 1956, Mary K. McCleary and Lido Anthony Iacocca were married by Father Michael McNicholas in Chester's St. Robert Catholic Church. At the reception no man, other than Lee himself, was happier or danced more than Nick Iacocca.

Because of Lee's promotion the honeymoon was necessarily brief. The couple came back to Chester, where Mary remained with her mother. Lee went on to Dearborn, eager to start his new assignment and to search for a house.

Charles Beacham had been significantly responsible for the transformation, so he was not surprised at the difference between the Lee Iacocca who had returned his Chester office nine years earlier and the well-tailored, confident Iacocca who reported to his office at Ford Division in October, 1956. Beacham was sure that this young man who had proved himself a wunderkind in the marketing of automobiles, an art vital to Ford at that time, was just the one to bring Ford sales back to respectability.

The Ford Motor Company had closed out 1956 with a market share 22.3 percent below that of General Motors and not quite 13 percent above Chrysler's share of the American market. The company badly needed a stimulating shot in its selling arm.

It was the kind of challenge Iacocca had hoped for. Only by doing the thorough job he had been doing— thus making himself visible—could he possibly come close to his pledge of a vice-presidency by his thirty-fifth birthday.

Those who knew of his aspiration called it an illusion, a grasping at shadows. An objective look at the situation made it an improbable, even impossible dream.

"A lot of us snickered behind his back," said one of his contemporaries. "He was such a gung-ho guy on the job, and he let you know it with his sharp duds and big cigar. What's his hurry, we said. As the new kid on the block, he had a lot of bodies to leapfrog. And no way could he shortstop any of the Whiz Kids."

"Whiz Kids" was a more dignified name for the group originally called the Quiz Kids, the same intellectuals who were privileged with brief indoctrination while Lee spent a full year as trainee. Lee was familiar with the achievements of a few, particularly Robert McNamara, now his top boss as vice-president of Ford and general manager of Ford Division. McNamara, along with Arjay Miller, Ed Lundy, Ben Mills, Francis Reith, and James Wright were indeed a formidable group.

Nothing could be gained by worrying about anyone else. The realities be damned—what he had to do was charge ahead. His nature thrived on seemingly irrational challenges. His dream might be called a fantasy, but even fantasies had a way of becoming fact. It counted for something that he had devotedly loved the Ford Motor Company as far back as when he sat in Model T's in his father's U-Drive-It. He had idolized the first Henry Ford for accomplishing what he had without an education and for having the courage to go ahead and do what he wanted. That devil-take-the-hindmost spirit of old Henry appealed to Iacocca.

He knew it would not be easy to reach his goal, which made it all the more exciting—as did the existing situation at Ford, with its up-one-year-and-down-the-next history.

During the first two decades of the twentieth century the Ford name had been synonymous with automobile. Ford was the royal family of the industry. In many ways the chronology of the company's activities over a half-century was a blend of genius and idiocy.

CHAPTER 3

People on seven continents know that the Ford Motor Company was given birth by Henry Ford. Strong parallels exist in the characters of Henry, a product of the nineteenth century, and the twentieth-century Iacocca, but they also had dissimilarities, such as those that existed between Iacocca and Henry Ford II.

Henry the first, no blueblood, although he came to see himself as the equivalent, began with only an idea and no money. From a humble start he built one of the world's best known organizations. Yet he all but destroyed the company through bad judgment and his increasingly obstreperous nature.

Henry Ford was born July 30, 1863, the eldest son of William Ford, who farmed a few acres just west of the city of Detroit. Because young Henry detested farming and was interested only in things mechanical, his father and two brothers, John and William, shared a dislike for Henry that verged on hatred as the years passed. Henry had as little regard for his father and brothers.

"John and William are all right," Henry's father once declared. "But I'm worried about Henry. I don't know what will become of him."

What became of Henry is history. He made himself the wealthy eccentric who changed the world's way of life by putting it on wheels. A man with the courage of his convictions and rare foresight, he was nonetheless the same Henry who also blundered and made almost as many turns down the wrong road as up the right.

He frequently refused sound advice. Too often he put his trust where it was not warranted, which proved to be his Achilles heel.

Henry's lone stabilizing influence, the one person whose judgment could override his own, was common-sensed Clara Bryant, the tiny, chestnut-haired girl he met at a square dance and married when he was twenty-eight. From the start of their courtship Clara, whom he always called "Mother," was his heart, mind, and often his voice. Characteristically, he did not marry Clara until she assured him that she, unlike his father and brothers, understood and appreciated his obsession with mechanics.

Henry Ford made the automobile an affordable means of transportation rather than a plaything of the wealthy, but he was not its inventor. Nor was he the originator or first builder of the internal combustion engine or the first to drive a "horseless carriage."

In April, 1866, two Germans, Nikolas Otto and Eugen Langen, were granted a patent for a gasoline-powered engine. Gottlieb Daimler and Karl Benz, also Germans, produced efficient engines as early as 1885. And in the United States, Charles Duryea, chugged through the streets of Springfield, Massachusetts, in his self-built gas-buggy on September 22, 1893.

Henry Ford was working for the Edison Illuminating Company in Detroit in 1893 when he was inspired by an article in the *American Machinist*, which described how to construct a gasoline engine. Henry built his machine in the basement of his home from an old piece of gas pipe and bits of scrap iron.

On Christmas Eve, 1893, about two months after his son Edsel was born, Henry carried his device upstairs to the kitchen. He connected a wire from the contrivance to an electric light to create an ignition. He started the engine with Clara carefully squeezing drops of gasoline into the pipe.

Henry worked in a small shed behind his home for another two and one-half years, refining his engine and building a four-wheeled cycle-type body. Early on the morning of June 4, 1896, he installed the engine in the makeshift body.

A happy Henry started the engine and prepared to mount the box that served as the quadracycle's only seat. Though it was after three in the morning, Clara could not keep him from taking the loud, clattering vehicle for a test drive. Henry started up to the seat and suddenly realized that his creation was far too big to pass through the shed's single door. Yet, galvanized by his inner excitement, Henry was not to be deprived of his ride. He grabbed an ax and demolished the front wall of the outbuilding.

Henry's quadracycle was a primitive contraption, boxy in appearance and without brakes. It had no reverse gear. Its deficiencies mattered little to Henry as he bounced through the rough Detroit streets, imagining himself building hundreds of cars at prices so low any working man could afford one.

But Henry had quit his job at Edison to work full-time on his quadracycle, and building cars would take money. He needed cash support, investors who had faith in him and in his dream.

His first patron was William Murphy, a Detroit lumber baron. Murphy believed in profits. Henry enjoyed tinkering with his "toy" rather than going into immediate production. The Detroit Automobile Company established by Murphy lost $100,000 in its first year, and Murphy went one way, Henry another.

Other investors came and went. Finally Murphy, who had not lost faith in Henry Ford's contraption, put together another group of investors, with Henry as chief engineer holding 1,000 shares of stock in the company. To keep Ford in line Murphy and his group hired Henry Leland, a highly respected engineer, to keep Henry enthusiastic about building cars.

Henry resented the intrusion. He ignored Leland and went along dreaming and not producing. He was, and would remain through his lifetime, a recalcitrant, iron-willed autocrat. "I'll do it my way or not at all."

It was too much for the Murphy investors, who bought Henry's shares for $9.00 each and then dissolved the Detroit Automobile Company. With Henry Leland as the new head, an organization was established as the Cadillac Motor Company. Henry's refusal to accept Leland was to cost the future Ford Motor Company. He not only lost the help of one of the most brilliant automobile minds the industry would know but would, in a few years, spend $8 million in Ford money to take over the Lincoln Motor Company eventually established by Leland.

The world mistakenly sees Henry Ford as an engineer with incomparable foresight, an organizational genius who built a worldwide industrial giant. Henry undeniably knew engines, and he did have the foresight to recognize a need for inexpensive automobiles. It was this latter fact which brought him his fame as well as his fortune. Despite his engineering know-how he was perhaps the most disorganized carmaker in automobile history.

Henry Ford could build engines, but his talents ended there. Someone else was needed to build the body and machine parts to precise specifications. This need brought about another of the freakish situations in which the Ford Motor Company would become involved.

John and Horace Dodge, hell-raising, heavy-drinking brothers who had come from Canada to open a machine shop in Detroit, were producing parts for Oldsmobile. They were approached by Alexander Malcomson, a coal merchant who delivered fuel for

77

the Ford fireplace, and became Henry's new financial backer. Malcomson asked the Dodge Brothers to provide Ford Motor with 650 full chassis a year at $250 each. They hesitated but finally agreed to leave Oldsmobile when Malcomson sweetened the pot with fifty shares of Ford stock for each brother.

With the Dodge brothers in the fold, the Ford Motor Company became a going concern. Within thirty-seven days the first Ford car, a two-cylinder dubbed the Model A, was sold for $850. By October 1 the fledgling company had delivered 195 Model A cars to show a profit of approximately $37,000 and orders began to pour in.

In the spring of 1903, Malcomson, excited by the potential, established a partnership that gave Henry his head and promised no interference. James Couzens, Malcomson's hot-tempered bookkeeper, would manage the Malcomson interests in a new company named after Henry.

The Ford Motor Company was established on June 16, 1903, capitalized at $150,000, with Henry Ford as vice-president and chief engineer. More than one-third of the original stock sold was held by John Gray, a Detroit banker, who was named president. With the filing of the corporate papers the Ford legend was born. The Ford name was on the way to international fame.

Henry, however, soon found Malcomson and other board members of the company bearing his name as difficult to please as William Murphy. Other automobile makers were building big cars, and the Ford directors soon understood that the bigger the car produced, the higher the selling price and the larger the profit margin. This did not fit Henry's concept. He wanted to build low-cost small cars that the average man could buy. He argued that building more and selling for less would balance out profits in the long run. The board would not agree.

Henry, realizing that he was at the mercy of the board, quietly began buying up stock. By October, 1906, he owned 58¹/₂ percent of all Ford stock and took over as president. He could now do what *he* wanted without question. The only man among the Malcomson group he retained was James Couzens, who later made millions thanks to Ford, yet subsequently, as a member of the United States Senate, fought Henry Ford at every turn.

Within one year, remembering the hard farm work he had hated, Ford introduced a mechanized tractor to ease the farmer's workload. Before the turn of the another calendar year, Detroit set eyes on his most memorable contribution to the world, a car people began writing about, singing about, and joking about.

It was Henry Ford's Model T, his fabulous "tin lizzie," the first production-built automobile model with the steering wheel on the left. Its cost was $850. Lizzie made her bow on October 1, 1908, Henry telling buyers, with a twinkle in his eyes, that they could have her "in any color they wanted as long as it was black."

The Model T sold well from the start, even though

the rest of the infant auto industry laughed at it and downgraded Lizzie behind Henry's back. They called it no more than a pile of sheet metal strung together with baling wire. But Henry had the last laugh.

He entered his Model T in a New York-to-Seattle endurance race open to all car-makers, giving its critics a field day. No way, they said, could this plain, ugly-structured horseless carriage make it from New York to New Jersey, much less across the continent.

Lizzie proved equal to the task. Twenty-two days after the competition got under way on June 1, 1909, she had conquered rutted dirt and mud-filled roads from the Atlantic to the Pacific, arriving in Seattle far in front of the few others able to withstand the rigors of the still primitive American roads. She had proved herself a durable, versatile automobile that people could depend on.

The success story of the tin lizzie is the success story of Henry Ford, a story too well known to bear repetition. In Henry's Highland Park Plant in 1910, 21,000 Model T's rolled off the newly designed production assembly line, where cars could be put together in minutes instead of days. Called the greatest of all engineering achievements, Henry's new line, which could assemble a complete car in ninety-three minutes, had cost more than $7 million. By 1912 the line was creating some 200,000 cars a year, and romanticists began calling it the eighth wonder of the world.

Henry Ford tossed another bombshell into the automobile industry on January 5, 1914, by announcing a $5 daily wage for eight hours work, earnings that more than doubled the industry scale of $2.34 for a nine-hour day. On January 6 10,000 laborers, including hundreds from General Motors, stormed the Ford plants for jobs.

Henry's only son, Edsel, married Eleanor Lowthian Clay on November 1, 1916. As a wedding gift Edsel was brought into the Ford Motor Company as secretary. Bright, intelligent, and already a carwise young man at twenty-two, Edsel was happy for the opportunity. His pleasure was short-lived, however. He had a title but no authority. What say-so Henry did not keep for himself he gave to Danish-born Charley Sorenson, his right-hand man. It was the start of a lifelong heartbreak for young Edsel, whose automotive expertise would never be acknowledged by his father.

It was also the forerunner of a series of other blunders by Henry Ford, almost all in the nature of disastrous ego trips.

One was his leasing a ship named *Oscar II* and sailing with a group of pacifists across the Atlantic to convince the Kaiser to stop World War I. The well-intentioned peace effort failed, and Henry never fully recovered from the fiasco.

On September 4, 1917, Edsel's first son, named Henry II for his grandfather, was born. Not long after that the Ford family was subjected to a trauma that plagues the wealthy. A man named Jacob Yellin threatened to kidnap Edsel in an extortion attempt. Though the man was quickly arrested and sent to prison, Henry, with the added worry of a new grandson, decided special security was needed, a bodyguard.

His choice was another horrendous mistake, one destined to bring the wrath of the workingman down on his family and the company. He hired Harry Herbert Bennett, ex-boxer, ex-navy man, a bully, and a trigger-tempered opportunist who quickly made himself indispensable to the "boss."

Bennett became untouchable at Ford, exempt from any responsibility and accountable only to the elder Henry, hired to serve as Henry's eyes and ears as to what went on within the company as well as to provide protection for the family.

Edsel, whose eagerness to work with his father in the company preempted his desire for a college education, continued to be ignored by his father, but persistence eventually brought him some responsibility. Henry finally permitted Edsel to hire Ernest Kanzler, his brother-in-law and friend, as treasurer. Edsel, feeling the company needed experienced men, also suggested hiring a tried and capable automobile man, William S. Knudsen, a thoroughly professional automobile executive with a genius for organization, a quality lacking in the Ford structure. Knudsen was hired.

Henry was pleased at what he perceived as his son's interest in the welfare of the company, but he was not convinced that Edsel had what it took to run the company once he was gone. He called in Charley Sorenson, telling him to "make a man out of Edsel."

Henry believed that Sorenson was ideal to put "guts and grit" into mild-mannered Edsel.

"Edsel's too soft," was Henry's appraisal of his only son and heir.

Henry Ford—interestingly—displayed the same toughness toward his son Edsel that Nicola Iacocca showed his Lido, but the important healing salve was lacking. The open, honest, and vital love and pride that Nicola always had for Lee was denied Edsel.

The Model T meanwhile had sent Henry's ego sky-high, transforming the introverted farmboy into a man in the world's spotlight. The name Ford, thanks to the Lizzie, had become a synonym for automobile. The Model T was busy doing what it was born to do, on the streets of Killarney, Glasgow, and Prague as well as on Broadway, State Street, or the backroads of Iowa and Kansas.

Henry Ford's spirit thrived on the international reputation brought him by the Model T. He came to believe that he could do anything, even run the United States government if need be, a fantasy given impetus by President Woodrow Wilson.

When World War I ended in 1918, Wilson was desperately trying to get congressional approval for American participation in the League of Nations. He invited Ford to the White House. Needing every possible Democratic vote to offset the isolationist bloc in the Republican Party, he told Henry, nominally a Republican, "You are the only man in Michigan who can be elected." Wilson knew how to appeal to Henry, who still felt the sting of ridicule from the Peace Ship failure. He added: "You can help bring about the peace you so much desire."

Henry went home to think it over. He had obviously made up his mind to accept when on January 1, 1919, he resigned as president of the Ford Motor Company and named Edsel to succeed him. It was a serious mistake, not because Edsel could not handle the responsibility, but because Ford assigned Henry Bennett to manage things. Edsel never had the authority that should have gone with the office.

Throughout the industry the paraphrased cliché became "Edsel proposes, but Bennett disposes." Everyone seemed to know. It was not Edsel, but Harry Bennett who actually piloted the ship.

During Edsel's first year as president Charley Sorenson proved to be as great a worry to him as Bennett. Charley was disappointed at losing the presidency and tried to undercut Bill Knudsen, who, with Edsel and Kanzler, was building a smoothly operating organization. Edsel and Kanzler soon realized what was going on and developed a plan to save the capable Knudsen for the Ford Motor Company.

To get Knudsen away from Sorenson's snooping and back-biting, Edsel planned to name Knudsen as manager of Ford's growing English subsidiary. Edsel intended to approach his father without Sorenson's or Bennett's knowledge.

The wily Sorenson had an ace in the hole: Henry's private secretary, Ernest Liebold, a Sorenson-Bennett stooge. When Liebold heard why Edsel wanted to see Henry, he put him off for a day to let Sorenson in on the planned reassignment.

Sorenson scurried to Henry's Fair Lane home. He, not Knudsen, Sorenson told Henry, deserved to head the British operation, if only on the basis of seniority. Henry, who always admired Sorenson's toughness and audacity, seldom denied him anything. He not only overruled Edsel's decision but also made another of his many tactical errors that kept Ford Motor Company foundering. He ordered Sorenson to fire Bill Knudsen.

To Henry's chagrin Knudsen went on to become one of the giants of the industry at General Motors, especially in his role as vice-president in charge of its Chevrolet Division. Before Knudsen took over Chevrolet, it had been so thoroughly smothered by Ford in the marketplace that GM seriously considered eliminating Chevy from the GM line.

In less than three years Knudsen had Chevrolet on the move. Within seven years he brought so much strength back into the division that Chevy sailed past Ford to become the best-selling car in the United States. Having listened to the toadying Sorenson rather than his own son, Henry gave his competition an edge it would never relinquish. Henry was ruining his business.

He seemed not to care. President Wilson's words had had a telling effort on his already inflated ego, and he was set to run for the U.S. Senate. He accepted the Democratic nomination to battle Truman H. Newberry, who had served as secretary of war in Theodore Roosevelt's cabinet.

It was a challenge without confrontation. Henry considered himself too important to stump and refused to campaign. His name, he said, was enough to engulf Newberry. Actually, inarticulate Henry dreaded making public appearances. He declared openly that "he would never make a public speech to get elected."

Even without campaigning Henry lost by less than 6,000 votes. His pride was strong as ever. Hadn't he proved the power of his name by coming so close without lifting a finger?

He did not leave well enough alone. He blamed the loss not on his failure to campaign but on the concerted efforts of "Jewish capitalists who made billions during the war." He also declared that he would show those "avaricious bankers and all America" the truth not found in the "capitalistic press owned or controlled by Jews."

Edsel was aghast at his father's escalating boorishness, but he could do nothing. There was no stopping Henry's purchase of a small weekly newspaper published near the Ford home at Fair Lane, a journal called the *Dearborn Independent*, which Henry boasted would quickly rival the *New York World* in circulation.

The May 18, 1920, edition of Henry's *Independent* carried a front-page editorial headed: "The International Jew: The World's Problem." It was the first of many anti-Semitic blasts to come.

The vicious editorials had their effect on Model T sales. Jews and Jewish organizations stopped buying

Fords. Thousands of non-Jews, including Christian businessmen who did not wish to alienate Jewish customers, boycotted the Ford Motor Company.

To improve sales Edsel suggested improved steering and braking and replacement of the four-cylinder engine with a six. But a six-cylinder engine was a horror to the farm-raised Henry.

"I've got no use," he snorted, "for an engine that's got more spark plugs than a cow has teats."

Henry forgot his disapproval of more spark plugs when an opportunity arose to turn the tables on an old adversary, Henry Leland, who had replaced Ford in the Detroit Automobile Company. Leland had built a luxurious car with a V-8 engine and incorporated his Lincoln Motor Company in early 1920. Now, his board of directors, led by one of Henry's former investors, was squeezing Leland out.

Desperate, Leland came to Ford for help. At the receivership sale Henry bought the Lincoln company for 8 million. In what seemed a magnanimous gesture at the time he named Henry Leland president, Leland's son Wilfred first vice-president, with Edsel to serve as second vice-president.

It was a short-lived, unhappy marriage. Soon Henry tried to force the Lelands out. Henry Leland, unable to face the loss of the company he started, sent his son to Ford with an offer to buy back Lincoln for the $8 million Henry had paid plus a fair interest.

"Mr. Leland," Henry said, "I wouldn't sell the Lincoln plant for five hundred million dollars."

With Edsel busy at the Lincoln plant Henry Ford

was relieved, at least for a time, of listening to his son's practical suggestions which he almost always turned down. But one day he recalled his son's solid arguments in favor of advertising as a means of getting more people to know and buy the model T. Henry had always been a confirmed and blatant publicity seeker if it cost nothing, and advertising cost money. Now he had what he thought was a better idea.

Henry had taken a number of camping trips with such good friends as Thomas Edison and Harvey Firestone, provider of tires for his Lizzie. Why not, he thought, invite the President of the United States, Warren Harding, to join them in a week of outdoor relaxation. A swarm of newspapermen would follow them.

Harding accepted the invitation, and the campers made for the wilderness in a cavalcade of Model T Fords. As Henry expected, the ruggedness and durability of Lizzie received as much attention as did the country's chief executive.

The trip brought Henry Ford the sales he expected from the free publicity. It also infected him with the germ of a new ambition. If a farmboy like Warren Harding—none too bright, as Henry saw him—could sit in the White House, there was no reason why he, one of the best-known men in the world, could not become President of the United States himself.

Harding was expected to run for a second term, but his chances for reelection began to dim soon after his return to Washington, as the country heard rumblings of "Teapot Dome," a scandal within the Harding cabinet. Almost simultaneously a "Henry Ford for President" boom got under way, sparked by Henry's secretary, Ernest Liebold, and by Charley Sorenson. Henry told Charley he would name him his secretary of war.

Ernest Liebold, doing double duty in public relations, got the word out. "Henry Ford for President" became a growing battle cry in rural America and spread into the cities. There were more poor in the cities than rich, and Henry had relentlessly cut costs so that a Model T was within reach of almost anyone. They would back him solidly.

But fate stepped in. What might well have been the tragedy of a Ford presidency was averted when Warren Harding, stung by the growing Teapot Dome scandal, died on August 2, 1923, and Calvin Coolidge was sworn in as President.

Coolidge had an appeal that transcended that of Henry Ford. He had a solid background in politics. His combination of homey simplicity, honesty, sincerity, and quiet humor made him an ideal candidate for the Republicans. The Ford balloon deflated quickly.

Edsel was still president of the Ford Motor Company and responsible, at least on paper, for all the company's activities. However, he had found himself happiest at the Lincoln plant. Only there did he have the semblance of a free hand. But whatever he planned, whatever he accomplished, Harry Bennett still haunted him. And now there was another concern: Ford's competition was picking up steam.

Chevrolet, under Bill Knudsen, was making worrisome inroads on Ford sales, turning out slightly under half a million units in 1923 and moving ahead rapidly. In June of 1924, when the 10 millionth Ford rolled off the assembly line—and even though the Model T still outsold Chevrolet by a million and a half cars and more—Henry finally listened to Edsel. He admitted that the Lizzie's days were numbered and gave his son the go-ahead to design a new car.

The last of more than 15 million Model T Fords came off the assembly line in May, 1927. On December 2 of that year its successor made its bow. The Model A—the second Ford to carry that designation—was a robust, stylish car for its day, with a redesigned four-cylinder engine that gave it more speed than Chevrolet. It included revolutionary new features such as the first laminated safety glass windshield ever offered as standard equipment.

The Model A was an immediate success. As many as 400,000 people placed orders, including cash deposits, within two weeks of its announcement. Before 1930 bowed out, four million had been produced, with model choices increased to nine. Edsel's green light for the Model A was taken so literally that a town-car version was produced, a car with chauffeur's seat and roof, isolating the passenger compartment, priced at $1,200. At the lower end of the price scale was the Model A Tudor at $500, available in gray and green as well as Henry's traditional black.

Even though the 5 millionth Model A was produced in 1931, a plunge in sales brought on by the nationwide depression led to the development of a new car. Henry Ford was ready for change with a revolutionary idea that proved a sensation. He introduced a V-8-engined Ford at a price only slightly higher than that of the four-cylinder Model A. This automobile carried Ford Motor Company into the next decade.

Despite the Depression the sales side of the Ford Motor Company ledger had held up. Even so, a storm was brewing within its offices. The aging Henry was slipping badly in judgment and losing his grip. Harry Bennett, the ex-boxer and bully whose rowdy nature contrasted severely with that of the sensitive and cultured Edsel Ford, took charge.

Thanks to Bennett, 1937 became a year not to remember, for it was one stigmatized by his abuse of power, the year of the infamous "Battle of the Rouge Overpass."

The United Auto Workers' Ford local, headed by Walter Reuther, had been granted permission by the City of Dearborn for a peaceful demonstration at the Ford Rouge gates the afternoon of May 26. Reuther, aware of Bennett's cadre of guards identified as "bruisers, ex-baseball and -football players and jail-birds," and of Bennett's impulsive, intemperate, violent reactions, had carefully planned the move on the Rouge.

Reuther and his volunteers, who included a number of women, arrived at the Rouge plant area about three o'clock to pass out their printed pieces during

Ford's 4:00 P.M. shift change. They headed for an overpass leading to a streetcar stop used by incoming and outgoing workers. At the other end a gate led into the Ford grounds, but the union organizers were to go no further than the middle of the overpass.

Reuther led his group up the bridgelike structure. Near the center they were met by a band of goons and musclemen led by Angelo Caruso, a known hoodlum hired by Harry Bennett.

"Get the hell out of here!" Caruso screamed. "This is Ford property."

Reuther wanted no confrontation. He ordered his people to back down toward the streetcar stop. They were faced suddenly with a second group of Ford bruisers, who began beating the retreating unionists with clubs and fists.

One grabbed Reuther from behind, knocked him to the ground, and, after kicking his head and body, flung him down the steel steps. Another unionist had his jacket pulled over his head to immobilize his arms and was then beaten. A woman was kicked in the stomach. Another union man had his back broken.

Newspaper photographers, who had gathered to catch the confrontation on film, were the next targets. They were beaten, and their cameras confiscated. But enough escaped to provide front-page coverage of the vicious assault for the next day's newspapers and for national magazines. Their pictures were so graphic that the National Labor Relations board found the Ford Motor Company guilty of using terror tactics to prevent union organization.

Henry accepted the government's decision with ill grace, blaming it all on the "capitalist" press as usual. But he refused to knuckle under. He bestowed greater powers than ever on Harry Bennett, ordering him to stamp out the least trace of union activity. Bennett obeyed with sadistic pleasure despite public disgust at the unneeded brutality. He was little concerned over the boycott of Ford products that sky-rocketed General Motors past Ford and dropped Henry's company into third place behind Chrysler.

Edsel was horror-stricken by his father's cavalier reaction to the brutality as well as by his refusal to honor the terms of the new labor law. It took four years of insistent pleading, and his mother's help, before Henry capitulated.

Clara was worried over Edsel's health and concerned over the corrosive and detrimental effect of the violence on the company. She declared to her husband that if he didn't do something about Harry Bennett's violence and sign the union agreement, she would leave him. That threat finally brought peace to the Ford Motor Company.

Henry's obstinacy, which Bennett encouraged during the lengthy strife, ate at Edsel's heart like the yet-undiagnosed cancer that was shortening his life. He worried about the workers in the plant, about the company's image, and about its plummeting profits. A compassionate man, he detested the useless violence triggered by Bennett's goons, which he was unable to halt.

There had never been much warm communication

between Edsel and his father. And when Henry suffered his first of two strokes, the rift widened. The old man refused to admit even to himself that he was incapable of running the company, and he continued making important decisions and interfering with the execution of almost every suggestion Edsel offered. Bennett was always at hand, ready and willing to relay Henry's orders. Too often they were not Henry's, but Bennett's, made in the old man's name.

Harry Bennett could do no wrong in Henry's eyes, but the wrongs Bennett committed had put the company well on the way to bankruptcy. The security men he controlled hauled tons of company property through the gates without a check. A inventory of parts and accessories taken later revealed shortages of over a million dollars.

One bright spot for Edsel in the last half of the thirties was the 1936-1939 four-year period in which Lincoln topped Cadillac in sales. Another was the completion of a personal car, built specifically for him, a Lincoln with the "long, low, continental" look Edsel so much admired.

Weakened by his worries over the slippage in Ford sales, the repercussions from the shameful incident at the Rouge overpass, and his unending and fruitless struggle with his father, Edsel visited Florida for a rest when the car was completed. Prenamed Lincoln Continental by him, the car was brought there in March, 1939.

From the moment it arrived, the stunning gray coupe caught the fancy of everyone who saw its fine craftsmanship. Edsel sensed the widespread interest and ordered it produced in a limited edition. It was introduced to the public in October, each car virtually hand built. America's reigning architect, Frank Lloyd Wright, described it as the most beautiful car ever made.

The hallmark of Edsel's Lincoln Continental Mark was the spare tire mounting at the rear of the car. Not a truly new concept, it had been commonplace in the 1920s but had gone out of favor in the early 1930s. Since the introduction of Edsel's car, any automobile with the tire so placed has been called continental. Years later Lee Iacocca would give the tire-placement image and the Continental name a new and meaningful success on American roads.

This Lincoln Continental may well be termed Edsel Ford's swan song. His illness, finally diagnosed as inoperable cancer, continued for another four years, though the bulldog in his father refused to face up to the seriousness of his son's condition.

It was only the "softness" in Edsel, Henry kept saying. If the boy would only toughen up like a man, he would be hale and hearty. Milk delivered directly from Henry's dairy farm to his son's home would make Edsel healthy and strong again.

Unfortunately Henry had a nature fetish that would not countenance pasteurization. When Edsel developed increased fever and pain and uncontrolled perspiration, doctors discovered that contamination in the unhomogenized milk was responsible for the undulant fever. Early on the morning of May 26,

1943, Edsel died at age forty-nine.

Edsel's wife, Eleanor, was never sure whether illness had caused her husband's death or whether heartbreak had brought on the illness. But she was grateful that he had lived long enough to see his oldest son, Henry II, marry beautiful and gentle Anne McDonnell, father a daughter, and be named a director of the Ford Motor Company. Henry II, who had been drafted into the navy with the outbreak of the Second World War, returned from the Great Lakes Naval Training Station for his father's funeral.

Once Edsel was buried, his family realized how serious a problem now confronted them. A meeting of the Ford board of directors was scheduled for June 1, at which Edsel's successor as president would be chosen. They were worried, and with good reason, that the aging and incapacitated Henry might order the appointment of Henry Bennett. In some way the Edsel Ford family was determined to maintain control of the board.

The block of stock bequeathed to Eleanor by Edsel enabled her to win a seat on the board before the members broke for lunch. Then, with Sorenson's help, she was able to maneuver the appointments of Henry II and her second-oldest son, Benson, to the board. But her victory was not total. Bennett and two of his cronies were also named directors.

Overall, the best the Edsel clan could do during the election of company officers was to have the older Henry restored to his earlier position as president, with Charley Sorenson as vice-president. B. J. Craig, a Bennett man, was elected second vice-president and treasurer.

Henry II had to return to his duties in the navy after the funeral, but he had seen and heard enough to disturb him. He asked Russell Gnau, Sorenson's secretary, to keep him advised of everything happening at the plant, unaware that he would learn only what Bennett wanted him to know. Gnau was another of Harry's many agents.

Bennett, realizing that the family plan was to move Henry II into his grandfather's position when the older Henry died, looked for ways to sidetrack the young heir. Bennett wanted to run the Ford Motor Company himself.

He asked the advice of I. A. Capizzi, a Ford attorney who had always been friendly to him, implying that Eleanor's brother, Ernest Kanzler, wanted control of the company. With so much voting stock in his sister's hands, Kanzler might easily succeed, Bennett pointed out.

Capizzi suggested a codicil to Henry's will that could clear Bennett's way by wiping out the Ford Foundation and its block of nonvoting stock. Then a trusteeship could be established to run the corporation for a period after Henry's death.

Bennett, pleased at the prospect, began composing a list of trustees. He would be secretary of that board. Others would include Capizzi, Ernest Liebold, and Frank Campsall, old Henry's current private secretary. Sorenson, however, could not be excluded, even though he also had his eye on the company presidency.

A drama of intrigue was in the making, and Harry Bennett was writing the script.

Ernest Kanzler, who had been ousted from his Ford position through Bennett's efforts, read Bennett's mind. He quickly sensed that a plan with ominous overtones for the Edsel Ford family was in the wind.

Kanzler was well aware that the company was in dire straits, its future resting in the hands of two men. One, Henry Ford, had been pronounced by his own physician, Dr. Roy McClure, to be too ill to leave his home or to be consulted on decisions. The other, devious Harry Bennett, wielded the actual power.

There was only one way, Kanzler decided, to deal Bennett a knockout blow. First he would need the combined support of Clara, old Henry's wife, and Eleanor, Edsel's widow. But just as critical to a successful sabotage of whatever Bennett had in mind was the presence on the scene of Henry II, whose release from the navy was years away.

Kanzler pleaded with Frank Knox, Franklin Delano Roosevelt's secretary of the navy. The deterioration in Henry Ford's physical and mental capacities, and his dependence on the ambitious and unscrupulous Harry Bennett, was reason enough to arrange a discharge from the navy for young Henry Ford. The company needed the strength of an untarnished, visible, and sane Ford to manage its government contracts and commercial future.

Knox agreed, and Henry Ford II won a naval discharge and came to the Ford Rouge plant in

August, 1943. At twenty-six he was thrust into a position he was hardly qualified to fill, and his playboy reputation provided little assurance that a young Henry Ford could do better than the senile old one.

Did he have the strength and talent to make order out of the chaos within the Ford Motor Company? Could he stand up to the wily Harry Bennett? It seemed too much to ask of someone whose life had been one of ease since birth, with never a worry or confrontation.

CHAPTER 4

What had perhaps been Henry Ford II's most significant exposure to the dominion he one day would rule had come at the age of two years and eight months, on the morning of May 17, 1920. Smartly attired, his chubby face topped by a hat made of beaver fur, he was brought to the newly built Rouge plant to christen its first blast furnace. Carried by his grandfather for the ceremony, little Henry couldn't handle the match to set the furnace ablaze. So it was the grandfather, not the heir, who struck the match.

Precociousness best describes Henry's growing years. He was never awed by rank, royalty, or fame. When Henry was six years old, Edward, Prince of Wales, heir to the British throne, was expected as a dinner guest at Edsel's home. Henry and his brother, Benson, four at the time, were promised a look at the future king of England.

Since their royal guest was late in arriving, Edsel's

wife asked her mother to take the boys to their bedroom, assuring them that the prince would come in to bid them goodnight. Sometime later Edsel escorted the English heir up the stairs to the accompaniment of snickers, chuckles, and booming laughter echoing loudly from the boys' room.

Edsel opened the door and looked around. His mother-in-law was nowhere to be seen. Flustered by the arrival of royalty she had taken cover behind a screen.

"What's going on?" Edsel demanded as Prince Edward preceded him into the bedroom.

Young Henry, unabashed by the royal presence, blurted out: "Benson was so excited he threw up." He then let out another guffaw and added: "You'll find grandmother hiding over there."

There is no denying the brilliance of today's Henry Ford II, but his prep-school years at Hotchkiss, the prestigious Connecticut academy for the sons of wealth, were unimpressive. Hitting the books was never the favorite pastime of this pudgy adolescent with a puckish sense of humor.

"He was not noted for his intellectual brilliance," is the evaluation of his headmaster of Hotchkiss.

However mediocre his Hotchkiss years may have been, Grandfather Henry and Grandmother Clara gave him a memorable graduation present, a trip to Europe. It was during this summer vacation, when he was nineteen, that he first met Anne McDonnell, the lovely and elegant blonde socialite who would become his first wife.

Henry's four years at Yale were even less noteworthy than his terms at Hotchkiss, except for his second meeting with Anne and his resolve to marry her. Otherwise his eight semesters at one of America's finest institutions of learning were a washout.

"I didn't learn anything, except maybe from my courses in sociology," Henry has admitted. "They were a bit of fun, and I took them because the guys told that sociology was a breeze, and I'd already flunked engineering. Hell, I also flunked sociology."

Henry failed his sociology course because his eagle-eyed professor decided the thesis he submitted was too well done to be Henry's own work. Confronted by the instructor, uninhibited, straightforward Henry made no excuse.

"I got some help," he confessed readily. "And when the prof said I couldn't get my degree unless I wrote a new thesis on a different subject, I said to hell with it. Besides, I didn't want to lose any time getting married."

There was a distressing hitch in Henry's prospect of marrying Anne. Grandfather Henry would have called it an unsurmountable obstacle, if he had only known in time. Anne was the daughter of William McDonnell, a Wall Street heavyweight. She was also a Roman Catholic.

A Wall Street connection was enough in itself to send the older Henry into a rage. But he also categorized Catholics with the hated Jews, Communists, and union leaders.

Edsel had no objections, but McDonnell family

details had to be kept from his father until it was too late. So careful were Eleanor and Edsel around old Henry that the remaining obstacle to the wedding was overcome without his knowledge: This was young Henry's conversion to Catholicism under the tutelage of world-respected Monsignor Fulton J. Sheen.

Henry Ford II and Anne McDonnell were married June 13, 1940, in what was reported as "the wedding of the year." Gifts from friends and relatives were worth over a million dollars. From Henry's parents the bridal couple received a palatial Grosse Pointe residence. Edsel, in addition, transferred to Henry, 25,000 shares of Ford stock valued at more than $3.2 million. With the stock came a note announcing that after his marriage Henry "will join the Ford Motor Company as your future business," and also noting the fact that Henry had been a director of the company for over two years.

Henry II arrived at the Rouge after discharge from the navy in the summer of '43 as guardian of his family's company. It was a weighty burden to place on the shoulders of a young man who had little or no experience in so competitive a business. He underestimated neither the importance of the job ahead nor the tangled skein that had to be unraveled. He had seen enough while on furlough for his father's funeral to realize that things were not right.

When Henry reported in for his first day, he had no definite assignment, not even a desk, much less an office. Grateful that Harry Bennett had made himself scarce, he roamed the plant asking questions of assembly-line workers and keeping his eyes open.

Finally Laurence Sheldrick, who had not been aware of Henry's arrival, took him in hand. Sheldrick, no Bennett hanger-on, had been Edsel's chief designer. He not only filled Henry in on what was going on, he also suggested a look at the Army Proving Grounds in Aberdeen, Maryland.

The trip didn't take place. Before they could start out, Sheldrick was summoned at Harry Bennett's orders to Sorenson's office.

"What the hell do you think you're doing?" Sorenson stormed. "Leave the kid alone, and don't go stuffing him with your crazy ideas about building modern cars after the war's over."

"All I've done," Sheldrick said, holding his temper, "is tell him about ideas Edsel was working on that he already knew about."

Sorenson's face turned red. "Then why did you go against Mr. Ford's wishes and take him to Aberdeen to make a warmonger out of him?"

Sheldrick's answer did him in. "All I was doing was showing young Henry that Ford's as much interested in helping the government as General Motors."

Sorenson exploded. "If GM's that goddamn good, why don't you go work for them!"

"All right," Sheldrick replied, "if that's the way it is, I'm through."

Sorenson had achieved what Bennett hoped, disposal of another of Edsel's few remaining loyalists. Furious as he was when he heard of it, Henry II held himself in check, biding his time.

Four months later, at a meeting of the board of directors, his family's votes brought him a vice-presidency, and Henry II moved into his father's old office. He kept Edsel's remaining staff and added a few of his own choices. Though he had to work closely with Charley Sorenson, he had little use for the man after the Sheldrick incident. As for Harry Bennett, Henry loathed his name and discounted Harry's egocentric claim to at-will entree to his ailing grandfather.

Henry II was not convinced that Bennett had his grandfather's ear and carte blanche to relay orders in the old man's name. He often had heard his father, Edsel, speak of Bennett's devious nature and was prepared to evaluate Bennett's manipulation of the truth.

"When an important policy matter came up," young Henry once reported, "Bennett would get into his car and disappear for a few hours. Then he would come back and say 'I've been to see Mr. Ford and he wants us to do it this way.'"

Henry did his best to maintain pleasant relations with his grandfather and visited him often. Old Henry would hear no bad word against Bennett. "He's a good man," he told his grandson. But young Henry did ask questions at appropriate moments and did get Bennett-damning answers.

"I checked with my grandfather," he said, "and found out that Bennett had not been to see him on the occasions he claimed."

Henry II knew only too well that something had to

be done about the older Henry, growing more senile and making decisions through Harry Bennett. He was ruling the company with passion rather than reason. More than a little frustrated, Henry II moved carefully, albeit his thinking was clear and incisive. In many ways he had the compassion and charm of his father. In others he exhibited the bulldog resolution of his grandfather.

Sorenson and Bennett cared little that Henry was a vice-president. They saw him as powerless, even during board meetings. As for young Henry, it grieved him to see his grandfather hobble in to the meetings against the will of his doctor, always accompanied by the inevitable Bennett. He was sure it was Bennett who insisted on the old man's attendance.

The board meetings were travesties. His grandfather would merely walk around the table, shake hands with each director, and then turn to Bennett.

"Come on, Harry," he would say. "Let's get the hell out of here. We'll probably change everything they do, anyway."

Henry II watched with growing contempt for both Sorenson and Bennett. Charley had engaged himself in an unequal power play, trying to outdo the well-entrenched Bennett in pleasing Henry's ailing grandfather. Both had eyes on the presidency that could never be theirs. The end result was a rash of firings, each guillotining qualified men he believed might be loyal to the other.

Bennett disposed of A. M. Wibel, a responsible and dedicated purchasing, production, and financial wizard, as well as Eugene Gregorie, one of the most capable designers in the industry. Sorenson already had drawn first blood by getting rid of Laurence Sheldrick.

Sorenson, who had been a loyal Ford man since 1905, was himself on the way out without realizing it. He had done an admirable job coordinating defense work, and now the Allies were gaining ground in Europe. Roosevelt, Churchill, and Chiang Kai-shek had met in Cairo for a strategy conference, and Roosevelt and Churchill had gone on to Tehran for a meeting with Joseph Stalin.

Sorenson was tired and badly in need of a rest, and there was little for him to do as 1943 wound down. He went to see old Henry.

"Everything's caught up," he told his longtime boss, "so I think I'll take a trip to Miami."

Henry's quick acquiescence should have been a warning, but tired as he was, Charley didn't read anything into the old man's hasty goodbye. He drove a company car south and had barely arrived when he heard that his office was being occupied by Ray Rausch, a Bennett crony.

Shocked and tormented by such treatment, a despicable trick in character with Harry Bennett, he burned up the telephone wires in vain. Henry refused to speak to him or return his calls.

Flustered and frustrated, Sorenson hastily drove back north. When he reached the gates of the Rouge, a Bennett security guard refused him entrance and took the car.

On January 23, 1944, Henry Ford II was elected executive vice-president of the Ford Motor Company. Despite the new title, which placed him second only to his grandfather, he was helpless in trying to alleviate the chaotic situation.

His grandfather remained in command, but his mind was fast deteriorating. He was too feeble to come to the office often. When he did, he could not remember the names of his most familiar executives and had to be reminded of their identity. All except the hovering Harry Bennett.

However hard he tried, Henry II could not pass the Bennett barrier. The confusion and mismanagement at every level made no sense. Bennett laughed off Henry II's concerns by pointing out that it was "always done that way."

Young Henry was also sickened by the brutality of the foreman in the plant. Bennett's reaction to his complaint was that it was necessary to keep lazy workers on the job.

His hands tied, Henry could do little more than shake his head, wondering how anything got accomplished. Good workers either rebelled at the harsh treatment and were fired, or they quit in disgust. They were losing too many good men, and not merely in the plant. Bennett's high-handed measures also disenchanted upper-echelon executives, who went off the payroll.

Not long after Henry II was elected vice-president, he made it clear that he did not have all the answers, that with his inexperience he needed all the help he could get. "One man can't do it alone," he said again and again. But, whether or not it was part of a Bennett-planned campaign, he was losing too many of the men who had tried to give him hand.

He became particularly upset when Harry Doss, Ford's capable sales manager, told Henry he could no longer tolerate Bennett interference. Bennett and his cohorts, Doss said, were putting the best dealerships in the hands of friends.

"I don't want to quit, but I've got to," Doss told Henry. "And I wouldn't if something could be done about Bennett's interference."

Henry tried to change Doss's mind, but without success. "I can't blame you one damn bit," Henry finally said. "There's not a damn thing I can do about it right now, but I guarantee you someday I will."

Henry discussed the problem with his uncle, Ernest Kanzler. He had to have a dependable, loyal, and able sales manager. Kanzler reminded Henry that the Doss resignation was hardly the first, and as a matter of fact, John Davis, whom Doss replaced, had taken a demotion to get away from Bennett. Davis, with Edsel's help, had remained with the company and was managing a branch office in California.

"He's the best man for the job in the country, if you can get him," Kanzler told Henry.

Henry phoned Davis, but Davis refused to come back to Dearborn. "I'll never do it if I have to deal with Harry Bennett again," he said.

Henry flew out to Long Beach, California, to talk to Davis. Strong-willed Jack Davis would not be budged, but Henry did not let him go. "I'll tell you what," he said. "Come on back. Hell, if Bennett makes trouble, you quit, and I'll quit too." Davis returned to Dearborn.

A month or so later Henry was approached by Leander Hamilton McCormick-Goodheart, then managing a small department called Personnel Planning. In 1939 McCormick-Goodheart had been about to begin his last year at England's Cambridge University when Germany invaded Poland, triggering World War II. A native American whose mother was English, McCormick-Goodheart had been refused a visa by the State Department to return to Cambridge because of the outbreak of hostilities.

McCormick-Goodheart's father had been a frequent golfing partner of Edsel Ford during Edsel's vacation periods at Bar Harbor, Maine. After graduation from the New York Institute of Photography, he was able, through Edsel, to join the Ford factory training program in September, 1940. He had worked himself up to his present position in the five intervening years.

"Mr. Ford," McCormick-Goodheart told Henry, "if I may suggest it, I believe it would be to the company's advantage to rejuvenate the student orientation program. The way it has evolved it has too many deficiencies, too many tool and die people and mechanics playing engineer. They're not professionals, which is really what the company needs."

Henry listened, liking what he heard. "Well, what are your ideas?" he asked. "What can you do about it?"

"I'd like to build the program back up," McCormick-Goodheart said. "I think it was an excellent program when it began, but it's become a dumping ground for Harry Bennett's pets, men who just spend time to pick up a paycheck. To me, that's most unproductive for the company. I'd like to revamp the whole program, streamline it, put some order and sense into it."

"How would you go about it?" Henry asked.

"I'd like to go to the major universities," McCormick-Goodheart replied, "and bring in some young professional engineers, hand-pick young men who are mechanical engineers because they want to be."

Henry was impressed by the loyalty and concern for the company evidenced by the young man about his own age. It was a practical, sound idea.

"Go do it," he told McCormick-Goodheart, little realizing the far-reaching, down-the-road impact it would have on the Ford Motor Company. Lee Iacocca was the brightest of the many gems McCormick-Goodheart discovered during that summer of 1945.

Harry Bennett, meanwhile, had done a little hiring on his own, adding an ingredient to his cadre that he believed was a necessary protective measure. He took on tough, vigorous John S. Bugas, a Wyoming lawyer who had been the head of the Detroit FBI office for about five years.

For the last of those years his office, because of the

war contracts awarded the Ford Motor Company, had kept a watchful eye on the company and had uncovered thefts of war matériel as well as the bootlegging and black market sale of parts. Bugas could not turn down the salary offered by Bennett to supervise labor relations for Ford.

Bugas had come in as a Bennett man, but to Harry's surprise Bugas was more his own man, honest and dedicated to his job. When he revealed his straight stripes by firing one of Bennett's cronies, Harry put him in a deep freeze. "Bennett had me as isolated as a tuberculosis bug," Bugas said.

Disgusted with Bennett's pattern of shortsighted, self-centered policies, Bugas became one of young Henry's best allies. Hiring John Bugas was to become Harry Bennett's passport to exile.

On June 28, 1945, the Ford Motor Company completed its war contracts when the last Liberator bomber was assembled at its Willow Run facility, ending a government assignment that had produced 8,600 bombers, 57,000 aircraft engines, and 278,000 jeeps and seeps (amphibious jeeps). Five days later Henry II ordered the resumption of passenger-car production, but he needed someone trustworthy to replace Ray Rausch, a Bennett confidant, as head of manufacturing.

The best man for the job, whom he could trust and who was not a Bennett stooge, was Mead Bricker, formerly Sorenson's assistant, now in charge at the Willow Run bomber plant.

First Henry wanted to sound out the only ones in

whom he had faith, John Bugas and John Davis, his sales manager. He decided to invite all three men to dinner at the Dearborn Inn, the posh hotel his grandfather had built for the convenience of visitors to Dearborn.

"My God, no!" Bugas exploded when Henry suggested the inn. "Every corner in that dining room is bugged."

They finally decided on a corner table in the dining room of the Detroit Club in downtown Detroit. As they sat down, Henry wasted no time in getting to the nub of the matter.

"I've asked you to come here because I have confidence in you," he said. "I want you to help me rebuild the Ford Motor Company."

Bricker, who knew the high regard in which Henry held John Bugas, realized he would not have been there without Bugas' approval. He let out a roar and turned to the former FBI man.

"You son of a bitch," he said to Bugas, smiling broadly, "I thought you distrusted me!"

"What the hell can we do?" Henry asked the other three men at the table.

His grandfather might have run the company single-handed, but young Henry knew he didn't have the experience to do it. Besides, times had changed. The day was long gone when a business like Ford Motor Company could be run single-handed.

Bugas had an answer. "First," he said, "get your grandfather to sign an order stating that nobody can get fired anymore without your permission." Bugas firmly believed it was the only way to water down Bennett's influence.

"All right," Henry agreed. "But then what?"

"Clean house," Bugas replied. "Better still, tell me to do it."

Henry shook his head. "If I did that," he said, "I'd be known around the company as a guy who passed the buck." Here Henry II exhibited a characteristic at odds with his grandfather's way of getting rid of the unwanted by not facing them directly.

At that time the Red Army had already taken Warsaw from the Germans and the Americans had crossed the Rhine at Remagen. By VE Day Henry was back at the Rouge with the order suggested by Bugas, signed by his grandfather.

The first firing salvo at Ford came when Mead Bricker entered Rausch's office to find that Bennett crony chatting with some of his lieutenants. In minutes after Bricker closed the door Rausch and his crew shot out into the corridor. Bricker remained inside, in charge.

The revitalization of Ford was progressing smoothly, perhaps too smoothly, since Henry was unaware of Harry's trump card, a codicil to his grandfather's will. It had been prepared by old Henry's lawyer, I. A. Capizzi, at Bennett's insistence. Suddenly rumors about this secret document, one that would put Ford Motor Company in control of a board of trustees after the aged Henry's death, began to float through the industry.

No one in the Edsel Ford family was aware of such

a document, but young Henry quickly realized that if indeed such a codicil existed, it would probably make Harry Bennett head man. The thought sickened and angered him.

Henry II sought out John Bugas. If the rumors were true, he told Bugas, he was going to resign and sell his stock. He would also recommend that Ford dealers dump their franchises. Better that there be no Ford Motor Company than one with Harry Bennett running it.

"Wait," Bugas suggested. "Let me find out from Harry if it's true."

Bugas charged into Bennett's office and confronted him. Redfaced, caught short by Bugas' obvious knowledge of the codicil, Bennett told Bugas to come back the next day and he would have the matter straightened out.

The next morning, when Bugas entered Bennett's office, Bennett was holding two legal-looking papers, one the alleged codicil to Henry's will, the other a carbon copy. He let Bugas see the original, then set a match to it. When it had been reduced to ashes, Bennett swept the ashes into an envelope.

"Here," he said, handing Bugas the envelope. "Take these back to Henry."

Bugas waited, his lips tight. Bennett finally handed over the carbon. There was no way of knowing whether the codicil had actually been signed by Henry Ford or if it was a clever forgery. But that mattered little now since the original had been destroyed.

Bennett continued to be Henry's prime hindrance in operating the company, and removing him while his grandfather was alive called for finesse. Yet the only way in which young Henry could exercise control was to send Bennett packing.

It was Henry II's mother, Eleanor, who tipped the scales. She made certain that old Henry was in full control of his senses before she made her move and visited the Ford patriarch.

She minced no words. In firm tones she told the bedridden old man that he must step down and that her son, Henry II, must become president of the company.

"If this is not done," she warned, emphasizing each word, "I shall sell my stock."

Old Henry had no choice. If Eleanor sold her stock, the Ford Motor Company would certainly pass from family control. On September 20, 1945, a tired, stringbean-thin Henry Ford sent for his grandson. In faltering words he told young Henry that he would be elected president the following day. The younger Henry made it clear to the older: He would take the job only if he had complete freedom to do what he felt necessary. The old man made no objection.

At the hastily called board meeting the next day old Henry and Bennett were both in attendance. The moment the secretary of the board began reading the aged Ford's letter of resignation, Bennett, his face flaming red, jumped to his feet.

"Congratulations!" he snapped angrily in young Henry's direction.

He started to leave the room but was held back by other directors in order to make the vote unanimous. The moment it was over, he bolted toward his own office. Henry Ford II was now president of the Ford Motor Company, and Bennett realized his hours were numbered.

The elder Henry Ford was helped from the meeting room. As the door closed behind him, the last page in a historical saga had seemingly been turned. Although Henry Ford lived on for another seventeen months, an unparalleled career in the automobile industry had come to an end. His grandson was now the man of the hour and the man with the power. As soon as the boardroom was clear, Henry II made his way to Harry Bennett's office. He found Harry in a state of shock.

"We've got to part company," Henry told Bennett. "I'll keep you on salary for a year and a half until your retirement pay begins, but stay off of Ford property."

Bennett, not surprised, took the news in his usually graceless manner. "You're taking over a billion-dollar organization you haven't contributed a thing to," he shrieked at Henry.

As he promised, Henry had not passed the buck, but he did leave it to John Bugas to see that Bennett left the premises by day's end. Aware that Bennett always had a .45 handy, Bugas holstered a .38 automatic inside his coat. He would be ready if Bennett tried anything.

Bugas opened the door to Bennett's office, entered,

and stood there for a moment as he closed it. Bennett sat at his desk, his eyes flaming. Bugas walked toward the desk, and as he reached it, Bennett leaped to his feet, pulling his blunt-nosed .45 from his desk drawer.

"You're behind all of this, you son of a bitch!" he screamed at Bugas.

Bugas waited, alert and ready, but Bennett's explosion seemed to have taken the steam from his anger. He unceremoniously dropped the gun on his desk and walked out. That same night he caught a train for California, never again to be seen at the Ford Motor Company. Soon after, as quickly as Henry could replace them, the rest of the Bennett squad disappeared from Ford.

Assuming the power of company president, Henry II had his hands full. He had inherited a crippled Ford Motor Company. He had an outmoded plant that would cost millions to modernize and millions more to retool for new cars. Losses were averaging about $10 million a month.

He had taken on a giant assignment, one he was unsure he could handle. The important thing was that he cared, cared for the company and for the thousands of people the company supported. His comparatively short time around the Rouge had made him aware of his priorities.

Fortunately cash was on hand for operating expenses, over $68 million dollars. His first priority was men, good, qualified men in tune with the times.

In November Henry received an enigmatic telegram. Its presumptuous, arrogant wording read, in part: "We have a matter of management importance to discuss with you." It was signed simply Charles Bates Thornton, Colonel U.S. Army Air Force, a name unknown to Henry or any of his men. But the telegram included as a reference the name of Robert Lovett, the secretary of defense.

Charles Thornton, who liked to be called "Tex," was reputed to be the only Air Force officer ever to reach the rank of full colonel by the age of twenty-five. He headed the Air Force Office of Statistical Control in Washington. To improve efficiency in that office he selected promising young officers and sent them to the Harvard Business School for quick courses in economics and business management. The brightest and most accomplished he brought back to Washington to serve on his staff.

As World War II wound down, Thornton selected his nine most brilliant aides. He told them that their exceptional and varied abilities could bring challenging and rewarding jobs in private industry. He also pointed out that since they all had worked together and knew each other's abilities so well, they could make a great splash in positions within the same company if they worked as a team of ten.

When Henry Ford II first received the telegram, his inclination was to throw it away. With the war over, even full colonels were a dime a dozen, and this Charles Thornton was an unknown. But he did know Robert Lovett well enough to give the telegram a second thought. He had one of his subordinates contact Thornton and invite him to Dearborn.

Thornton arrived with seven of his ten men in tow. Henry was flabbergasted, not only by the number of men, but also by the demand that all ten would have to be hired en masse. He was willing, however, to listen.

He had inherited a company badly in need of bright new men, and while he was being offered a most unconventional deal, it was worth exploring. The "rah-rah, let's-get-the-job-done" attitude of Thornton and his men was contagious. Despite his own problems at Yale Henry had been impressed by the dedication of the "genius types" in his classes. He decided Ford could use some of the do-or-die spirit that this infusion of new blood might bring the company. If only one of them made a contribution to help restore Ford leadership in the industry, it would be a profitable investment.

"Thornton came up with ideas that made a lot of sense to me," Henry said. "He convinced me that he and his men could make military management systems work in private industry, and improve cost-efficiency. That kind of talk appealed to me. So I hired 'em all."

The Thornton crew reported for assignment in Dearborn on February 1, 1946. In addition to Tex Thornton they included George Moore, J. E. Lundy, Wilbur Andreson, Charles E. Bosworth, Ben Davis Mills, Francis C. Reith, James O. Wright, Arjay Miller, and Robert S. McNamara. Their wide-ranging knowledge covered business, law, economics, and finance. Not one had an automobile background.

At the start they were given an abbreviated version of the in-plant training received by Frank Zimmerman, Lee Iacocca, and other McCormick-Goodheart discoveries. An orientation period followed to learn the business side of automobile production as well as the structure of the Ford Motor Company. They were given carte blanche to roam the vast Ford complex, to move from one department to the other, asking pertinent questions as they went.

For a time they were a thorn in the sides of department heads and their personnel. Some considered them company spies or, at best, young, wet-behind-the-ears, inquisitive meddlers. They soon earned the nickname "Quiz Kids," a term they resented.

"I hate it," one of them complained. "We aren't kids and we're not quizzing anybody. We're just asking questions because that's the only way we can get the information to do a good job."

As they became better known and respected for their abilities, the hated appellation was varied to "Whiz Kids," a name that suited them better. Henry Ford was pleased with their dedication, for within four months they proved themselves to be indeed "whizzes" who knew considerably more about Ford Motor Company operations than employees of twenty years' service. He had little doubt that more than one of the ten would play major roles in the future of Ford.

Henry also realized that their inexperience in the

automobile industry meant it would be years before
they could make major contributions. His immediate
need was a solid automotive-oriented man who could
work closely with him.

He found the ideal candidate with the help of his
uncle, Ernest Kanzler, then a director of the Bendix
Aviation Corporation. The man was an ex-General
Motors executive, Ernest R. Breech, president of
Bendix. Breech, reluctant to leave Bendix where he
was happy as top man, at first refused Ford's offer,
then accepted it as a challenge despite the pitiful
conditions he knew existed at Ford.

Five months after the Whiz Kids bowed in, Breech
joined Ford as Henry's executive vice-president. It
was July 1, 1946, a date most automotive experts call
the day of first salvation for the Ford Motor Company.

In September, 1945, when Henry Ford II took over
the company presidency, he had said that his one aim
was to make Ford number one among American
automobile manufacturers. Now, in July, 1946,
Ernest Breech let it be known that he had taken what
appeared a thankless job with one thought in mind,
that of helping Ford become "the leading automobile
manufacturer in the United States." It was an off-the-
cuff excuse for his leaving Bendix, so far as reporters
were concerned. Who in his right senses would leave a
secure position for such a doubtful future?

The press was wrong. Breech knew what he was
doing. He had analyzed the situation at Ford, knew
what he had to do, knew how to get it done. Ford was

trying to bridge the gap between wartime and peace-time production, and this was the kind of challenge Breech enjoyed. In the interim between accepting Ford's offer and actually joining the company he made important decisions as to the people he needed.

One must be a forward-looking, innovative, yet down-to-earth chief of engineering. He had in mind Harold T. Youngren, a top-notch chief engineer with Borg-Warner, who had earlier been at the Oldsmobile Division of General Motors. Youngren, unhappy that he was doing more desk work than engineering, readily gave both Breech and Henry II an unqualified yes.

Finance, in as much a muddle as engineering, also needed a man of high caliber. Breech wanted Lewis Crusoe, who had been controller of GM's Fisher Body Division and assistant treasurer for General Motors itself. Crusoe had retired and only recently had come to Bendix as Breech's assistant.

Mead Bricker and Logan Miller had been doing an acceptable job in manufacturing, but Breech saw that a more hard-driving chief with up-to-date knowhow could move Ford forward faster. He made his feelings known to Henry and told him that Delmar S. Harder, who had spent some years supervising production for GM, would supply the experience needed. After some reluctance, and with the offer of a five-year contract, Harder joined the Breech team.

Even before he began his reconstruction at Ford, Breech knew it would take more than changes in high-level management. One vital problem was worker morale, which he'd seen at first hand on a chance visit to the Rouge plant. He and Mead Bricker were taken on a tour by a production supervisor. At one point, as they passed between the machines silent during the lunch break, they noticed a young man reading a newspaper. Unceremoniously the supervisor kicked the newspaper from the worker's hands and screamed at the surprised employee: "Get out! Don't you ever let me see you in here again!"

Later in the tour another worker who had not seen them coming accidentally blocked their path. Without a word the supervisor picked up the young man and flung him out of the way. Seething, Bricker fired the supervisor on the spot.

As they left the building, Breech told Bricker that he thought Henry II had outlawed the plant brutality for which the company had become infamous. Bricker agreed that Henry had.

"But you can't change some of these men," Bricker said. "The fact is that five years ago supervisors would have been fired if they *didn't* act that way."

On November 15, 1946, not long after Lee Iacocca began his training period in the Rouge plant, Breech brought all supervisors and department heads together. He had in his hands an Elmo Roper report on employee impressions of working conditions at Ford. Almost 85 percent of the near 25,000 who responded criticized the treatment by their foremen and supervisors. In addition over 81 percent expressed dislike of what they considered management's attitude toward hem.

Breech made it clear that the supervisors in front of him had to stop their abuse of men on the line, whose work was as important, maybe even more so, than that of the supers who abused them. The Ford Motor Company was not an army encampment, he told them.

"We won't have an 'officer caste' here," he emphasized. "We won't have any brass-hat-ism."

Backing Breech to the hilt, Henry II made it equally clear that while the Ford Motor Company had operated on, and exploited, the fear of its workers during the past twenty years, those days were gone.

"No company," he said, "can operate when relationships inside the company are predicated on fear." He also pointed out the waste that came from working under such conditions, that cars could not be built as cheaply as when good human relations existed inside the company.

However imperious and obdurate Henry II may have been in later years, he was no autocrat as he went about restoring the company left ravaged by his grandfather. He knew his limitations, admitted them, and sought the help of men knowledgeable enough to keep him on the right track. He read business publications, books, and magazines, searching for the surest and quickest course to make Ford competitive in an industry made more complex by government rulings.

A czar or a young Caesar would have feared a strong, dominant, and dedicated Ernest Breech, but

Henry trusted Ernie and leaned heavily on his experi
ence. He immediately agreed that the company's
most conspicuous need was a decentralization o
authority; that no one man could oversee the hydra
headed monster into which the Ford Motor Company
had evolved.

No longer was there only a Model T production t
manage. Now there were Fords, Mercurys, Lincolns
There were steel mills, rubber plantations, soybea
farms, and dozens of sidelines begun as his grandfa
ther's avocations. Some were millstones that shoulc
be discarded. The others needed single-authority
management to ensure efficient control of productio
and cost-efficiency.

Under Henry I the only consideration had beer
overall profit. Little attention was given to losse
sustained by one or another of the widespread enter
prises. Good sense dictated keeping and making th
winners more productive while disposing of the non-
essentials and the losers. Company losses were hold
ing at about $10 million a month. Selling th
off-shoots not germane to building cars would hel
cut losses, perhaps even provide operating cash.

Henry II went down the line with an ax. Ford
owned shops that turned out nuts, bolts, gauges
wheels, and other components were sold. The Brazil
ian government bought the Ford rubber plantations
which had amassed losses of $20 million and more
Soybean farms and processing plants went on th
block.

With Breech at his side Henry charged ahead with

a vengeance, but he had so much to do and so little time in which to get it done. High in priority was the production of the company's all-new 1949 model. The postwar cars already built were little more than the prewar 1942s offered the public. Something striking and totally different would be their salvation, a product the public would flock to as they had to the Tin Lizzie, one that would be a blockbuster in the marketplace.

It had to be a car without the "tin" connotation of old Lizzie, one strongly built, whose doors would close with the solid but soft thud that indicated quality construction. Henry was obsessed with the belief that only such a car could bring substantial profits.

In 1946 Ford sustained a $50 million loss. A price increase of $62.50 per car approved by the OPA brought a $5 million profit in September, enabling the Company to post a modest $2,000 profit before year's end.

Henry also realized that it would take more than good-quality construction to sell cars. He remembered his father's firm declaration, never agreed to by his grandfather, that a car also had to be pleasing to the eye. The new 1949 had to offer both.

Autmobiles were no longer being made directly from design prints as in the days of the first Henry Ford. Now the company followed a multistep procedure before a car was actually produced. Small-scale models were made to vividly show the styling concept. When they were approved, full-size models were constructed from wet clay, enabling the stylist to make minor changes in the car's exterior lines through the use of a spatula.

Old Henry would have been shocked, but he was too ill and too unconcerned as his mind continued to deteriorate. Clara had taken her husband to Georgia for two months in the warm sun and brought him back to Fair Lane in April. He died in his bed of a cerebral hemorrhage the night of April 7, 1947. He was eighty-three.

Young Henry and Ernie Breech—while also finalizing plans for the new 1949 Ford—had restructured the company. Each major facet of the company's operations would be called a division, with a single executive responsible for each; every division head was answerable to the policy committee, which in turn reported to Ford and Breech.

The various divisions, each to be managed by a vice-president, were automotive engineering, industrial relations, manufacturing, purchasing, finance, and sales. A Lincoln-Mercury Division, headed by Benson Ford after his father's death, had been set up in late 1925. Ford Division had not yet been formed but was being considered.

As the finishing touches were being applied to the 1949 Ford, styled by Henry's new designer George Walker, Benson Ford, vice-president in charge of the Lincoln-Mercury Division, had his new offerings ready. On April 11, 1948, the 1949 Lincoln and Lincoln Cosmopolitan were introduced to the public. Eighteen days later, on the 29th, Benson revealed his personal pride, the stylish and comfortable 1949

Mercury.

None of the Lincoln-Mercury cars received the introduction fanfare accorded the new Ford when it was unveiled on June 10. For this gala event only the gold-and-white grand ballroom of New York's Waldorf-Astoria would do.

The New York showing was lavish. Before the grand opening for the public, radio, television, and newspaper reporters enjoyed a preview complete with music, champagne, and a miniature replica of the 1949 Ford presented to each member of the media in attendance.

They saw the first of the totally new postwar automobiles, for Ford had the jump on the competition, and the car was hardly recognizable as a Ford product. It was lower to the ground, neatly designed with minimum chrome trim, offered greater seating capacity than previous Fords, and had a larger windshield with more side glass for increased visibility. The running boards had vanished.

Throughout the six-day show the Waldorf-Astoria ballroom was jammed with the curious, thousands ready to buy. Before the books were closed on the '49, more than 800,000 were sold. Total Ford Motor Company passenger car sales, which included Lincoln and Mercury units, broke the million barrier. Henry Ford II had the company back on its feet.

The 1949 Ford proved, however, not to have the high-quality construction Henry had envisioned. The body did not fit solidly to the chassis, and dealers began to relay buyer complaints of dirt and water seeping into the interior. After talking it over with Ernie Breech, Henry decided that the time had come to form a separate division to oversee Ford vehicle production. On February 11, 1949, Ford Division was organized to handle all aspects of production, assembly, and marketing of all passenger cars and trucks bearing the Ford nameplate. Lewis D. Crusoe, who had headed planning for the contemplated organization for two years, was named vice-president in charge. He was to supervise the division as a totally separate function, a company within the company.

Crusoe and his assistant general manager at the new Ford Division, staid and scholarly Robert S. McNamara, were both cost-conscious executives. Tex Thornton had resigned, and McNamara was top man among the Whiz Kids. McNamara, with his roundish face, rimless glasses, and straight hair flat against his scalp, hardly fit so playful a term as "whiz kid," but he had an incisive, finance-oriented mind.

Both men, Crusoe in particular, felt the 1949 Ford was too expensive to compete with Chevrolet. John Davis, the sales manager, was not so sure.

"Remember," he pointed out, "that when we were first in sales Chevrolet took our leadership away from us even when their car cost a hundred dollars more than ours. They made real profits because they had a good gross margin."

Crusoe and McNamara believed that higher grosses came by reducing production costs. They had their engineers dismantle Fords and Chevrolets, then compared the parts from both cars as to size and number and actual cost, getting the figures down to within one cent.

"You know," Crusoe said, "this is a nickel-and-dime business. If we save a dime on each of a million units, we've saved $100,000 in production costs. I'll tell you, we'll practically cut your throat around here for a quarter."

His final comparative figures had shown him that a Chevrolet was less costly to produce than a Ford, about $84 cheaper. He and McNamara set about to lower that differential, but it would take time.

The outbreak of the Korean War in June of 1950 upset their timetable. While automobile production was not halted, a crimp was put into making cars by government restrictions on aluminum and steel. Not until after the end of the conflict, three years later, could they get back into high gear.

Planning for war's end, Ford Division was ready in 1953 to surprise the market with a new series of two better styled cars that offered roomier interiors and better handling and roadability. One, the lower of the two in price, was the Ford Mainline. The second, which would take its place among the company's more successful products, was the Ford Fairlane. Sales of the 1954s hit 267,799, only 25,280 less than Chevrolet. They had made the kind of inroads Ford had hoped for.

In the meantime Ford was making great strides with its overseas operations. What had started as far back as 1904 with the granting of a franchise to sell Fords throughout Europe to a man named Percival

Perry, had later been broadened into Ford of Britain acting as a holding company for facilities developed in Germany, Denmark, Spain, Holland, and France. In the early fifties Ford bought out minority interests in their foreign subsidiaries to form Ford of Europe, with headquarters in London. The company was now literally worldwide.

General Motors and Chrysler also had highly successful European operations. Inevitably the European manufacturers began testing the waters of the American market. The little MG Midget began it in 1946, with Jaguar following soon after, its XK120 at around $4,000 hitting it big from the start. Americans were not only talking about, but also buying, cars that were winners at LeMans and in European Grand Prix races.

The minor flood of sporty imports opened the eyes of the American automakers. Their designers began emulating the imports, scrapping the big, high-off-the-ground styling, lowering the overall height and rounding out sharp body corners to minimize wind drag.

Chevrolet beat Ford to the draw, unveiling its dream car, the Corvette, at the 1953 Motorama. Its most unusual features were body construction of reinforced fiberglass on a conventional frame, with seating for only two. It was acclaimed as the most striking American sports car since the classic Stutz Bearcat, which had died in the Depression.

Lewis Crusoe was not to be outdone. On October 22, 1954, less than two years after the Corvette debut,

Ford answered the Chevrolet challenge with its Thunderbird two-seater. It offered a full range of transmissions—automatic, manual syncromesh, and overdrive—and the availability of options such as power brakes, power steering, and power seats.

Corvette, in the $5,000 bracket, had first-year problems in performance and maneuverability that were quickly corrected. However, its first-year production totaled only 300, while Thunderbird hit the road with 11,000 during its initial year at a basic price under $2,700.

On February 1, 1955, changes were made in the corporate structure of the Ford Motor Company. One of the executive promotions more than likely triggered a reversal in the temperament of Henry Ford II, while another proved significant to the future of Lee Iacocca. Ernest R. Breech moved up from executive vice-president to the newly established post of chairman of the board. While Breech and Ford continued handling major management decisions together, the titles in effect made Ernie Breech Henry's superior.

The position of executive vice-president was filled by Lewis Crusoe, who was replaced as the head of Ford Division by Robert S. McNamara.

Ford Division designers had no totally new car on the drawing boards for the 1956 model year when Bob McNamara took over. However, new models for 1956 were introduced in late 1955 for the Mercury and the Lincoln/Continental divisions. Mercury brought out two, the more luxurious of which was the Monterey, planned to compete with Buick and Oldsmobile. William Clay Ford, Henry's brother and head of Lincoln/Continental, offered the Continental Mark II.

McNamara's most serious concern at Ford Division in his first year as its head was to try to close the widening gap between Ford and Chevrolet. In 1954 Ford had closed in on Chevy, coming within 17,013 units after a disastrous 1953, when Chevy had beaten Ford by 226,213 sales. In 1955 the hopes of the previous year were dashed as Chevrolet retightened its lead to the tune of almost 67,000.

Lee Iacocca's fabulous promotion for the Philadelphia district, "56 for 56," had set new records for the area. McNamara was impressed by the sales in Philadelphia and picked up the "56 for 56" idea for national use. Although sales increased by some 72,000 sales that might not otherwise have been made, Ford's 1956 model year was disheartening. Chevrolet's edge had stretched to 190,056 over Ford.

It became obvious to Bob McNamara that his Ford Division needed a heavy charge. He was hopeful that the young marketing genius in the Chester office, who had just been promoted to head the Washington district, was the man to turn things around. He sent Charley Beacham to Chester during the week of Lee Iacocca's wedding to bring the young man, nurtured by Beacham, back to Ford Division headquarters in Dearborn as Ford's new marketing manager for trucks.

CHAPTER 5

Jubilant as a newlywed, and hopeful that his career was on the rise, Lee Iacocca arrived in Dearborn on November 1, 1956, to take up his new duties. He was confident that here, in the thick of things at Ford, he could make his mark in the big leagues of the automobile business. He checked in with Charley Beacham at Ford Division, the low-rise structure less than a mile south of Ford's new twelve-story world headquarters. The imposing Glass House had been dedicated just three days before his marriage to Mary McCleary.

The ebullient spirit of his strikingly beautiful and understanding wife had increased his own zest for life and his love of the challenge ahead. He missed her tremendously, and his first priority had to be finding a home so that she could join him.

With Beacham's help good luck came his way within a week. Another Ford executive was being transferred, and his house was available. Lee, certain that Mary would like the rambling ranch house on Orchard Lake, about twenty miles north of his Dearborn office, rented it. Mary arrived by the middle of the month.

When he first stepped into the Ford Division offices, Lee found the Ford complex in an upbeat state. The previous year had set a record in car and truck production. More than 2.5 million vehicles had rolled off the assembly lines despite the company's slippage in its battle with General Motors and Ford Division's inability to close in on Chevrolet. Amazingly, Ford had paid out over $1 billion in wages to 180,000 employees in the one year.

On March 7 the Ford Motor Company had become a public corporation when the Ford Foundation released 10 million shares for sale. No longer was it a wholly family-owned company, even though the Fords still controlled a majority of the voting stock. The day Ford shares went on sale, the floor of the New York Stock Exchange was a madhouse. Ford's first annual report, reflecting a $437 million profit, made investors eager to buy pieces of the pie. Over 235,000 individuals bought one or more shares of stock within a week.

The year 1956 had begun and progressed right into fall as a year of milestones. On June 19 a Ford had set the 500-mile stock car record at the Indianapolis Speedway. The world took note, and Ford stock went up. Then, on September 28, the day after Lee heard of his promotion, Ford had received even more worldwide publicity as it made its first public showing of cars in Moscow. Henry Ford II had been there, capitalist or not, to be regaled by the Soviet communist leaders.

On November 16 Henry presided over another big Ford event, one that—unsuspected at the time—would become one of the company's biggest flops. It was the introduction of the Edsel.

The Edsel was named for the first Ford who believed in the value of automobile styling. Edsel's father had not agreed, but now Henry II was bringing out an automobile that he confidently expected would become the styling sensation of the decade.

It was not. The Edsel had been designed in group sessions, with too many fingers leaving their mark on its identity. It came to life, as one wag put it, like a camel, which is really a horse created by committee.

The Edsel did have a different, innovative style, much too different for the times, and it came on the market with three strikes against it. The car had been rushed through and had far more defects than the normal few usually expected in new automobiles. Its front end was strange looking with a "horsecollar" grille that turned off many buyers. And the Edsel was offered in so many models at such varying prices that prospective purchasers were confused.

The Edsel was also unlucky. It made its bow just before a recession hit the nation, so that even later refinements in its styling and correction of its defects could not save it. An expensive fiasco—its tooling and production costs were estimated at $350 million—it died an ignominious death soon after its second birthday.

The optimism Lee sensed when he first arrived had

137

turned to ashes, but with his new responsibilities he could not let the pall that hung over the company affect his work. He attacked his job head-on, not conservatively and feeling his way as most newcomers to responsibility are wont to do. For him today was already yesterday if he were to reverse Ford's bad second in truck sales to Chevrolet. A look at the charts revealed that Chevrolet had averaged 50,000 more sales a year for each of the last five. Ford had come closest in 1954, when it had been only 25,280 behind.

Iacocca quickly discovered that the source of the problem nationwide was little different from what he had found in the Philadelphia district. Dealer apathy had relegated truck merchandising to the status of stepchild in relation to cars. Most dealerships who sold both cars and trucks found selling five or more automobiles easier than making a single truck sale, and few urged their salesmen to give equal emphasis to trucks.

The solution, then, lay in dealership-level training. Both dealers and salesmen had to be sensitized to the importance of truck volume to their own profitability. Iacocca would have to reemphasize the specific knowledge needed to sell cargo carriers in contrast to those necessary for passenger car sales.

Lee went into the field himself. He paid hard-sell visits to dealers. He held forceful seminars for salesmen, speaking his mind toughly and tersely, sure that only a get-with-it honest approach could succeed. He organized a task force to follow up his personal visits and check on progress.

His program worked. In his first year as truck marketing manager he chopped Ford's truck sales deficit to within 14,000 of Chevrolet, an astounding success when balanced against the miseries of the five previous years.

This startling turnaround was not lost on Robert McNamara, and before the year's end he promoted Lee Iacocca to marketing manager for cars.

Lee could hardly contain himself. It was a giant step toward his goal, and he could not wait to phone his father. Nick's Italian blood raced with pride. He had always said there was no stopping his son, and he urged Lee to go for the top.

Lee swung into his new assignment with his usual total commitment, giving more evidence of his ability to cope with the demands of the increasingly complex automobile business. In 1957, for the first time in twenty-two years, Ford new-car registrations topped those of Chevrolet. In one year Ford Division shot 50,000 units ahead of the enemy. It was a master achievement, a historic landmark for the Ford Motor Company, and one that helped ease the agony over the Edsel.

The normally imperturbable McNamara was enthusiastic in his praise. His protégé had achieved a long-sought goal. Ernest Breech came by personally with a salute. Even Henry Ford II phoned to congratulate Lee. If cloud nine exists, Lee Iacocca was riding it.

A few days later Lee had a more personal cause for celebration. Mary had returned home from a visit to her doctor to say she was pregnant. Lee's spirits sky-rocketed, looking ahead to the one blessing that out-weighed his progress at Ford.

It was not something for him to delight in alone. Nick and Antoinette would have to come. So, too, would Mary's mother. And, he told Mary, it was time that they bought their own house, since his promotion made it financially feasible. A finer, larger home was found in Birmingham, the suburb north of Detroit that housed many of the industry's executives.

Back at his desk in Ford Division, Lee busily prepared for the introduction of McNamara's brainchild, the Ford Falcon. The more McNamara saw of Iacocca, the more he liked the straightforward, dogged honesty of the young man from Allentown. He was particularly impressed by the fact that Iacocca was no sycophant. If he disagreed with something, he spoke up, even when his position was counter to that of his boss.

McNamara had planned the Falcon, the first American compact, as a car that would enable Ford to beat all other major carmakers in offering a smaller-sized automobile, and he wanted a solid marketing strategy for its introduction. McNamara told his planning committee that he thought "safety" was the basis on which the new car should be sold. He was concerned over the public's perception of the automobile as a killer since congressional hearings on the subject began in 1956. In his view the public would react favorably to positioning the safety features of the Falcon as the base of its promotion and advertising.

"Safety won't sell cars," was Iacocca's unhesitant reaction.

Safety, he was convinced, would only rub salt in an already festering wound and make the buyer more wary. Besides, legal problems might accrue from advertising safety. An accident victim might prove a case against the company, claiming that "advertised safety" was tantamount to a guarantee against injury. McNamara saw the point and dropped the idea.

Lee and his staff plunged full speed ahead in search of a promotion so electrifying it would receive broadscale coverage in newspapers as well as on radio and television. It was a trying time for Lee, spearheading the structure of the promotion while spending as much time as possible with Mary, now in her ninth month of pregnancy.

Lee's father and mother arrived from Allentown, and Mary's mother from Chester, to help. On June 29, 1959, less than five weeks before the unveiling of the Falcon, Kathy Iacocca introduced herself to the world at Detroit's Henry Ford Hospital. The tiny girl had upstaged the spectacular Lee was planning for Ford's newest car.

When Mary came home with the Iacocca firstborn, holding the beautiful, dark-haired baby girl became a source of competition between Lee and the grandparents. Never was a child more loved and coddled, and no home echoed more with happiness and joy.

The exultation at the Iacocca home in Birmingham was in sharp contrast to the fretful spirit that marked the Henry Ford II mansion in Grosse Pointe. Anne,

the dazzling socialite Henry had given up his college
degree to marry, had wearied of him. She had given
Henry two daughters—Charlotte, born in 1941, and
Anne, in 1943, as well as a son, Edsel II, in 1945—but
had enough of Henry's peccable ways.

The beginning of the end had come when Henry
met Cristina Vettore Austin, an Italian divorcee at a
Parisian party given by Ernest Kanzler's fourth wife.
With the once rhapsodic union of Anne McDonnell
and Henry Ford II turning sour, Henry was hardly
aware of the plans for the presentation of his newest
automobile.

Bob McNamara enthusiastically approved the Falcon introduction promo, conceived by Iacocca, and
gave Lee a hearty go-ahead. The setting was to be a
small town in the center of the United States, Flora, a
city of 5,000 population in the heart of the dairy and
farming area of southern Illinois.

On a bright, hot day in August a procession of new
Falcons paraded into the usually quiet town, now
festooned with flags and bunting heralding the honor
bestowed on it by the Ford Motor Company. On their
arrival the Falcons were distributed among the towns-
people, one for each family in Flora and the adjacent
area, and one for each single adult.

Throughout the morning and afternoon Lee
Iacocca moved among the citizens and business estab-
lishments of Flora, asking their personal opinions of
the cars they drove. What did they like about them?
What didn't they like? Would they suggest any
changes? It was an attention-getter never before expe-

rienced in the automobile industry, and it was enjoyed vicariously by all America via television.

Flora's gala day sparked a Falcon sales record unequaled in the industry, with first-year registrations of 417,174. A testimonial to the skill with which Lee Iacocca executed the campaign, it was also a triumph for Robert McNamara, who described Lee Iacocca as a man worth his weight in gold. It had not been easy to sell Henry Ford II on the value of offering the American public a smartly styled, low-priced, six-cylinder car as a choice against the gas-guzzlers of the day.

Less than three months after his phenomenal success at Flora, Lee Iacocca celebrated his thirty-fifth birthday. He experienced a tinge of disappointment at not having earned a vice-presidency by then, but his regret was alleviated by the happy birthday greetings at home and by tiny Kathy, not yet four months old. He also took solace in the fact that he had come a long way in a short time.

Unaware that Henry Ford II was sharpening his guillotine for a series of decapitations, Iacocca continued to work hard. Henry had felt for some time that he had had enough of Ernest Breech, that the time was ripe to bid him goodbye.

Breech had been more instrumental than Henry himself in saving the Ford Motor Company after the death of the first Henry Ford. Henry II had leaned on his knowledge and expertise and had given Breech the post of chairman, a step higher than his own as president. For Henry this was no longer a healthy situation.

Henry had been usurping many of Breech's prerogatives as chairman. With private innuendos he began downgrading the man who had done so much for the company, while in public utterances he continued to praise Breech. Increasingly Henry exhibited traits that reminded his associates of his grandfather.

In the summer of 1960 he finally let Ernie Breech know that he was no longer wanted. The professional and tactful Beech quietly submitted his resignation to Henry in mid-July. In the subsequent corporate realignment Henry II served for a time both as president and chairman.

Soon, however, the burden proved too great for a man with an impending divorce who was drinking more heavily. Robert McNamara was named president, which created an opening in the post of vice-president and general manager of Ford Division.

On the morning of November 11, 1960, Lee Iacocca was summoned to Henry's office in the Glass House. The job was his. He had achieved the vice-presidency, not by his thirty-fifth birthday as he had predicted so long ago, but less than two weeks after his thirty-sixth.

Lee returned to Ford Division as its boss. Driving the short distance back from the Glass House, he realized that his takeover of Bob McNamara's office was bound to breed bitterness and animosity. He had leaped past older men with longer tenure. Keeping them in line would take strong, unsubtle measures.

"Get with it," he told the men now under his command. "You're being observed closely. Guys who

don't get with it don't play on the team after a while."
It worked because, as Iacocca says, "all of a sudden a
guy is face to face with the reality of his mortgage
payments."

From the moment he returned to Ford Division as
its head, Lee Iacocca set about to get a firm grip on
everything affecting his responsibilities. He made certain that he knew all that happened in the ranks, and
he let his men know he knew. He developed an evaluation process for his department heads, preparing what
came to be known as Iacocca's "black book"—a journal that held each department chief's objectives for
the quarter ahead. At the end of each three-month
period he graded each man on the extent to which
those objectives had been met.

He stretched his people to their limits and threw
himself into the battle with equal intensity, spurred on
by an ego that matched his position. He had a large
group of varied and conflicting personalities to manage and control. Those who knew and respected his
integrity were inspired by his dedication. Any who
harbored resentment at his meteoric climb were pulled
quickly in line by the force of his magnetism or were
soon gone.

Lee Iacocca's toughness and resoluteness of purpose brought distinction and panache to Ford Division. "So much panache," said Hal Sperlick, a
product planner and engineer at Ford since 1957,
"that along with John Kennedy, who hit the world
about the same time, he was like a breath of fresh air.
They were both young for the responsibilities they

were to have. They brought a little bit of Camelot, Kennedy to Washington and Iacocca to Ford Division. With Lee's young, new kind of management, things were pretty exciting."

Excitement was the norm throughout the Ford Motor Company during the final months of 1960. President-elect John F. Kennedy wanted the man who was president of Ford in his cabinet.

Despite having been given the choice of heading the Treasury or Defense departments, Robert McNamara was reluctant to leave Ford so soon after attaining its presidency. Sargent Shriver, sent by Kennedy to make the offer, persisted, but McNamara refused the Treasury appointment, claiming no expertise in fiscal affairs or banking. Nor did he want Defense. He did, however, promise to meet with John Kennedy the following day.

It took a second meeting with the President-elect before McNamara accepted the post of secretary of defense. He submitted his resignation to Henry Ford II, and John Dykstra, not Lee Iacocca, was named to succeed him at Ford.

Early in 1961 Lee Iacocca stirred up excitement at Ford with a dynamic promotion that overshadowed the pageantry of the pilgrimage to Flora, Illinois. He had added a convertible to the Falcon, giving the line a sporty flair that included bucket seats. The Falcon's inaugural at Flora had been all-American. This new Falcon with touches of European styling deserved a continental presentation.

On New Year's Eve two airliners with more than

200 men and women aboard, including Lee Iacocca, Gar Laux, Walter Murphy, Wes Small, and Tom Kierney of Ford Division, as well as Bill Winn and Bob Castle representing Ford promotion agencies, took off for Europe. Also aboard were a variety of Ford automobiles, not the least of which were several new Falcon convertibles, and 120 press people, which included representatives of prestigious magazines such as *Newsweek* and *Time*.

The entourage arrived at Monaco, the tiny principality overlooking the Mediterranean, at six in the morning New Year's Day. The all-night ride, spiced by many beverages, was a loud, happy, and wakeful one. The hour of arrival, however, allowed little time for freshening up, much less a catnap. A reception was scheduled for ten o'clock at the royal palace of Prince Rainier and Princess Grace.

In the great hall of the palace, awaiting the appearance of the royal family, the Ford people and the news people were served champagne in huge beer mugs. "The last thing we needed after that plane ride," Walter Murphy said. At ten o'clock sharp huge golden doors opened, framing Princess Grace, former American movie star.

Princess Grace, followed by Prince Rainier and three-year-old Prince Albert, greeted Lee Iacocca and the entire American group. There was an instantaneous rapport between Iacocca and the ruler of the world's smallest principality. They talked at length about automobiles. Rainier, Lee discovered, had a well-rounded knowledge of engineering.

Iacocca presented His Serene Highness with a new Ford Thunderbird and Princess Grace with a Ford station wagon for her Red Cross charity. To their heir, Prince Albert, he gave a specially handcrafted, miniature Thunderbird.

The unveiling of the new Falcon convertible and other Ford products to the press was scheduled for that afternoon in the grounds of the Place du Casino de Monte Carlo, high above the Mediterranean, and although Monaco has no more than sixty days of rain in a year, that day it poured. A large tent was erected on the Casino grounds for the product presentation presided over by Gar Laux.

At the conclusion of the formalities members of the press took part in a ride-and-drive exercise to give each an opportunity to evaluate the car. Starting at the casino, a seventy-five-mile route road-rally course had been laid out that took the riders through the town and out into the Maritime Alps.

Lee Iacocca rode in a Falcon piloted by Timo Makinen, a Finnish race driver. At one point as they made a turn in the mountains, the driver lost control momentarily. For seconds the car seemed headed off the crest of a mountain into a gully hundreds of feet down.

The car was righted just in time and brought to the finish line undamaged. "Well, I at least found out what the car can do," was all a still-shaking Iacocca could say as he stepped out of the Falcon.

In the evening most of the Ford and press people congregated in the world's most famous casino. As he stood watching the milling crowd, Walter Murphy, Iacocca's public relations chief, was approached by a dark-haired, dark-skinned man.

"My boss would like to talk to your boss," the man told Murphy in broken English.

"Who's your boss?" Murphy asked. The request seemed strange, coming at such an inappropriate time.

The man pointed toward the entrance where Murphy could see a dignified, gray-haired, smartly attired, obviously well-to-do individual. "It is Mr. Aristotle Onassis," the man explained.

Knowing that Iacocca did not stand on protocol, Murphy indicated the table at which Lee stood. "There's my boss," he told the man. "Take him over and introduce him."

It was definitely not the way of Ari Onassis. "No! No!" the dark-skinned man said almost fearfully. "It is not right. You must introduce him."

Murphy shrugged his shoulders. The man must be one of the Onassis's servants or bodyguards, he decided. He agreed to introduce the famous Greek shipping tycoon to Lee Iacocca, vice-president of the Ford Motor Company.

Once he had done the honors, Murphy walked out onto the balcony overlooking the basinlike harbor of Monte Carlo. Moored there, far below, was the Onassis yacht—as big as the *Queen Mary*, Murphy thought—festooned with strings of sparkling lights from prow to stern, which illuminated a huge banner bearing a welcome to Ford and Lee Iacocca.

Lee found Ari Onassis a charming and enchanting conversationalist. He was fascinated by this Greek who had spent little time in the United States, yet knew more about American history than he did. Onassis began with the causes of the American Revolution and ticked off, in year-by-year chronology, historic events through the election of John Fitzgerald Kennedy.

The stay in Monaco lasted two weeks. During that period Ford cars were entered in the annual Monaco Grand Prix, the twisting, treacherous, around-the-houses race now a fixture on the Grand Prix circuit. The Ford cars were not expected to win—they were entered only as a test of the cars' durability for the benefit of the press. The race was won by England's great driver, Stirling Moss, in a Lotus-Climax.

Ford automobiles also took part in the Paris-to-Monaco leg of the Monte Carlo Rally, one of the oldest and best known of all rallies. The principal purpose was to get film footage of Ford cars in action, with Bill Winn supervising the crew that photographed the full run. This time a Falcon won in its class.

The Ford session in Monaco and its entries in the Grand Prix and Monte Carlo Rally received worldwide attention and so was judged an overwhelming promotional success. Once back in America, Lee Iacocca had other attention-getters ready for the same model year. One, designed to add zest to the Falcon's introduction to Ford dealers, made a new Falcon convertible available to airline stewardesses who had a day off between flights in cities where Ford dealer meetings were being held. The stewardesses had the car for their personal use and visited the ceremonies presenting the Falcon to the Ford dealers.

It was also in 1961 that Lee Iacocca produced another promotion that would continue bringing prospects into Ford dealerships. This was the highly motivating Punt, Pass, and Kick program, providing youngsters nine through thirteen the opportunity to show their abilities in three facets of football. Produced in cooperation with the National Football League, the Punt, Pass, and Kick competition began in local Ford dealerships.

Winners at the local level went on to compete in district challenges. District victors met other district winners for zone competitions. The latter were held during half times of scheduled NFL games, with the champions in each age group going on to vie for national honors during half time of the Super Bowl.

Youngsters qualified for PP&K participation by visiting their local Ford dealership in the company of fathers or related adults, a factor that in itself packed a powerful promotional punch. Over the fifteen-year span of the program more than 20 million car buyers visited Ford dealerships with PP&K hopefuls, a good percentage of whom might not otherwise have been exposed to a Ford product. No valid estimate can be made of the probably many thousands of sales that were generated.

Punt, Pass, and Kick exemplifies Lee Iacocca's perception of what stimulates public interest and produces sales. It also reflects his awareness of what it takes to stir public interest and excitement. In this instance the passion of young America for sports competition could become an asset for Ford because Iacocca understood the public as well as his relationship to those who implemented the programs.

No one else in the industry came close to achieving the success of the promotional themes conceived by Lee Iacocca. His campaigns combined good, practical, utilitarian sense with drama.

In methodical, systematized fashion Lee Iacocca went about planning for automobiles that would carry his personal totem. When he took over Ford Division, he had to work with automobiles conceived by others. He gave McNamara's Falcon a few new touches, added the successful convertible to the line, but a car that was distinctly an Iacocca creation would take time. In the automobile industry an incubation of three years was necessary to take a car from design to final production.

Moving from the first scratches on the drawing board to a finished automobile is a long, laborious, and tedious process that in more recent years has been speeded up by computer and other technological advances. First is the planning. What kind of car will have public appeal? What dimensions? What power? What basic features are needed to make it an attractive buy at a marketable price?

Only after most of these fundamentals have been resolved, production costs estimated, is the next step—designing—taken. This in itself is no simple, one-time go-through. Refinements and adjustments in styling lines, often in the preset dimensions and other elements, are made, altered, and realtered until the powers are satisfied. Then prototypes are constructed of wood and clay. And again changes may be needed. At the same time dies to make the body components are created. All this is necessary before a driveable prototype can be built, because the final product represents an investment of millions of dollars.

Lee realized that Ford could not afford another bomb like the Edsel. Planning for his own car of the future had to begin with positive indications of its viability in the market. Meanwhile, business had to proceed as usual.

He supervised the final touches on the new Ford Fairlane series, which entered the market with some success on November 16, 1961, as one of the Ford entries for the 1962 model year. For 1963 he restyled the Falcon and the standard Ford model rooflines to provide a more contemporary look, and he added a V-8 to give Falcon better performance. To give the "new-look" Falcon exposure Iacocca had it driven to college campuses throughout the country accompanied by a "Hootenanny Folk Sing."

Iacocca was also determined to dispel the public's image of Ford cars as stodgy, unimaginative vehicles and to give the cars' fresh, modern styling and improved performance more visibility. Where better, he thought, than on the racetrack?

European Fords had done their part over the years. In 1936, 1938, and 1953 English Fords won the Monte Carlo Rally and other races on the continent. In 1955 another English Ford won the rough, tough, East African Safari through Kenya and Uganda.

Before 1960, the year in which the American automobile industry agreed not to sponsor racing events, American Fords had done extremely well. The 1,913-mile

Pan-Americana race through Central America was won by Lincolns in 1952–53–54, and from 1956 through 1959 Ford racked up hundreds of wins in NASCAR (National Association for Stock Car Auto Racing) competition. And in 1962 an unsponsored Ford-powered car won the three-hour continental race at Daytona.

Iacocca looked on the three-year-old agreement as an exercise in hypocrisy. Many manufacturers still clandestinely underwrote race expenses. He believed Ford should come out in the open with company sponsorship and approached Henry Ford II with his idea. Automotive racing attracted more people than baseball and football combined, making it ideal for the exposure of Ford cars.

Henry was enthusiastic. He had already been excited by the nearly endless Grand Prix and LeMans wins by Ferrari, so much so that he had tried to buy Enzo Ferrari's company and make Ferrari director of operations for automobiles that would be called Ford-Ferraris.

Ferrari had turned him down, irritating Henry. A few weeks later Ferrari changed his mind, but Henry took no chances on a second rebuff. He refused to buy. He gave Lee Iacocca carte blanche to get into racing, especially to build Ford cars that would whip Ferrari's best.

Henry's quick agreement may have been triggered by other matters that occupied his mind. For one thing he made it clear on May 1, 1963, that uneasy would lie the head of anyone he made president of the Ford Motor Company. He announced that John Dykstra had been replaced by Arjay Miller, one of the original Whiz Kids. Miller took office as the seventh president in the history of the company, the fifth to hold that office in the seventeen years since Henry II took over.

The following months were especially troublesome for Henry. His marriage to Anne had finally collapsed. His affair with the Italian divorcee had become too much of an embarrassment to Anne McDonnell Ford. On August 3, 1963, she and Henry had legally separated, she to go her way, he to pursue the indomitable Cristina.

Lee went back to work not only to prepare the Ford Motor Company for racing wars, but to make final decisions on his personal contribution to the Ford line, a car to be called—after many other names were discarded for one reason or another—the Ford Mustang.

CHAPTER 6

Unaware that he was creating a legend, Lee Iacocca initiated plans for the first automobile he could call his own. His primary objective was to give American car buyers the kind of automobile they wanted. Iacocca was determined that his new car would be something special. It had to be, for he sensed that the American public had become more demanding and more quality conscious, that a change in public tastes was in the air.

A significant factor in Iacocca's thinking were the imports, which were eating up an increasingly larger share of the American market. The import invasion had begun after World War II when England's manufacturers returned to car production before their counterparts in the United States were given the go-ahead by Washington.

The perky and sporty MG led the way, sending one-third of its 1946 production, 500 cars, across the

Atlantic. Jaguar quickly followed. American GIs in Europe had been exposed to the sportier styling of British and European cars, many of which, like the MG, were smaller that U.S. models, and they had earned to like them. Given a choice between a used American car and a new European model, many opted for the latter. In no time MG's most profitable market was the United States. Jaguar also found a bonanza on the western shores of the Atlantic. When its XK120, a stock car that sold for about $4,000, was delivered in the United States, it became an overnight sensation among fine-car buffs.

By 1948 the imports had achieved the modest American market penetration of 0.46 percent. It was so small, compared to GM's more than 40 percent, Chrysler's over 21 percent, and even Ford's near 19 percent, that American carmakers had not been concerned. Nor were they worried in 1956, when the import share climbed to 1.65 percent of American sales, even though it was more than double that of the previous year.

Volkswagen's Beetle and its smart Kharmann-Ghia coupe had hit American buyers in 1955, accounting for the sharp rise in import sales. Toyota and Datsun, from Japan, followed in 1957 and 1958, respectively. By the end of 1959 imports had achieved a startling 10.17 percent of American car sales, taking just over 4.25 percent from General Motors and over 2.5 percent from Chrysler. Thanks to Falcon, Ford earned a 1.68 percent increase.

A sharp diagnostician, Iacocca found further rein-

forcement for his concept of a new car in the sale
figures for 1960, a year in which both GM an
Chrysler introduced new compact cars to increas
their shares of the American market at the expense o
the imports and Ford.

Just a few months before Lee Iacocca's promotio
to general manager of Ford Division—a pressure
laden responsibility since Ford Division produced 8
percent of the company's car—Chrysler had brough
out its compact Plymouth Valiant, with a 101-horse
power, six-cylinder engine and a revolutionary electri
cal alternator. The new Valiant helped boos
Plymouth sales by 55,486 in 1960.

At about the same time GM's Chevrolet Divisio
offered its air-cooled, independently sprung, rea
engined Corvair. Corvair sold surprisingly well—i
would be some time before Ralph Nader's boo
Unsafe at Any Speed would deal it a death blow—
boosting Chevy's 1960 sales 277,794 over the previou
year.

One factor in Corvair's sales charts particularl
intrigued Iacocca. The highest number of Corvai
sales went to its sporty version called Monza, a ca
that to a great degree reflected the styling of th
European imports. But Lee was not totally convince
that the Corvair Monza provided a barometer fo
what Americans hungered for in an automobile. Cer
tainly, Monza's success indicated that Ford Moto
Company's lack of sportily styled automobiles ha
caused its decrease in 1960 of more than 50,000 sale
while Chevy registrations shot up over a quarter

million. Yet Iacocca felt that sportiness alone was not the complete answer.

A somewhat clearer picture emerged from a survey taken of the extra equipment ordered for Ford Falcons. A great percentage of buyers had paid extra for more powerful engines, automatic transmissions, power features, and decorative items such as paint stripes and white sidewall tires. Americans, it seemed, did not want plain, unexciting cars.

Nonetheless, the picture of trends in American buyer wants in automobiles was still cloudy. Iacocca needed a sharper focus to avoid an Edsel fiasco. The Edsel's styling had not been thoroughly researched.

To get a handle on public preference Lee gathered a staff of twenty young researchers and put them on a crash schedule. He told them to find out what kind of car Americans wanted. How big or small? How much power? What kind of styling? What special equipment?

His researchers polled students, young marrieds, the middle-aged, Korean veterans, even Monza buyers. Surprisingly few interviewees cared for anything then on the market. Some pointed to the small, jazzy Europeans as "maybe" their kind of car. Most said only that they would like "something different."

Early on in his new position Lee Iacocca had put together a staff of capable aides, specialists in engineering, product planning, styling, and merchandising. Hal Sperlick was one. Gar Laux, Don Frey, and Joe Oros were others. Together with Lee they analyzed the research results in depth.

159

They soon noted that a new market segment, with its own buying patterns, had been growing gradually among young buyers, the eighteen- and nineteen-year-olds ready for their first car, as well as the young marrieds who were then taking on family responsibilities at an earlier age. They wanted a car with flair in its styling.

As the Iacocca team dug further, it discovered that this same sportiness was desired by a sizable percentage of the middle-aged and older, the "young at heart" who wanted to express their youthful spirit in a car with gusto. Television had proved to be the foundation of youth that washed away the stodgy and dull in their lives and instilled a passion for excitement and adventure.

The research revealed another important factor. A growing economy was producing a more affluent middle class. The number of two-car families was growing, and they preferred a smaller, personalized automobile for their second car.

These multiple findings established a profile of the automobile Lee's intuition told him would please American buyers. This would be his first contribution to the Ford product line. Plan a car that is easy to handle, he ordered his team, a car styled with zip and class, lower and longer in front than other American makes, and shorter in the rear deck. Make it an automobile that performs with dash, that can go from zero to sixty in seven or eight seconds. And, very important, he emphasized, produce a car affordable for young America.

"Lee was very much personally involved in every phase of the car right from scratch," Hal Sperlick said. "He wanted to pave some fresh ground as the new vice-president of Ford Division. He wanted this car to hit a ready market and make the statement that Ford really was back in the mainstream of the automobile business."

Iacocca was not looking for a small car per se, Sperlick made clear. "There were some small cars out, like the Falcon and Monza," he said. "But Lee was looking for a distinctive kind of car. From cars already on the market you could buy only either a big car or a smaller, plain kind, and there wasn't a really nice smaller car available. If you wanted a nice car, you had to buy a Lincoln or Cadillac, but that was it."

In late October of 1961 Iacocca approved the specifications for the car as recommended by Sperlick and his product-planning team. It should weigh no more than 2,500 pounds and be no more than fifteen feet (180 inches) in overall length. And its retail price should be $2,500 or less.

The next step was to create a clay model based on the specifications. Lee discussed the matter with Eugene Bordinat, Ford Motor Company's chief designer. Bordinat arranged a competition between the company's three design studios, the Ford Division, Lincoln-Mercury, and Corporate studios. Each would take the specifications and come up with one or more clay models reflecting their individual conceptions of how the car should look.

Within two weeks the studios had seven clay models ready for inspection by Iacocca and his team. The one designed by Joe Oros, Ford Division's head stylist, had the lines and smart styling Lee wanted. It was a different, unique breed of automobile that measured less than twenty-nine inches from the ground to the top of the hood and only 154 inches in overall length, twenty-six inches shorter than the original specifications called for.

Lee was pleased with Oros's design at first sight. His initial plan had been a two-seater, much like the original Thunderbird, but he had changed his mind, asking that a small back seat be added. His gut reaction as he examined the clay model of a convertible was that they were on the right track.

But what about Henry Ford II? How would he look on this project, which had been put together secretly? It would take many millions of dollars to tool up for and put into production such a car, and Henry's yes or no meant its life or death.

Protocol demanded that Iacocca approach Arjay Miller, the company president, before going to Ford, the board chairman. But Lee, impatient at any small delay, went directly to Henry's suite in the Glass House. Henry all but literally threw him out of the office. He had absolutely no interest.

Lee returned to Ford Division undismayed. He knew he was right, and however long it took, he would prove it. In a week he was back at the Glass House, trying to persuade Henry that the market was ready for this type of smaller car. An angry Henry again showed Lee the door, making it clear he was not interested in a small car.

A third and fourth trip found Henry gradually weakening, showing a bit of interest, but still opposed. But Lee, realizing that he was developing a sort of inevitability for the success of his project, persisted. The fifth time at Henry's office he was able to outline details of the research he had conducted. Henry finally agreed to at least come and take a look.

At the Styling Center, surrounded by Iacocca, Sperlick, and other Ford Division men, Henry still shook his head. Neither Lee Iacocca nor Hal Sperlick could convince Henry, however aggressively they sold the concept of the new automobile or the need for it in the marketplace. Henry was nervous over the failure of the Edsel and the resulting cash drain on the company, yet he finally agreed to think it over.

Iacocca already had set himself a timetable that would be shattered if he had to wait for Henry's final decision. He took a chance and gave his team a go-ahead to proceed to the next phase, building an actual-size model from laminated hardwoods.

He had good reasons for his seeming impatience. As vital as secrecy is in the highly competitive automobile business, where every security caution possible is taken, word of activity on anything new does leak out. Lee already knew that Chevrolet was considering a scaled-down version of the successful Corvette, and he was determined to beat them into the market.

Lee also realized that rumors were buzzing around

Detroit about an unusual new two-seater sports-type car on the Ford drawing boards. He hoped that these fast-spreading but unconfirmed reports would not send Chevrolet into a crash program that would upset his own schedule. He had to have a prototype ready the moment Henry approved funding for production—if, indeed, he gave the go-ahead.

Speculation about the new one from Ford escalated throughout the industry, and Lee had a plan to feed those rumors. Dependent on Henry II's decision, he intended to unveil a prototype of some kind during the annual running of the 1962 American Grand Prix at Watkins Glen, New York, on October 7.

Meanwhile Iacocca and his team busied themselves with deciding on a name for his creation. The name of a new car is vitally important to its marketability and sales success. In order to stir buyer enthusiasm it had to be catchy, memorable, and meaningful in terms of the car's image, a name that could be translated into advertising impact.

Merely for identification Iacocca's team referred to the new automobile as the Special Falcon. But nothing like the name Falcon was to be considered. Falcon was a Bob McNamara offering, and the all-new concept had to be perceived as an Iacocca production. Lee ordered the Ford Division advertising agency, J. Walter Thompson, to suggest names. The agency reported back with a list numbering more than 5,000. On the list were Colt, Bronco, Cheetah, Torino, Cougar, and Mustang.

Joe Oros had referred to his clay model as Cougar,

and for a time that name was considered. Then a decision was made to call the car Torino, since it had a Ferrari flavor and Ferrari was built in Turin, a city the Italians call Torino. Torino was considered so seriously that J. Walker Thompson prepared potential advertisements using that name.

Despite all the pre-preparation the name Torino was suddenly dropped. One Ford executive said that the name had become an embarrassment since Henry Ford II was at the time pursuing Cristina all over Europe while his divorce was still pending. Iacocca, it was said, feared that the press would play the Italian connection to the hilt, making a mockery of the car's introduction.

Gar Laux, who was close to Lee throughout the car's development, is inclined to discount that story. "Look at the car," he said. "Look at the first proto-type, then the second, and finally the car that was introduced. It looked, that first little one at Watkins Glen, like an Italian import. But when the car went on the market, it was all-American. Its looks had changed, so the name had to change. It became the Yankee-doodle car, and a name like Torino didn't fit. Mustang did. Made you think of wild charging horses and the wide-open west. The name and the car, they were both as American as all hell!"

Getting the approval of Henry Ford II to build Mustang took time and some doing on Lee Iacocca's part. As structured under Henry Ford II the Ford Motor Company was heavily financed-oriented, in sharp contrast to the fiscal looseness of the company under his grandfather. As a result every major investment was a difficult sell. Henry was not about to commit millions of dollars to produce anything but a sure hit. Undismayed, Iacocca collared Henry at every opportunity, either alone or with Hal Sperlick's backing. Sperlick was as confident in, and as excited about, their planned car as was Lee. But Henry continued to hold out, demanding solid facts and figures to justify spending millions.

Yet, when Lee and Sperlick provided the facts and figures and peppered Henry with the results of their surveys, Henry remained opposed. Sure of his ground, Lee did not give up.

On September 10, 1962, Lee made another trip to the Glass House office of Henry Ford II. He again presented his case for a car that his gut feeling told him would bowl over the industry.

This time Henry, obviously weakening, agreed to take another look. He went with Lee to the Styling Center and examined the prototype from bumper to bumper. Finally he opened the passenger-side door and sat in the rear seat.

Henry, as the story goes, frowned for a moment. The back seat did not have enough room, he said. The car should provide an additional inch of space in the rear.

Iacocca, Sperlick, and the design team surrounding the car disagreed. Adding even that inch of space would destroy the styling, they all agreed. Henry would not listen. It had to be his way or there would be no new car.

Losing a small battle was better than total defeat. The designers and stylists added the extra space. Iacocca's persuasiveness had paid off at small cost. Henry approved an appropriation of $51 million for production of the new Mustang.

Iacocca and Sperlick were jubilant as they rushed back to Ford Division, but they had little time to savor their victory because a lot of work remained before the blue prototype could be shipped under wraps to Watkins Glen. After nearly a month's work around-the-clock, everything was ready.

The afternoon of October 7, 1962, 35,000 race buffs filled the Watkins Glen grandstand as a hard rain swept across the oval. They were there primarily to see some of the world's greatest race drivers compete in the American Grand Prix, but for hours curious eyes were focused on a platform in the infield where something was shrouded in canvas.

After Scotland's champion driver Jim Clark swept across the finish line as winner in his Lotus-Climax, the tarpaulin was removed. There it stood, now identified as Experimental Mustang I. In minutes thousands of spectators sloshed through mud and wet grass to get a close-up view of the little blue car with a Ferrari flair.

Standing no higher than a baby's crib, it had a long, sloping front end that ended hardly a foot from the platform floor. It had no headlights. It was equipped with a V-4 engine installed, not under the hood like most American cars, not at the rear like a Volkswagen Beetle or Corvair, but in the middle like many classic European cars.

It had been planned as a smoke screen, a showcase car displayed to throw all competition off base, one with just enough of the future Mustang to whet the appetite—if indeed American car buyers reacted with pleasure. It was there to give Iacocca the assurance that he was on the right track.

At the unveiling Lee knew he was. The enthuiasm of the thousands crowding around the platform oblivious of the torrential rain gave him his answer. The hundreds in the crowd trying to place orders immediately buttressed his confidence.

Of course it was impossible to take orders, however loudly the crowd clamored. The real Mustang would not be ready for sale for almost two years.

After his return to Dearborn Iacocca realized that a way would have to be found to maintain and nourish the astounding interest generated at Watkins Glen in a car not yet ready for final production. A means had to be found for placating the media, which was bombarding him, Walter Murphy, and his Ford public relations staff with questions.

Iacocca could not afford to dampen this mounting Mustang momentum. Since he was not ready to release details about his final product, he decided on preparing another red herring to keep curiosity boiling. He ordered the building of a second Mustang prototype.

The front and back ends of Experimental Mustang I were chopped and pointed fenders added to give the new showpiece a different look. Since Mustang I, with its aerodynamic front end, had no headlights, recessed headlamps with glass covers were installed. Experimental Mustang II was also given an open-mouthed grille in which was centered the soon-to-become-ubiquitous galloping pony emblem.

Iacocca was playing a cloak-and-dagger game to give himself time to produce the real Mustang while throwing competition off. So he created Experimental Mustang II as another hybrid, part real Mustang and part fantasy, though less a phantom of the mind than the first.

No secret was made of the plan to reveal the new prototype. It was sent off with panoply and fanfare to the 1963 Watkins Glen American Grand Prix. Unlike 1962, this showing was not intended as a sneak preview. Newspapers, television, and radio reported the upcoming event. Journalists speculated as much about the car as about the race itself. Not surprisingly, attendance at Watkins Glen was far greater than in 1962.

Iacocca had hoped for a large crowd, for the reaction of the thousands at Watkins Glen would reassure him that his new car had what would be needed to crowd Ford showrooms once the real Mustang was introduced.

Iacocca need not have worried. A hungry, eager crowd swarmed excitedly about the platform displaying his four-wheeled offspring. Not only young people, but men and women of middle age and older, shouted at anyone who appeared to be a Ford representative demanding, as hundreds had done the year before, to place orders.

The usually impassive Iacocca could not suppress a smile. If only Henry Ford II, who had fought production of Mustang for so long, were there to see.

Back at the Ford Division offices Iacocca Sperlick, Laux, and others on his Mustang team sat around a conference table relishing their victory. They had many things to discuss, including the refinements that would transform Experimental Mustang II into the real thing. Just as important was the matter of Mustang's introduction.

New car models were at the time normally introduced in the fall, which would mean a year's wait. Iacocca was not about to have Mustang's debut diluted by other car intros. He put production on an all-out basis. "Make Mustang happen," he told his staff. "And make it quick."

Lee Iacocca had involved himself in all levels leading to the creation of the Mustang, a rarity in the industry. Now his primary efforts could be directed toward promotion and marketing, at which he was a master. The two exposures at Watkins Glen were just the forerunners of a promotion blitz unequaled in any area of the business world.

Lee did not permit any letdown after the smash success at Watkins Glen. Within weeks he had his staff invite fifty young, middle-income couples to the Ford Styling Center as a means of confirming consumer reactions to Mustang. They came in small groups, they looked and admired. Almost to a couple their only negative reaction was to what they believed such a fine car would cost. Their estimates ranged from $4,000-$7,000, hardly practical for middle-incomes of the time.

When they heard that the base price was somewhat under $2,500, they expressed amazement and disbelief. At such a price, all agreed, Mustang was a car that they would like to own. This simple master stroke sent 100 voices out of the Ford Styling Center to spread the word of Mustang through fifty American cities.

To further bridge the gap before Mustang's official introduction, Iacocca brought 200 of the nation's most listened-to radio disc jockeys to the Ford test track opposite Ford Division. Each test-drove a Mustang, and each was promised the use of a Mustang for a week after his return home. All any d.j. needed to do was contact the local Ford dealer and pick up the car.

At the turn of the year, Iacoca brought in Frank Zimmerman, who had joined Ford as a trainee just before Lee himself, to work with him as general marketing manager. As Mustang Day neared, promotions were stepped up. Mustangs were displayed at 200 Holiday Inns and in major airport terminals, shopping centers, and business lobbies.

On Monday April 13, 1964, Mustang Introduction Day, a press preview preceded the public showing in the Ford Pavilion at the New York World's Fair. Newspaper, radio, and television representatives from the United States and Canada heard briefings on Mustang and then participated in a road rally that

171

took them from the pavilion to Ford headquarters in Dearborn, Michigan.

A reporter at the Ford Pavilion asked Lee Iacocca how many Mustangs he expected to sell in its first year.

"How many Falcons were sold?" Lee asked.

The automotive journalist rattled off the Falcon sales record, as yet unequaled in the industry. He told Lee, "417,174."

"Mustang will go 417,175," Lee said. (Actual sales figures for Mustang's first year were 417,800!)

Mustang mania took hold of America when the car was officially introduced to the public on April 17 at the New York World's Fair. Visitors packed into the Ford Pavilion in near hysteria. That same evening a Mustang served as pace car for a race in Huntsville, Alabama. More than 7,500 enthusiasts leaped over the retaining wall to form a phalanx around the Mustang, holding it in place and delaying the race for over an hour.

Car buffs swarmed into Ford dealerships from coast to coast in such numbers that business was halted. A Ford dealer in Pittsburgh was unable to get a Mustang off a wash rack because of people crowding around the car. In Chicago a dealer was forced to lock his doors, the crush of Mustang lookers was so great.

Henry Ford II was on hand at the Ford Pavilion, but Lee Iacocca was the man in demand. His picture made the cover of the April 17 issue of *Time*, and the cover feature of *Newsweek* was the Iacocca story. He had produced a spectacular car with a name that would soon be familiar in Rio, Rome, and Rangoon as well as Racine.

Mustang was quickly perceived as the all-American, all-purpose automobile. It could be seen at country clubs, outside famous restaurants and churches, as well as at drag strips and on boulevards. It was the right car at the right time, a sizzler with four-on-the-floor that appealed to a full spectrum of drivers from eighteen to eighty.

Such terms as "Mustang mystique," "Mustang mania," and "Mustang generation" became everyday expressions, the latter first used by a California real estate developer named Howard Ruby. In brochures advertising apartments for young singles he offered "A country club atmosphere catering to the champagne tastes of the Mustang generation."

Mustanging became a way of life in America and throughout the world, and erased the dull and the humdrum replacing them with glamour and excitement. It was a Cinderella slipper on wheels, magically converting reserved Walter Mitty types into debonair men-about-town, as pictured in one of the early television commercials approved by Iacocca.

In the one-minute commercial Henry Foster, staid and prim in rimless pince-nez spectacles, derby hat, and dark suit, was seen leaving his shop. He was carrying something in a brown paper bag. He turned the sign that read "open" to "out to lunch" and securely locked the door. In the background was a wispy old lady who operated a nearby shop. "Have you heard about Henry Foster?" she asked.

Henry then walked stiffly until he turned the cor
ner. There, in sight of his new red Mustang he
became a different man. Off went his pince-ne
glasses, his derby hat, his dark suitcoat. On went
bright plaid hat, red vest, and dark goggles, all taken
from the brown paper bag. As he got behind the
wheel of the Mustang, the old lady's voice was heard
saying: "Something's happened to Henry."

The screen then showed Henry braking his Mus
tang in a park area as a soft, seductive voice said, "A
Mustang's happened to Henry." On a grassy plot in
the park a sexy young woman waited with a picnic
basket and bottle of wine. Henry leaped from his
Mustang to join the young lady, now totally uninhib
ited, happy and laughing.

"Mustang made it happen" became the battle cry
of the "in" people of the mid-sixties, whatever their
age. Lee Iacocca's desk at Ford Division was flooded
with letters from young and old telling how much
Mustang was loved. One forty-four-year-old bachelo
from Texas wrote that he had a "pony V-8 in Rangoon
Red with accent paint stripes, molding, and air
conditioning, and man, this is the greatest. A widow
with seven thousand acres came sixty miles so I could
take her riding in it."

It was a Mustang world from its first day in the
showroom, and Lee Iacocca took every advantage to
keep the magic full force. The day Mustang was born
he agreed to cooperate with the newly formed Na
tional Council of Mustang Clubs headquartered in

the shadows of Ford Division. It was an extension of the firmly rooted car club traditions in Europe.

The National Council of Mustang Clubs brought the hundreds of such clubs throughout the United States under one umbrella, sponsoring activities that ran the gamut of motorsport action. Its big day through the following years was April 17, a nationwide celebration of Mustang's birthday.

On that day rallies were held by the hundreds of clubs associated with the National Council. From the final results of each year's rallies a national winner was determined and presented with a new Mustang. All the proceeds generated by rallies supervised by the National Council on that day were donated by the individual clubs to local charities.

Club activities took place year-round. On any weekend one might find a beach gathering in Florida or California. There would be local slaloms, gymkhanas, and hill climbs almost anywhere. The National Council even developed a "Braille rally" for youngsters at schools for the blind. Club members would bring their Mustangs and each select a blind boy or girl to serve as navigator using instructions prepared in braille.

Iacocca also created the Society of Mustangers, a no-constitution and no-by-laws groups of Mustang owners brought together about the time the millionth Mustang came off the assembly line. It was established only after Mustang owners in Chicago, Philadelphia, and Los Angeles were mailed a brochure explaining the plan and asking their reaction.

The only obligation, as stated in the brochure, was a two dollar annual fee, for which members would receive quarterly issues of *The Mustanger*, a magazine that would serve as the official voice of the society, as well as a membership card and a decal for their car. Other incentives were discounted tour and travel rates; hotel, motel, restaurant, and nightclub discounts; specially arranged Mustanger pleasure trips; and quality merchandise items at about half the normal retail cost, all explained and displayed in *The Mustanger*.

The recipients of the brochures were asked only to mail in a "no" or "yes" indication of their interest in this type of organization. So strong was the magnetism of Mustang that not only were "yes" votes unexpectedly large, 16 percent of those answering also included two dollars, even though the society had not yet been established. One month later an actual solicitation mailing was made, and over 35,000 Mustang owners became members of the Society of Mustangers.

One of the surprising facts discovered in the creation of the society was that as many as 8 percent of members were between fifty-five and sixty-five years of age, and 2 percent were over sixty-five. As was expected, 67 percent were under forty-five. Not expected were such revealing figures as those that showed 51 percent had annual incomes of $10,000 or over, and 36 percent were professional or managerial types. The college educated accounted for 58 percent.

Lee Iacocca had stunned the automobile industry

with his Mustang, the car that made its debut at a time when America was ready for an automobile with a change of pace in styling and performance. General Motors, Chrysler, and American Motors were not about to stand by stoically watching Mustang sales spiral steadily upward without doing something.

Chevrolet had a similiar car on its drawing boards when Mustang exploded on the market, but it did not make its bow for two years. Mustang sales had soared past a half-million before Chevy brought out its Camaro, another jazzy, sleek machine that symbolized youthfulness.

To a degree the 1967 Camaro was a Mustang copy. It fit the long-hood, short-deck design and came on the scene gunning for Mustang's record. While 100,000 Camaros did hit the road within seven months, Chevy's entry was unable to outsell Mustang in any one sales period for almost three years.

General Motors tossed another competitor into the ring with its Pontiac Firebird. Chrysler entered the sports car field about the same time with refined versions of the Plymouth Barracuda and Dodge Charger, neither of which was a completely new car. A year after Camaro American Motors produced two "muscle" cars, as Mustang types were being called, the Javelin and the AMX. None came near matching Camaro, and Camaro was hard put to come close to Mustang in popularity.

The phenomenon that was Mustang, especially with spirited, powerful engines offered as options, could not be restricted to the street scene. Inevitably it progressed from street to drag strip and from drag strip to racing oval.

"Race 'em on Sunday, and sell 'em on Monday," was Lee Iacocca's philosophy. Mustangs raced and sold.

On drag strips, where it takes brute horsepower to eat up 1,320 feet of hot asphalt in the shortest time, Mustangs were fierce competitors, thanks to Iacocca's support and a supercharged 427-cubic-inch single overhead cam engine. Mustangs won class championships in the spring nationals of the National Hot Rod Association. In the American Hot Rod Association winter championship races a Mustang equipped with a 429-cubic-inch Cobra jet engine achieved an estimated 114 miles per hour, turning in an elapsed time of 12.5 seconds for the 1,320-foot dash.

From drag strip to road racing is a natural progression, and there, too, Mustang could not be denied. The Sports Car Club of America opened the door when it established the Trans-American sedan series. In a "24-hours at Daytona" race Mustang blew its Trans-Am competitors, including Camaro, figuratively into the Atlantic as it finished first in class, and fourth overall, behind three Porsche 907 coupes.

Ford Motor Company's reentry into the racing scene actually had taken place early in the summer of '64, two months after Mustang's introduction. Henry Ford II, anxious to upstage Enzo Ferrari after the Italian carmaker's initial refusal to sell the Ferrari plant to Ford, had pressured Iacocca's Ford Division

eam to produce a car for the 1964 LeMans twenty-
our hour race.

Iacocca's engineers produced three cars dubbed the
Ford GT40 for the confrontation with Ferrari. The
first Ford-built, Ford-sponsored cars ever to race on
an international circuit, they were equipped with 4.2-
liter (256-cubic-inch) V-8 engines. Their GT40 designation deceived few at the famous French race. Most
saw them as experimental Mustangs with special
bodies.

Also included among the fifty-five starters in the
competition were two cars with 427-cubic-inch Ford
Cobra Jet engines. Neither was an official Ford Motor Company entry. Enzo Ferrari's entries included
two new V-12 Ferraris with 3.3- and 4-liter displace-
ment. Triumphs, Porsches, Alfa Romeos, and Jag-
uars were among the other racers ready for the
twenty-four-hour run.

As far as the press and the public were concerned,
the focus of the race was on the Ferrari-Ford confrontation. Henry Ford II, in typical fashion, pulled no
punches. He was out to humiliate Ferrari, and he was
confident it could be done. In substance the race had
developed into a struggle between American cars and
the European.

For the first hour after the fall of the starter's
flag—and despite two of the Ford GT40s being boxed
in by other cars—the third GT40, driven by Richie
Ginther and Gaston Gregory (both Americans), held
the lead over a Ferrari 330P, handled by Lorenzo
Bandini of Italy and England's John Surtees. Before

it was over, however, all three GT40s had broke
down, and Ferrari ran away with the honors.

It was a bitter defeat for Henry Ford II, tempere
little by the fact that one of the unsponsored Cobr
Jets had won first place in the GT category. Henr
vowed to be back next year.

The defeat at LeMans in no way tarnished 1964 a
Lee Iacocca's year of glory. Before year's end th
Mustang was acclaimed an international succes
visible almost everywhere in the free world. An
everywhere the Ford Motor Company was perceive
in connection with Lee Iacocca as much as Henr
Ford. Iacocca was lauded as Mr. Mustang.

Everyone close to Lee Iacocca knows, however, tha
the birth of the Mustang was not his most treasure
memory of 1964. On July 16 Mary Iacocca ha
presented him with his second daughter. She wa
named Lia, after her now famous father.

Walter P. Chrysler, founder of Chrysler Corporation (*National Automotive History Collection Photo, Detroit Public Library*)

Lee Iacocca, the new president of the Ford Motor Company in 1970 (*National Automotive History Collection Photo, Detroit Public Library*)

Lee Iacocca, Frank Sinatra, and Leo-Arthur Kelmenson during discussion of Sinatra's TV appearances for Chrysler Imperial (*Photo courtesy of Kenyon & Eckhardt Public Relations*)

Iacocca and the first K-car off the assembly line (*Photo by John Collier,* Detroit Free Press)

Iacocca answering questions at a news conference (*Photo by John Collier*, Detroit Free Press)

A moment at home with younger daughter, Lia (*Photo by John Collier*, Detroit Free Press)

Lee Iacocca with wife Mary and daughter Lia in the living room of their Bloomfield Hills home (*Photo by John Collier*, Detroit Free Press)

Lee at home in Lido's Lounge, as wife Mary and daughter Lia watch a news report showing a televised Iacocca appearance before a congressional committee (*Photo by John Collier*, Detroit Free Press)

Henry Ford II as he took over the Ford Motor Company after discharge from the Navy in 1946 (*National Automotive History Collection Photo, Detroit Public Library*)

The first Henry Ford in his original Model A (*National Automotive History Collection Photo, Detroit Public Library*)

Lee Iacocca on his arrival at Ford headquarters in 1956 (*National Automotive History Collection Photo, Detroit Public Library*)

Lee Iacocca (*right*) with Bill Winn during the Cougar introduction in the Caribbean (*Photo courtesy of Bill Winn*)

Experimental Mustang I, the red-herring prototype exhibited at 1962 Watkins Glen Grand Prix *(National Automotive History Collection Photo, Detroit Public Library)*

Experimental Mustang II, the second smokescreen prototype exhibited at 1963 Watkins Glen Grand Prix (*National Automotive History Collection Photo, Detroit Public Library*)

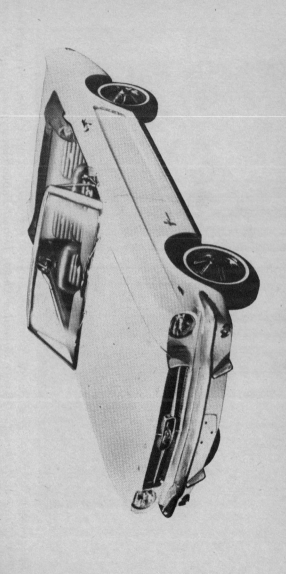

The real first Mustang as introduced at the New York World's Fair in April, 1964 (*National Automotive History Collection Photo, Detroit Public Library*)

Left to right: Bill Winn, Lee Iacocca, Frank Zimmerman, and Larry Domegal (Ford's fleet and lease manager) at a cocktail reception following a Mustang introduction *(Photo courtesy of Bill Winn)*

CHAPTER 7

For Lee Iacocca the birth of his second daughter had a bittersweet tinge. Tiny Lia, with reddish hair and pretty features much like her mother's, seemed likely to be their last child, an unhappy prospect for a man so family-oriented. But Lee was worried about his wife. Mary Iacocca had been a diabetic for some time, and recently her condition had worsened.

Lee's devotion to his wife of more than two and one-half decades was in the classic, biblical mode, a total commitment that places her welfare above his own. For him she was a friend, companion, and confidante. And he was her balm during hours of pain, anxious when he must leave town without her, and making contingent plans before he did leave. Friends like Bill Winn and Gar Laux were always ready if an emergency arose. Both tell of rushing her to a hospital in a diabetic coma when Lee had been away.

Time and again Lee had left important meetings abruptly after getting word that Mary has been stricken. At a most critical moment during the Chrysler Corporation loan-guarantee hearings in January, 1979, he left Washington the moment his secretary notified him that Mary had suffered a heart attack, rushing to the hospital in Boca Raton, Florida, the site of their winter home, where Mary sought relief from the bitter Michigan cold.

Lee also accompanied his wife on all her visits for tests or treatment at Boston's Joslin Clinic for Diabetes Research. He was dedicated not only to helping her get well, but also to helping solve the problem of diabetes. For some time he contributed a significant part of his salary to the Joslin Clinic. He also served on the board of directors of the President's Advisory Council of the American Diabetes Association.

"Some of the men he works with call him the Iron Chancellor or the Ayatollah at the office," Mary said with a laugh, "but around the house he's a lamb. He calls Kathy 'Olive Oyl' and Lia 'Sweet Pea.' They call him 'Wimpy.' "

Iacocca is proud of his role as a dedicated father. Though his two daughters, Kathy and Lia, seem to have the world on a string, both know the value of money and like to do things on their own. The spirit of independence and the emotional drive to be a doer, inherited by Lee from his father, is also apparent in the two girls.

When twenty-one-year-old Kathy went to work at Chrysler as part of a college course, she insisted it be without pay. She was not only concerned over her father's being accused of nepotism but felt it wrong when Chrysler workers made sacrifices to keep the company going. Yet, when her six-week course took her into sales and she joined the sales staff of a Chrysler dealership away from the Detroit area, she accepted commissions for cars she sold.

"She moved four cars in one week's time," the dealer reported. "More than my best salesman, so she earned it."

Just before turning seventeen Lee's youngest daughter, Lia, also wanted to earn her own money during summer vacation. To go to work at Chrysler in a depressed economy and with people out of work was unthinkable. She did ask her father to help her get work at Kenyon & Eckhardt, Chrysler's ad agency. Lee said no, that would not be proper, at the same time wondering if she understood his refusal to help.

Lia did understand. On her own she found and took a summer job with an art studio as an apprentice and messenger.

Understandably, since Lee is so much a reflection of his father, his family is close-knit. On Sundays when Mary's health permitted, all four may have been seen together at St. Hugo of the Hills Catholic Church for mass. Holidays, birthdays, anniversaries, any special occasion within the family, were spent together as a foursome.

Lee allowed no circumstance, however urgent, to interfere with a promise to Mary or the children. On one occasion while he was president of Ford a mixup in the scheduled date of a high-level meeting with Henry Ford conflicted with an afternoon off on which he had promised to take the children on an outing.

As he prepared to leave his office for the day, his secretary told Lee that he was expected at the meeting.

"I'm not going to the meeting," he told her.

The secretary reminded him of its importance. "Mr. Ford said . . ." she insisted.

Lee cut her off. "I don't really give a damn," he said. "I promised my daughters I was taking them out, and I'm going to take them. This damn place could burn down before I'd break my promise."

With Lee Iacocca his family comes before everything else. "He is very protective of us," Mary Iacocca said. "Maybe too much so. He telephoned every day, maybe three or four times. And it doesn't matter where he is, at a dealer meeting in California or over in Europe. He was also that way with Kathy when she was at college in California. And his mother, too. At least once a week he phoned Antoinette to see how she was."

Iococca has always had an abiding preference for his home fireside. On normal days he makes every effort to leave his office as soon after six as possible. And, unlike many of his contemporaries, he never stops at some watering place on the way home. Eager to get there, he immediately headed his car north on the Southfield Freeway, heading for the comfortable, quietly elegant nineteen-room home in Bloomfield Hills.

There was peace and serenity in the very location of the house, sitting back from the road and framed by tall and stately trees. Its large sunken living room with huge picture windows overlooking the green of a Michigan spring or summer, the multicolored leaves of fall, or the white snows of winter, was not furnished for show but for easy conversation among friends and family.

Iacocca's home life was easy, happy, and uncomplicated, except for his continuing concern over Mary's health. There was no formality even when Mary and he entertain, no fancy feasts. Most dinners, even when such close friends as the Bill Winns are there, have a family flavor reminiscent of those in the Allentown row house when Lee was a young man.

When Lee arrived home, he was most likely pulling off his tie as he walked in the door. Relaxing before dinner he may have had a bit of cheese, a glass of wine, and perhaps a few moments alone. More often than not he would sip as he helped in the kitchen, for at the Iacocca's getting dinner was a family affair.

Naturally, pasta was a frequent fare, Lee and Mary would jointly get it ready, as Lia—when Kathy was away at school—made the salad and set the table. Noodles for the spaghetti were Mary's own home-made. The sauce varied from time to time, but Lee's preference was one without tomatoes, with the noodles simmered in broth and topped with a creamy sauce over which grated cheese and crumbled bacon was generously sprinkled.

After dinner it may have been just casual conversa-

tion in the living room, a game of gin with Mary, or—
as Lee so much enjoys—an hour or two alone in his
den, which was located on a lower level. Iacocca
called this fully equipped haven Lido's Lounge. It
was filled with mementos of his life, pictures of his
family and friends, a game table, and a soundproof
booth holding a sixteen-millimeter projector for Sat-
urday-night showing of carefully chosen motion pictures. There, too, was Lee's special pride, an excellent
stereo system.

Lido's Lounge was Iacocca's "think tank" hide-
away. One of his greatest pleasures was to lie back in a
comfortable chair and listen to tapes of the music he
loves best, the big-band sound of the forties era,
Tommy Dorsey, Les Brown, Paul Whiteman.

"Lee has always been a jazz buff," says Bill Winn,
who shared an apartment with Lee in his earliest
Ford days. After Lee completed his training period
and began work at Ford's Philadelphia District office, Winn visited Iacocca. "We went to New York for
a weekend," he says. "Lee really wanted to see the
Andrea Doria, which was then making its maiden
voyage. After all, it's an Italian ship and was docking
at New York and allowing visitors aboard."

Winn and Iacocca did board the *Andrea Doria* and
were impressed, but the most memorable event of the
weekend was their stop at a small club where the
great Dizzy Gillespie was featured. "Once Lee knew
Gillespie was there, we had to go," Winn says.

They arrived at the club so early that no one was

there but Gillespie himself, sitting on the bandstand with his horn. The sweet Gillespie tones mesmerized Iacocca, according to Winn, but only until Dizzy began eating a sandwich while he played.

"We sat there, I don't know how long, just waiting for part of the sandwich to come blowing out of that horn," Winn laughs. "It's something Lee has never forgotten. And Dizzy Gillespie has been a favorite ever since."

Their beautiful home notwithstanding, the Iacoccas did little socializing. A dinner out now and then when Mary felt well enough, and a gathering of their closest friends once in a while. When not in Washington fighting government regulation, or away on other business inside or outside the country, Lee's evenings were spent quietly at home.

Except Friday. That was Lee's night, reserved for a friendly game of poker either in Lido's Lounge or at the home of one of the other men with whom he played. Even during the most amicable game Lee's shrewdness was evident.

"You can never get by with a bluff with him," says Gar Laux. "That computer mind of his has your hand pegged from your first raise. But he's really a softie, a good human being under that hard-nosed exterior. It's not in his nature to hurt a person's feelings."

Laux himself was a volunteer aide in helping solve a problem caused by Lee's inability to harm someone who had served him well. For some weeks Laux had seen that Lee's secretary, an older woman who had been at the job for years, had become too slow to keep up with Iacocca's fast-charging dictation. He finally suggested that it wasn't fair to keep the woman in a job for which she was no longer suited, that it would be best to let the secretary go.

"I just can't do it," Lee told Laux. "I haven't got the heart to hurt her."

"You know, you're not being mean to the woman," Laux pointed out. "She's a nice lady, but she's having a hard time. If you can't do it, would you like me to handle it?"

Lee nodded. "But be sure she's transferred to a job that pays at least the same," he said. "Something she can hold until her retirement."

Men like Gar Laux, Bill Winn, Hal Sperlick, and Leo-Arthur Kelmenson, who have known Iacocca and worked closely with him for thirty-five years or more, describe him as the most loyal and protective of his friends of anyone they have ever known. Each always is careful to point out that he shouldn't be looked on as a saint, a man without blemish who never makes a wrong judgment.

"Sure he does things wrong," Gar Laux is quick to say. "We all do. The only guy who didn't died on a cross, and the world has seen only one of those. But hell, he's right so damn much more than he's wrong." Rough and gruff himself, Laux holds nothing back. "He's the roughest s.o.b. I've ever worked for," he adds. "In a second he can make you feel like shinola if you've goofed somewhere. A minute later he's asking you how's the wife! Or reminding you about

Friday night's poker game."

On the job Lee Iacocca is tough and uncompromising. He expects much and demands much of the men who work with and for him. What his people learn from him is to keep reaching, never to stop reaching. He is never satisfied with a man just doing his job, even if he does it well. A man must reach beyond the limits of his immediate work.

He preaches two philosophies. One is that he doesn't pay any man on his team merely for what he does. More important is what the man gets others to accomplish. Anyone working for Lee at a supervisory level has to give management of subordinates his highest priority. In a business as complex as the automobile industry no department can be a one-man operation and run smoothly. And that leads to Iacocca's second doctrine, the need for management development.

Lee is adamant that his department heads not only manage their people but they also develop personnel who can climb up the corporate ladder, individuals who at the very least can replace their immediate supervisors.

Each of his department heads is required to turn in quarterly evaluation forms of the people they manage. If he receives a form indicating that a worker in the department has remained too long in one capacity, Lee's reaction is that the department head has not done his job in bringing the subordinate along.

"That's one of the keys to Iacocca's success," Gar Laux says. "Even if a man is an expert in one phase of the business, he wants him to progress to another and become equally expert. Everybody working for him has to move forward, expect to be the head honcho someday."

Iacocca also instituted a requirement that department heads submit quarterly plans indicating what they intend to accomplish in the following three-month period. At the end of each quarter he expects an evaluation by each individual of his own work. He is more likely to accept total failure if the man evaluates his accomplishment as zero and can explain the reasons, than if one says 50 percent and has managed only 40 to 45 percent. He is that tough a taskmaster. He wants honesty at all times and from everybody, whether employees or suppliers.

Leo-Arthur Kelmenson discovered this Iacocca characteristic the first time they met. Kelmenson had just joined Kenyon & Eckhardt and arrived at Lee's office to introduce himself and assure Iacocca that he would carry on the advertising agency's work on behalf of Ford with the same high level of quality as his predecessor. After an hour of give and take Kelmenson said goodbye and started for the door.

"Kelmenson!" Iacocca called as Kelmenson reached the door. Kelmenson turned and waited. "One thing," Iacocca added. "Don't ever bullshit me."

Kelmenson, a positive-thinker and doer in his own right, answered: "Okay, that's a deal. But you don't bullshit me either."

Based on a more-than-twenty-year working association through good times and bad, one that brought about a close-knit family-to-family relationship, Kelmenson draws a graphic picture of Lee Iacocca. He sees him as a farsighted, hardheaded, often abrasive executive, and a bit of an egomaniac.

Iacocca's biggest problem, in Kelmenson's view, is people who don't really do their work as they should and do only what they think he wants. He is a man who abhors sycophants, who wants his people to fight with him and take a position, to be strong and smart and prove they are right in their stand.

"He's enigmatic, he's wild, he's a hip-shooter, a dreamer," Kelmenson says, "but in spite of all those things he's pragmatic as hell. If he has fifty, a hundred, or a thousand ideas, he knows they're not all good. He knows some are disastrous. But he expects people around him to tell him. But there are far more brilliant strokes of genius that come out of those ideas than from any other man I have ever met."

Iacocca has indeed proved his brilliance again and again. The broadness of his capacity to store information is awesome, as is his ability to use it in daily conversations, speeches, and meetings. He has made himself one of the easiest to listen to, most persuasive public speakers in the industry.

Almost to a man those who have worked with him at Ford, and who now make up his team at Chrysler, say he is an easy leader to follow, an inspiration to do their jobs. He never asks a man to do anything he can't or won't do himself. They also emphasize his phenomenal memory. Make a slip, and at one time or another he'll drag it out of his brain and slap you with it. But they insist, he does it always in a man-to-man confrontation. He never embarrasses a person in public.

Hal Sperlick, who has worked directly with Iacocca longer than any other single individual—he was at Iacocca's side as product planner throughout the development of Mustang—makes an interesting observation about Lee. "There is a piece of him that is General Patton when he's at work," Sperlick says. "Cocky and a great leader, he's the kind of man men follow through hell and high water."

Sperlick also describes Iacocca as a blend of many other personalities, an unusual character aside from his enormous business strength. There's a piece of him that's kind and very, very gentle, a gentleness not only with his family, where he is extraordinary, but with the men he works with.

You see both sides of his character in business, Sperlick elaborates, the very concerned, gentle man and the tough, hard-riding general. And it's a truly interesting kind of man who can be both at the same time. Cars are Iacocca's life. He's a car man through and through. "He awakens in the morning with the car business, and he falls asleep at night in the car business." Sperlick further thinks that what creates a man of such diverse natures would take a mind-boggling depth of psychology to fathom.

Jay Dugan has a somewhat different assessment of the Iacocca character. Other than Bill Winn, Dugan has known Lee Iacocca longer (and knew him earlier in his career) than any of Lee's other contemporaries. Dugan calls Iacocca's "genius a simple genius," the ability to design cars and marketing campaigns that are ahead of his time.

"He is always thinking way ahead of anybody," Dugan says. "It's not as if he gets messages carried by angels. His ideas are simple damn things, but they're so simple they're good, and you wonder why you didn't think of them yourself."

On the more personal side Dugan says that he has never met anyone who has had personal contact with Iacocca, worked for him or with him or was a social friend, who had anything but admiration for the man. "That's rather unique in today's business," Dugan says, "because you've got to be pretty iron-butt, bash in a lot of heads and kick a lot of asses. With it all Lee still has the capacity to engender respect and admiration."

There are those, however, who do not share the near hero worship Jay Dugan, Hal Sperlick, and Gar Laux feel for Iacocca. A good number—all former colleagues at Ford, most of whom came along for the Chrysler ride—disagreed in their evaluations of Iacocca as a man and as a boss, although all attested to his phenomenal ability.

One former vice-president of Ford said, "Unless you were one of Iacocca's inner circle, you always got the short end of the stick. As an executive I expected being called down for serious mistakes, but for even the smallest, often insignificant error, there was a viciousness in his eating out that was humiliating and abusive. You had to take it without a word of rebuttal or you'd find yourself knocked down a few notches."

"Lee was never what you'd call a jolly, warm kind of guy," another said. "But he was on the friendly side when he first came to Ford Division. The minute he was named vice-president of the company in charge of the division, an icky kind of ego seemed to mushroom overnight. He'd walk by you with that big cigar as if you didn't exist. One thing I'll say for Henry. He always had a nod or a smile."

Two other interviewees said they felt demeaned when Iacocca kept them cooling their heels in an outer office after calling them in. "Maybe he was busy," said one of the two, "but it happened too often. After all I had work to do, too."

One former high-level Ford executive who was put through this "wait" routine turned the tables on Iacocca in early 1982. Ben Bidwell, who had headed both Ford car divisions at one time or another and rose to vice-president in charge of Ford's North American car and truck operations, gave Iacocca a dose of his own medicine.

Bidwell left the Ford Motor Company in 1981 and took over the presidency of the Hertz Corporation. In January, 1982, Iacocca paid a visit to Bidwell's Madison Avenue office in New York. He was there to convince his old employee to add more Chrysler-built cars to the Hertz inventory. Iacocca was kept waiting for some twenty minutes in an anteroom of the Hertz headquarters before Bidwell signaled his secretary to usher in his former boss.

Bidwell, a pleasant, pixieish man with a well-known sense of humor, looked up with a smile, as the story goes, and said: "Sorry, Lee. It was the devil made me do it!"

Two others were sharply critical of Iacocca's role in the Pinto rear-end collision crisis. "It was hell around the Glass House in early 1978 when the Pinto problem hit high C," said one. "Pinto sales pooped out like a deflated balloon, and Pinto was really Lee's baby. He got all the kudos when Pinto hit the market, but he never acknowledged any blame for the big trouble we had."

"The Pinto problem would not have happened," the second of the two pointed out, "if the company hadn't tried to save seven or eight dollars a car. Iacocca was the boss, so it was his responsibility. The money it cost Ford could have paid the bill to make two million Pinto gas tanks safe in a rear-end collision. We saved the money and lost the war."

However one views Lee Iacocca, the fact remains that because of Mustang he burst on the world scene as an automotive sage, a rare species in the manner of a Karl Benz or Enzo Ferrari, a farsighted innovator ahead of his times. The often incompatible images of Iacocca drawn by his contemporaries paint him as a hard-driving, often cruel, sometimes sadistic entrepreneur or as a demanding taskmaster fair in his treatment of subordinates, a loyal friend, a warm and loving husband and father.

Too tough though he may be, and sometimes impatient and uncomfortable with those he deems unimportant, the fact remains that, on the job at least, he is in a class by himself. He handles his team like a sharp quarterback, running his offense with imagination and courage.

Unlike his counterparts at other automobile companies Iacocca is publicly perceived as a lively, spirited man and a battler. He maintains a visibility the others lack and has made himself a national—even international—personality. When it is to his advantage, and when the spirit moves him, he can be a humorous, warm, and winning individual, "a guy who can charm the hide off a bull elephant," as one Ford vice-president expressed it, a man at ease with the likes of high-powered types like Gay Talese, Frank Sinatra, and George Steinbrenner.

Incompatible as the varied images of him drawn by his contemporaries may be, he is a loyal friend, an affectionate and dedicated husband and father. For him, his family remains his first priority.

To understand Iacocca the man one must begin with the shy youth, the teenager in a sickbed doing his homework so as not to lose time from his classes. One must then place him in proper perspective as the son of a strong, imperious, often arrogant, loving, overprotective father, as a son who idolized that father and absorbed much of his drive, ambition, and determination.

CHAPTER 8

The year 1965 began on a high note for both the Ford Motor Company and Lee Iacocca. Figures released on January 2 revealed that the company had set a record in worldwide sales—3,952,727 automobiles, trucks, and tractors. Of the more than 2.5 million units sold within the United States, Lee Iacocca's Ford Division had accounted for about three-fourths, an undeniable affirmation of the Iacocca marketing magic.

This achievement deserved recognition and promotion, and Iacocca received both. On January 15, Henry Ford II appointed Lee vice-president of the corporate car and truck group. This step up the corporate ladder also meant a move to world headquarters, an office in the Glass House.

In this new position Iacocca's responsibilities were broadened extensively. He now had overall supervision of planning, production, and marketing of all vehicles offered by the Lincoln-Mercury and Ford divisions. He also would control the advertising and promotion activities of Kenyon & Eckhardt, the advertising agency for Lincoln-Mercury, as well as those of J. Walter Thompson, the agency for Ford Division products.

The promotion brought Lee Iacocca within a step or two of the company presidency. This high on the ladder of succession he certainly would be more vulnerable than ever to demoralizing snipings of fearful or jealous executives. He was aware that in just such a way the dismissal of a good and capable man had been engineered during his second year at Ford Division.

James J. Nance, who had been president of the Packard Motor Car Company, had been persuaded by Ernest Breech to leave that post and come to Ford as vice-president of marketing. Breech, thinking of Ford's future, wanted an experienced man available to replace him.

At that time, Robert S. McNamara, one of the original Whiz Kids, held the position to which Lee Iacocca had just been promoted. Some of McNamara's associates considered Jim Nance a roadblock to their own progress and searched for means to remove him. With the probably unwitting help of Charles F. Moore, Jr., vice-president for public relations, they maneuvered Nance into a newspaper press conference and then accused him of violating Ford policy by not getting prior approval. Henry Ford II, who was soon to dispose of Breech, probably welcomed the opportunity to fire Nance, which he did.

To protect himself Iacocca surrounded himself with men he could trust, including Hal Sperlick, Gar Laux, Frank Zimmerman, and Walter Murphy. He installed John B. Naughton as general manager of Ford Division, Matthew S. McLaughlin to head Lincoln-Mercury, and Theodore Mecke, Jr., as vice-president for public relations. All three were graduates of the Philadelphia district office at Chester, where Lee had gotten his start.

Iacocca had been long aware that too many car buyers harbored an unfavorable perception of Ford Motor Company engineering. In his newly expanded role he now could do something about correcting that impression.

From its earliest years Ford had been the most innovative of carmakers in America. An extensive list of firsts to enhance driving performance, convenience, and safety began developing as early as 1904. The innumerable innovations, which were later utilized by other manufacturers, included Ford's production of the two-door body type, application of a baked-enamel finish for bodies, safety-glass windshields as standard equipment, and the one-piece windshield.

Ford had also been first with the fingertip, push-button starter; first to position passengers between axles rather than over them, for better riding comfort; first with a three-speed torque-converter automatic transmission and with an all-synchro three-speed manual transmission. In more recent years the company had introduced power front-disc brakes, self-adjusting brakes, rack-and-pinion steering for American cars, and many other innovations that the public took for granted, without knowing they originated with Ford.

Iacocca was determined that the public know. He called on Kenyon & Eckhardt for a campaign that would focus on Ford as the industry's foremost innovator. In the process of planning this advertising campaign one of the most memorable slogans in automobile history was created.

A group in the New York office of K & E headed by Ronald DeLuca developed an appropriate concept and produced a number of ads stressing Ford as the company that had conceived and implemented many of the most important refinements in automotive engineering. While working on one of the many ads produced for the campaign, a copywriter in DeLuca's group came up with a phrase that ranks with the previously most memorable of all time: "Ask the man who owns one," which had been conceived for the long-gone Packard. The new slogan, "Ford Has a Better Idea," still serves the company well after more than sixteen years.

Iacocca's appointment of Matt McLaughlin to head Lincoln-Mercury Division fitted in with another of his priorities, to give Lincoln-Mercury greater significance as a division within the company, and to restore it to the status planned for it by Henry's two brothers, Benson and William Clay. For too many years the division had been little more than a company stepchild. To a great degree it had been a dumping ground for Ford Division executives who were deemed incapable of future progress, or a farm club for men believed to be promising material for Ford Division.

Lincoln sales were usually about one-fifth of those of Cadillac, Lincoln's prime competitor. And Mercury was always beaten substantially by Buick and Oldsmobile and by more than two to one by Pontiac. Iacocca could not stomach that situation. He knew that the fault lay in product quality. Mercury had neither good looks nor a comfortable ride.

The reasons for the division's position were obvious. Sufficient money was never allocated to improve product quality, and Lincoln-Mercury advertising budgets were kept too low for effective merchandising. Further erosion had resulted from complacency among Lincoln-Mercury dealers.

"Iacocca took the necessary steps to make Lincoln-Mercury a significant division," according to Leo-Arthur Kelmenson, president of Kenyon & Eckhardt. "He committed the resources to improve product quality. To whatever degree he could, he was the one who supported a clear separation of the two divisions by making the cosmetic and engineering changes needed to give Lincoln and Mercury cars their own image and justify making Lincoln-Mercury a totally separate division within the company."

Iacocca encountered little resistance from Henry Ford II in his efforts to revitalize Lincoln-Mercury and in the appointment of his experienced loyalists to important positions. For one thing, in early 1965 Henry was busy trying to placate his mother, who made no secret about her displeasure over Henry's insistence on marrying Cristina Vettore Austin. Henry became even more preoccupied when he was actually married to Cristina by a District of Columbia justice the night of February 19. The couple went off on an extended honeymoon to England, France, and Switzerland.

Henry was unable to remain long around the Glass House even after his return to Dearborn. During the honeymoon he had set the stage for another family problem by inviting his two daughters, Charlotte and Anne, to come to Europe and get to know the new Mrs. Henry Ford II. While there Charlotte met Stavros Niarchos, the Greek multimillionaire.

The romance that blossomed was not much to Henry's liking. Niarchos was not only eight years older than Henry himself, but he was already married. Henry spent much time flying to New York and to Europe to dissuade his daughter, but to no avail.

Meanwhile Lee Iacocca pursued his ambition to improve Lincoln-Mercury's share of the car market quite unhindered. He directed his product-planning group headed by Hal Sperlick to work toward two new cars far different from the dull, unimaginatively styled, and hard-riding products then being offered by the division.

At the same time he had his racing team at Ford Division make refinements on the Ford GT40 that might bring Henry his desperately wanted victory over Enzo Ferrari at the 1965 LeMans, to be run June 19 and 20. The fleet of GT40s headed for LeMans were to carry the further designation of Mk.2.

Seven GT40 Mk.2 prototypes were sent to LeMans for the round-the-clock race. Hopes were highest for one powered by a seven-liter V-8 and driven by Philip Hill, the first American ever to win a Grand Prix Championship.

During practice sessions Hill's Ford lapped 5.1 seconds faster than the quickest Ferrari, and also set a lap record during the actual race. Through the first half of the twenty-four-hour competition a happy Henry Ford II anxiously awaited the checkered flag. Unfortunately the Ford V-8 engine poured out too much power for the car's transmission and clutch, which broke down.

Enzo Ferrari had turned back Ford for the second successive time and, to embarrass Henry further, had not only done it with a smaller (3.3 liter) engine, but had had his Ferraris finish one-two-three. Irritated, but still stubborn, Henry promised to be back with a winner.

It was an angry Henry Ford II who returned to the Glass House demanding that the Ford racing cars be ready for the 1966 running of the LeMans twenty-four-hour race and placing the burden of getting the job done on Iacocca. Even though Lee was deeply involved in the planning of cars for both Ford and Lincoln-Mercury three years into the future, as well as in completing production of the two Mercurys for introduction in 1966, he could not let Henry down.

He worked with the Ford racing team to produce a fleet of GT40 Ford cars capable of giving Ferrari a run for his money. Exhaustive tests were given each racer to make sure that transmission and clutch performance were compatible with the power of the 427-cubic-inch V-8 engines installed in the cars. Heads would roll if Henry had to eat crow for a third time.

Iacocca further strengthened the 1966 assault on the twenty-four hours of LeMans by approving the signing of three of the finest race-driver teams available. Ken Miles, who had won with a GT40 at Daytona, was paired with Denis Hulme, a Grand Prix champion from New Zealand. Two other New Zealanders who were also Grand Prix winners, Chris Amon and Bruce McLaren, would drive another Ford entry. A third would be handled by Dan Gurney, one of America's greatest drivers, and Jerry Grant, another American.

It was a confident Ford team that arrived in LeMans. In practice sessions before the race Dan Gurney's GT40 Mk.2 turned in the fastest officially timed lap, 142.5 miles per hour, but since Phil Hill had about the same record the year before, Henry Ford II—who was in attendance—reserved judgment. After all there were fifty-five starters in the race, seven of which were Ferraris, three of them new P3 models with four-liter V-12 engines equipped with fuel injection.

Henry should not have worried. While one Ferrari held the lead briefly during the night, the Fords swept

he boards, finishing first, second, and third.
'orsches took the next four positions. Only one of the
even Ferraris was able to finish.

Having earned some measure of revenge for the
'errari snub of three years past and for the drubbings
n the two previous years' races, Henry was happy but
autious. Remembering that Ferrari had beaten him
wo in a row, he was determined to even the score. He
old Iacocca to have Ford entries ready for the 1967
eMans.

But in his World Headquarters office Lee finished
reparations for the introduction of his new Mercury
ars. One was the Mercury Marquis, a luxurious car
lesigned as a full-sized, middle-priced competitor to
3uick, Olds, and Pontiac, and Mercury Cougar,
America's first luxury sports car.

Earlier in the year, in order to build dealer enthusi-
sm for the new Mercurys, Iacocca had called on Bill
Winn and Bill Fugazy and asked them to produce the
nost unusual and dramatic dealers-only introduction
n automobile history. Both men were trusted friends
nd capable entrepreneurs. Winn was a creator of
pectaculars, Fugazy a developer of exciting travel-
ncentive programs.

Lee had added some personal touches to the intro-
luction plans and approved them before leaving for
eMans. On his return he found that Fugazy had
mplemented a competition among dealers to select
he group which would be present for the two-car
ntroduction. And Bill Winn had hired Bob Castle
nd a crew from Wilding Division of Bell & Howell to

handle the introduction staging.

Iacocca had planned to reveal the new Lincoln-Mercury products to the public on September 30 1966. The dealers who had met their assigned sales quotas, and thus were to participate in the preview spectacular, would see their new '67 products two weeks earlier.

In mid-September Iacocca, his Lincoln-Mercury team, the selected dealers, and the staging crew boarded the luxury liner, S.S. *Independence* at New York. Their destination was the Caribbean. However as the ship entered tropical waters, a little more than halfway from New York, she was turned so the stern faced the sunset. Her engines were then silenced.

As the sun slid low on the horizon, the dealers assembled at the stern of the ship. There they saw a mound of helium-filled balloons that was some ten feet long, five feet wide, and five feet high. Suddenly to a fanfare of music, the balloons were released to reveal the 1967 Mercury Marquis, one of the two cars that were to bring Lincoln-Mercury Division back to a semblance of respectability.

Matt McLaughlin and Lee Iacocca described the car and its features. The dealers cheered. This car they agreed, was what they needed. Once the ceremonies were concluded, the S.S. *Independence* reset a course for St. Thomas, one of the American Virgin Islands. Two days later it docked at Charlotte Amalie on the island's southern shore.

The first full day at Charlotte Amalie was spent in playing golf and tennis, swimming, and sightseeing

The second day everyone was bussed to the island's north side, bordering the Atlantic Ocean. There, along the rounded end of horseshoe-shaped Magens Bay, discovered by Christopher Columbus in 1493, a luau and beach party was laid out.

Throughout the afternoon members of the entourage swam and, between dips in the bay or the ocean, discussed with Iacocca and other Lincoln-Mercury officials their high expectations for the Marquis and the division. Each conversation usually included an assurance that there was more to come.

As evening approached, the group enjoyed an outdoor cookout of barbecued ribs and chicken. Local people made tours through the area leading mules, each of which carried two bottles of brandy around its neck. As it turned dark, five hundred torches were lit.

Suddenly the sounds of an engine came from the middle of the bay, and what looked to be a banana boat soon appeared. Actually, it was World War II LST covered with leaves and banana stalks and outfitted with lights. The landing craft came right to the beach and lowered its front end.

A bright new automobile rolled out of the LST, over the beach, and up a six-foot-high ramp onto a thatched, hutlike structure that had been erected at the center of the bay's curve. As the car came to a stop on stage, the interior of the thatched hut came ablaze with lights.

Out of the car stepped Vic Damone, who introduced the new Mercury Cougar to the attending dealers in song. Damone had become a friend of

Iacocca's in 1964 while starring in an NBC network program called *The Lively Ones*, which was sponsored by Ford Division for Iacocca's record-breaking Mustang.

Returning to the United States by plane, the Lincoln-Mercury dealers were unstinting in their praise for Lee Iacocca. They were impressed by the theatrics that introduced Marquis and Cougar, but even more so with the cars themselves. Iacocca made it clear, however, that a division that had lain dormant for so long would not spring back to life overnight.

It would, and did, take a few years of intensive planning and hard work before the Lincoln-Mercury Division reached an appreciably profitable stage. The buying public had to be convinced that the quality, so long missing, was back. It took the concerned efforts of Lee Iacocca, Matt McLaughlin's Lincoln-Mercury staff, and Kenyon & Eckhardt.

Marquis, as a full-size family car appealing primarily to older buyers, had to be positioned as a dependable, smooth-riding automobile, something previous Mercurys had not been. After much trial and error Iacocca approved a memorable campaign that in time accomplished what he wanted.

Kenyon & Eckhardt chose television as the medium for this new approach because of its high visual impact, and the agency produced a commercial promoting the comfort and smoothness of the Mercury Marquis ride. It portrayed a Dutch diamond cutter riding in the back seat of a Marquis. He was about to split a large, precious gem while the car traveled over rough roads. The diamond, after moments of suspense, was precisely cut without difficulty.

Shown across the nation for a year and more, it was one of the most effective, most talked-about commercials ever produced, one so well known that it earned a spoof on *Saturday Night Live*. In the tricked-up version an imaginary car called the "Royal DeLuxe" was seen on the same type of rough roads. However, the diamond cutter was supplanted by a man posing as a rabbi performing a successful circumcision on an infant.

Promoting Mercury Cougar was another matter. Cougar was a different automobile, a sporty type aimed at the youthful and youthful-feeling who wanted luxury in their automobiles. Its buyers were similar to Mustangs, but more affluent.

The assignment was so challenging to both Kenyon & Eckhardt and the Lincoln-Mercury promotion staff that to ease the tension, Frank Zimmerman at Lincoln-Mercury suggested to Lee Iacocca that he hire a trained orangutang to drive a Cougar from New York to San Francisco. The animal, said Zimmerman, tongue in cheek, would be trained to sit behind the wheel and simulate driving. A man hunched under the dash would use specially installed equipment to do the actual driving.

Think of the drama in such a situation, Zimmerman said, the perception it would give people of how simple and safe it is to drive a Ford-built car. As he made a hasty retreat out of the office, he reminded Lee of the hundreds of newspaper reporters and camera crews followed the car from coast-to-coast.

The idea, ludicrous as it was, triggered a stroke of marketing genius. Why not a real cougar to suggest the image of the new car?

The idea that the cougar is the most graceful of all large cats in the New World could be used in advertising to reflect the smoothness of the car's ride and its ability to conquer American roads with a touch of elegance. The silken sleek look and fluid motion of the cat could be suggestive of the Cougar's ride. And the growl might well symbolize the power of the car.

The go-ahead from Iacocca placed the responsibility for implementing the concept on the shoulders of Bill Suchman, creative director at Kenyon & Eckhardt's New York office. Suchman recommended that the cat be used not only in print and broadcast advertising to identify the new Cougar, but also to symbolize the Mercury line of the Lincoln-Mercury Division. The latter could be accomplished by placing the animal atop the sign identifying dealerships.

Finding the suitable trained animal was one thing, but getting it up on the sign to photograph was something else. It took weeks of work and more than a few dangerous scrapes, but the animal's trainer finally managed to get the animal up and to emit the desired growl. It was another Iacocca-inspired triumph. "The Sign of the Cat" became a nationwide trademark, and despite the change in advertising agencies from Kenyon & Eckhardt to Young and Rubicam in 1979, the cat continues to give an identity to Mercury automobiles.

The two new Mercurys, Marquis and Cougar, helped Iacocca bring profitability to the Lincoln-Mercury Division as well as recognition within the Ford Motor Company. Nevertheless it did not, and probably never could, match Ford Division in sales. But where Lincoln-Mercury sales had seldom topped 300,000 annually, they began to nudge the half-million mark, cutting into the market shares of Buick, Oldsmobile, and Pontiac.

It was a fine start toward a meaningful increase in market penetration, the symbol of success in the auto industry. Chrysler was so far behind it could be discounted, but Iacocca knew that to battle General Motors for further increases both the Ford and Lincoln-Mercury divisions needed new and salable competitors for Chevrolet in particular, and all GM divisions in general. The gulf between Ford and General Motors was too wide to expect miracles. But Iacocca had narrowed the gap between Ford Division and Chevrolet. Even though Chevy was still ahead by 167,291 registrations in 1966, Ford Division had gained over a quarter-million in that one year.

That made Chevrolet Iacocca's prime target for the upcoming 1968 model year. He gave both Ford and Lincoln-Mercury divisions products aimed to fight Chevy head-to-head. They were Ford Torino and Mercury Montego, each already in production. But in those early months of 1967, Iacocca had another important responsibility.

The twenty-four-hours at LeMans was scheduled for June 10 and 11, and Henry Ford II was determined to defeat Enzo Ferrari for the second year in a row. Lee had to keep an eye on the refinements being made for the new GT40s, which would be designated M4. He had ordered the horsepower increased and the GT40 Mk4s made heavier than the Mk2s of 1966. He also had the new versions equipped with cast-iron cylinder heads instead of the aluminum used the previous year. The cars were also given larger brakes to compensate for their increased speeds.

A win at LeMans would not only make Henry happy, it also could lead to greater sales in the 1968 model year. It had always been Iacocca's contention that more people watch automobile racing than baseball, football, and basketball combined, and those millions would have their attention focused on LeMans in June.

He was determined to leave as little as possible to chance and he authorized the managers of the racing group to hire the finest teams of drivers. Signed for LeMans were Dan Gurney and A. J. Foyt as one, Mark Donahue and Bruce McLaren for the second, Mario Andretti and Lucien Bianchi as a third, and Roger McCluskey and Jo Schlesser as a fourth team. All but Bianchi, McLaren, and Schlesser were Americans.

Both Henry Ford and Lee Iacocca were on hand for the start of the race on June 10. The four GT40 Mk4 racers for Ford were backed up by three Mk2s that had been modified. Seven Ferraris were among the fifty-four starters, which also included Chaparral, Matra, Peugeot, and Renault.

All the Fords and Ferraris got away well when the starter's flag was dropped, with the Chaparral, driven by America's Grand Prix Champion Phil Hill, in close pursuit. Two Ferraris soon moved in ahead of the Chaparral. The hours passed with Fords and Ferraris alternating in the lead. After midnight three of the GT40s were in front, a Ferrari was fourth, the Chaparral fifth. The closest other Ferrari was running seventh.

Suddenly serious trouble hit the Ford teams. The McLaren-Donahue car developed clutch trouble and was forced into the pits. Lucien Bianchi, in another Ford, came in and turned the driving over to Mario Andretti. Andretti snapped on his helmet, goggles, and harness and sped out onto the road. He took his GT40 up a rise and started down the hill at about 160 miles an hour.

As he approached a series of S-turns, he jammed on the brakes too quickly. The left-front brake locked, and the GT40 skidded around. It hit the bank on one side of the road, then skidded across to bounce off the opposite bank into the middle of the road, where it stalled. Alarmed that other cars would soon be bearing down on the GT40, Andretti leaped from the car and ran clear off the road.

Within a half-minute Roger McCluskey's GT40 came barreling over the top of the hill. Fearful that the driver might still be in the cockpit of the stalled car visible in his headlights, McCluskey rammed the GT40 into the road bank.

A few seconds later Jo Schlesser's GT40 caught the

two disabled vehicles in its headlights as it came over the hill. Schlesser made a valiant effort to drive between the two disabled Fords and missed, crashing into McCluskey's. Three out of the four most powerful GT40s were out of the race.

The one remaining Ford GT40 Mk4, driven by the Dan Gurney-A. J. Foyt team, managed to slide by the damaged threesome. It was the only hope for a Ford victory. Gurney and Foyt were in the lead, but two more power-laden Ferrari P4s were after them. As the Ferraris passed their pits, they were signaled by Enzo Ferrari to speed up. His strategy was to get close to the lone Ford, driven by Gurney, and tease him into an all-out race that might punish the Ford engine enough to disable it. One of the Ferraris pulled up beside Gurney's Ford. Gurney, aware of a ploy he had often used himself, merely smiled and waved the Ferrari on. But the second the Ferrari passed his GT40, Gurney jammed the accelerator to the floorboard and roared past the Ferrari driver. Gurney did not let up and opened an increasing lead each second. He completed the 3,200-mile course and crossed the finish line more than thirty miles ahead of the nearest Ferrari.

Iacocca stood by silently as Henry accepted the honors. If it was revenge over Enzo Ferrari that Henry wanted so badly, it was his. He had defeated the Italian master two in a row, which really amounted to a standoff, since Ferrari had also defeated Ford twice.

LeMans 1967 was Ford's last company-sponsored

European race, though the American racing schedule was carried on for the balance of the year. Thereafter the money spent on racing was to be diverted to achieving the emissions and safety standards required by the government. Iacocca returned to his Glass House office and a heavy workload, soon to be made heavier as the Detroit area, and the auto industry, experienced an unexpected blow.

The disastrous summer of 1967 race riots, which almost wrecked Detroit, also took their toll on automobile production. New-car registrations for each of the Big Three dropped substantially from 1966 with almost every car line suffering equally, except for one surprising difference. GM's Cadillac and Chrysler's Imperial divisions revealed appreciable increases. The one luxury car line showing a loss was Ford's Lincoln, dropping almost 15,000 sales from 1966.

Ford Motor Company suffered another blow during 1967, one not shared by the other automobile manufacturers. The Arab-Israeli war brought about a boycott of Ford products in all Arab countries because Ford Motor Company operated an assembly plant in Israel. This exclusion of Ford products was destined to last at least into the eighties and barred all Ford cars from Lebanon, Syria, Saudi Arabia, the Arab Emirates, Yemen, Iraq, and Egypt. It meant a tremendous loss in revenue, since Ford products, especially Mustang, had been favorites in the Middle East.

For Iacocca 1967 was a debilitating year even though he had introduced two new cars to the public.

Ford sold about 500,000 fewer units in 1966, and its profits dropped proportionately. In midsummer the United Auto Workers called a strike that closed all Ford plants for fifty-three days, an action that intensified the problems caused by the race riots.

As if that was not enough, shoddy workmanship by Ford plant workers produced another business setback. About one-third of all the cars built, including every one of 447,000 Mustangs, had to be recalled to correct various defects. Over and above the cost of repairs Ford Motor Company paid out a quarter-million dollars in postage fees to notify owners to return their cars.

Iacocca had yet another problem as the year ended. Henry had insisted that the Mustang planned for the following year be longer and heavier, and Lee now deeply regretted that he had let himself be persuaded. The car that had knocked the industry on its ears in 1965 was no longer the smart little muscle car that reflected the spirit of American youth.

It was almost a tradition in the industry to enlarge successful automobiles, lengthening them, increasing their overall size and weight, and adding to their cost to increase profit. With Mustang, this idea backfired. Sales dropped. Individuals trading in their original Mustangs complained about the new models.

Iacocca felt something had to be done. He could not bear to see his classic little pony fade from the scene through impractical design. He had to find a way to convince Henry that the old premise—bigger is better—no longer held true, at least to the medium-

and lower-priced cars.

In analyzing the market over the previous few years, Iacocca had noted a resurgence in the luxury-car segment. Ever on the alert to taking advantage of market changes, he was ready. The new car he had waiting in the wings not only should please Henry, it should also soften his resistance to downsizing the Mustang.

Planned for a 1968 introduction, the new Mark III was an up-to-date version of Edsel Ford's Continental Mark discontinued some years earlier. Iacocca had predicted a return to prominence of luxurious automobiles as early as 1965 and had his product planners design a car that would compete with Cadillac's Eldorado.

The Mark II Continental had been discontinued in 1957 even though many acknowledged it the most beautiful, as well as the most expensive and heaviest, car on the road. Other luxury cars were overstyled and ostentatious, but the Mark had a classic simplicity, with good taste in its design, an understated dignity and elegance. However, the mid-fifties had proved to be bad years for a car that sold for $10,000.

Iacocca saw the market in the late sixties as being just right, and how better to make an impact in the luxury-car field than with the revival of an acknowledged classic? Cadillac's Eldorado needed an American competitor, and Iacocca wanted to improve the Lincoln's market share, which had rarely been better than 4 percent.

Henry Ford II found no fault with Iacocca's plan

to revive the Continental Mark. He endorsed it heartily as a worthy successor to his father's Mark I and the Mark II in which his brother William Clay was so thoroughly involved.

Iacocca's star glittered brightly along the corridors of the Glass House as 1967 came to a close. Executives at all levels below Lee's executive vice-presidency were giving odds that the next president of the Ford Motor Company would be none other than the man from Allentown. With Henry's unpredictability a change might come at any moment.

Lee himself felt certain that he would not be overlooked when the time came for a change. He had proved himself the most capable man in the history of the company. Businessmen throughout the nation considered him the most important man in the entire automobile industry. There was no doubt in his or anyone else's mind (except perhaps Henry II) that the Ford presidency would go to him soon.

Mercurial Henry Ford II did have a different, if not a better, idea. It was one made possible by the sudden resignation of Semon E. (Bunkie) Knudsen as executive vice-president of General Motors. Bunkie, whose father had been fired by Henry Ford I and then gone on to become president of General Motors, expected to follow in his father's footsteps.

In the normal course of events the new president of GM would have been Bunkie Knudsen. But for some reason Edward Cole was named. To bypass a man in direct line for promotion is tantamount in the automobile industry to telling the skipped-over executive that he has reached his peak. Knudsen, realizing this, resigned.

Henry Ford II had just returned from a vacation with Cristina in the British West Indies when he heard of Bunkie's resignation, Knudsen, of course, was no stranger to him. During Bunkie's thirty years at General Motors their paths had crossed many times, and Henry felt that Ford could use a man with Knudsen's experience. Besides, Henry had his hands full with some outside interests.

Earlier in the year President Lyndon Johnson had asked Henry to chair his newly created National Alliance of Businessmen, the stated function of which was to hire and train about a half-million ghetto youths. It was a three-year assignment and would demand much of Henry's time, visiting businessmen throughout the country and getting their pledges to make good use of the millions of dollars appropriated by Congress. Yes, Henry decided, he needed Bunkie Knudsen.

He phoned Bunkie and asked to meet with him. Knudsen quickly agreed to come to Henry's home in Grosse Pointe, but Henry wanted to keep the meeting secret, and Grosse Pointers have a way of learning too much too soon. It was decided that Henry would visit Bunkie at his home in Bloomfield Hills. He arrived there in a rented GM car to throw off any nosy neighbors.

Bunkie Knudsen was willing to come to Ford, but he knew Henry too well. He accepted a salary and bonus comparable to Henry's, but he was not about to make himself a well-paid sacrificial lamb. He said yes only after Henry agreed to give him a protective contract. Besides, Knudsen couldn't help but wonder why Ford needed him with Iacocca in the wings. Was it because Henry felt Bunkie could really help the company? Or was it a kind of atonement for the treatment given his father by Henry's grandfather about four decades earlier?

The morning of February 6, 1968, Henry Ford II held a press conference to announce the elevation of Arjay Miller (a token promotion to ease the way for his resignation) to vice chairman of the board, and the appointment of Semon E. Knudsen as president of Ford Motor Company. During the press conference Henry praised his new second in command.

"Today the flow of history has been reversed," Henry told the assembled reporters. "Another Knudsen, having left General Motors, has been elected president of the company his father helped build. I am delighted to have him because he is a strong and resourceful executive, brought up in a great automotive tradition. He will be a fine asset to to management at Ford."

The unexpected announcement was a blow to Lee Iacocca's ego. Bringing in an outsider to fill a position he felt eminently qualified for—and entitled to—was infuriating. Reporters, wondering whether Iacocca might resign, didn't leave Henry off the hook.

"Why?" they asked the Ford chairman. Henry weaseled. His unconvincing answer was that Iacocca was still needed where he was. Besides, he added, another year or so of experience would make him even more valuable when his time came.

Henry's reasoning seemed downright ludicrous. If Lee Iacocca had not yet proven himself capable of running the Ford Motor Company, he never would. Had Bunkie Knudsen done as much for General Motors as Lee had for Ford? Nobody with knowledge of the inner workings of the industry bought Henry's lame excuse.

Possibly Henry had begun to fear Iacocca's strength within the company. Or maybe Henry had decided on this way to let Iacocca know that he was not indispensable, to pierce what many at Ford were calling an inflated ego.

"Lee had become as imperialistic as Henry himself," said one man who was close to Lee at Ford. "He had become, well you might say a little big for his britches. He was a good and brilliant man, no doubt about that, but what bothered a lot of people was that he let you know it."

Another Ford executive, now retired, said, "Lee had changed quite a bit from the time he hit it big with Mustang. At one time he had a smile and a good word for lower-echelon people, but all of a sudden he would walk by them, ignore them, his head held high like a royal personage expecting a curtsy. He gave you the feeling that you didn't exist, that the only ones who mattered were the men on his team. None of the rest of us were surprised when Henry detoured around him to name a new president."

Iacocca's reactions to Henry's appointment of Knudsen have been kept within him. Perhaps Henry's statements to the press, holding out hope for another day, may have mollified Lee. Whatever his feelings, he decided to bide his time and returned to work no doubt determined to make Henry regret the Knudsen appointment.

Two months after Knudsen took office Iacocca presented America's luxury-car buyers with the Continental Mark III. Lee had supervised its design and production, taking it through all channels—market research, design reviews, marketing and advertising strategy—and with appropriate panoply and fanfare introduced it as an automobile of distinctive personality on April 5, 1968. The car had an attractively sculpted low profile, a hood longer than any other American car, and a short rear deck distinguished by a continental spare tire reminiscent of the early Marks.

Powered by a 460-cubic-inch overhead-valve, V-8 engine, the 1969 Continental Mark III was a rarity among heavy luxury cars, able to get from zero to sixty miles an hour in nine and one-half seconds, from zero to ninety in under twenty-one. Iacocca positioned it as a personal luxury car available in one body style, a two-door coupe.

The Continental Mark III did what Iacocca hoped it would, increasing Lincoln's prestige in the luxury-car market by outselling the Cadillac Eldorado by 30 percent in its first year. It also helped achieve the highest single-year sales for Lincoln in 1969, despite a depressed economy in 1970 and 1971, the car also enjoyed increased sales in those years.

Iacocca had another car ready for the 1969 model year. September 27, 1968, he brought out the Marauder to give the Mercury line a shot in the arm. Marauder offered some of the luxury of Marquis and a bit of the sportiness of Cougar to attract the older buyers who wanted a performance image in their car.

Overall, 1968 was such a good year that Iacocca was able to forget the humiliation of being passed over for Bunkie Knudsen. Henry was away so often that Lee had few problems from that quarter. The chairman was enjoying his fling in the political arena despite his unhappiness over Lyndon Johnson's having announced in March that he would not seek reelection. With a strong distaste for Richard Nixon Henry immediately supported Hubert Humphrey for the nation's highest office.

The year was also a comeback year for the Ford Motor Company and the city of Detroit. By June indications were strong that Ford would top the 2.25 million mark in new-car registrations in the United States. And Detroit was rebounding from the calamitous effects of the previous year's race riots.

In fact a spirit of oneness developed between whites and blacks as Detroit's professional baseball team, the Tigers, charged toward the American League championship. Al Kaline, Mickey Lolich, Willie Horton, and Gates Brown helped propel a team to a world's championship in defeating the National League's St. Louis Cardinals, which pointed up

Iacocca's farsightedness. He had established a sports panel for Lincoln-Mercury that included Al Kaline, a contender for the Baseball Hall of Fame.

Looking ahead, Lee was concerned over government standards for the automobile industry as well as the mushrooming sales of imports. To help satisfy one and offset the effects of the other he began plans for small cars with improved mileage. One, for Ford Division, would be all-new, with a name that would have a marketing rub-off from Mustang, the Pinto. The second, for the Mercury line, was a newly designed car along the lines of Pinto, and on a Pinto chassis, that would retain the somewhat successful name Comet. Later it would become Mercury Bobcat.

Pursuing these ideas, Iacocca again locked horns with Henry Ford II, who had little interest in small cars. Lee argued that Ford had to bring out fuel-efficient cars to combat imports. In the previous six years, he told Henry, imports had doubled their share of the American market, from under five percent in 1962 to a near 10.5 percent in 1968.

Henry, as he usually did when Iacocca initially suggested a policy change, disagreed. He reminded Lee of the Mustang as well as another car smaller than other Ford models ready for the following year, Lee's own 1970 Maverick. Maverick, Lee countered, would be a fine car and a good seller, but it was not the kind of car to match Volkswagen or compete with Toyota. Henry remained unconvinced.

As he had done with Mustang, Iacocca kept at

Henry, often backed up in his arguments by Hal Sperlick. "Our insistence that small cars were the wave of the future led to Iacocca and Sperlick not being much admired by Mr. Ford," Hal Sperlick says. Admired or not, Henry finally gave in to the two men and agreed to fund production of Pinto and the restyled Comet, both of which were introduced as 1971 models on September 11, 1970.

Bunkie Knudsen, meanwhile, had stormed into his presidency at Ford like a lion on the loose. Henry Ford II had described him to the press as "strong and resourceful," and he was all of that. He looked into everything—planning, styling, engineering, production—and made changes, often without consulting Henry, much less Iacocca.

At General Motors Knudsen had shown himself competent in managing GM's international operations, which were smaller than Ford's. So he made himself visible throughout the thirty-odd countries where Ford owned business. He was an obsessive achiever, perhaps too much like Iacocca himself. Morning, noon, and night he could be found in the foundry, at the styling center, anywhere in the Ford empire, suggesting a change here, a change there. He made at least one design variation that had the styling center up in arms, placing a GM-type grille on the Ford Thunderbird.

No one could deny that Bunkie Knudsen was a sincere, hard-working Ford man, but perhaps he worked too hard, so hard that Henry, remembering the dedication of the Ernest Breech he had ousted, began to fear him. Rumors began floating about the Glass House that Henry indeed was concerned and that his fears were being fed by some members of Lee Iacocca's team.

Knudsen, unintentionally, made one serious mistake. As April 17, 1969, introduction day for the new Maverick approached, Bunkie began singing the praises of the fine new Ford entry, which might possibly give Mustang a run for its money in sales. Then, on introduction day, Bunkie was there in the forefront answering reporters' questions and being very presidential, as though he were offering the new Maverick as his creation, not Iacocca's.

In early summer Glass House corridors echoed with whispers that about a dozen Ford men—Iacocca stalwarts?—had prepared a list of Knudsen misdemeanors for presentation to Mr. Ford. True or not, early on the morning of September 1, Ted Mecke, an Iacocca man who had been promoted two weeks earlier to vice-president of public affairs, visited Bunkie Knudsen at his home.

The word is that Mecke went to alert Knudsen that Henry Ford II was going to fire him that day. And Knudsen says that the following day Ford came into his office and told him that "things had not worked out" as Henry had hoped and that he would be fired.

Knudsen was speechless for a moment. Perhaps his mind focused on the day when he was about ten or eleven and his father was just as summarily fired by the grandfather of the man who was now giving him his walking papers. He asked Henry II to give him a eason. Henry did not. Maybe, as in previous such ircumstances, he couldn't.

Within two weeks Henry Ford II called a press onference and announced that his board of directors ad voted to terminate the nineteenth-month presi-ency of Semon E. Knudsen. Even though Knudsen vas absent, reporters made it rough for Henry, asking or reasons. Bunkie Knudsen was no ordinary execu-ive to be brushed off so easily.

Henry had trouble answering. It was not a resigna-ion—he had made that clear. In fact, as Knudsen aid later, Ford had not even given him a chance to esign, although if he had, Knudsen would have efused it. As reporters kept hammering for a reason, Ienry finally said only that "sometimes these things lon't work out."

Bunkie Knudsen, however, had an answer to ex-lain Henry's arbitrary maneuver. "Henry was afraid f losing his Tinkertoy," he told friends the night of he firing.

Whatever the reason for Knudsen's dismissal, it ost the Ford Motor Company a bundle of money. According to the settlement Knudsen would continue o receive his $600,000 salary until the end of 1972. n addition he would also receive his 1969 share of the nnual bonus given Ford executives, a figure that ould approach $500,000. Knudsen also retained the 5,000 shares of Ford stock he received on joining ord and kept options to purchase, if he wished, nother 75,000 shares at slightly less than $50 each.

For Henry Ford II and his company the severance

proved expensive, but, as might be expected, i
brought jubilation to the Iacocca camp. They had n
doubt that now their champion would get his jus
reward. As for Lee himself he remained priml
guarded as to his inner feelings. When reporter
asked how he felt about the Knudsen firing, hi
answer was "I've never said 'no comment' to yo
before, but I'll say 'no comment' this time."

Iacocca wanted to be certain that his time ha
come, even though it was definitely his turn to serv
as second in command to Henry Ford II. But Henr
had another surprise up his sleeve.

He did not name a new president for the For
Motor Company, he named three men to handle th
duties of the office. Iacocca was one, with the title o
executive vice-president of the Ford Motor Compan
and president of Ford's North American automotiv
operations. The other two were Robert Stevenson
president of Ford's international automotive opera
tions, and Robert Hampson, president of non-auto
motive operations. The three were to operate a
equals in authority, all answerable to Henry Ford II

This unusual and strange turn of events was a
bitter pill for Iacocca. Not only did this three-way
split deprive him of the office he believed he deserved
it also represented a watering down of his authority. I
mattered little that as president of Ford's Nort
American operations he headed the most importan
phase of the company's activities. He actually ha
occupied that seat for the past two years, so Henry'
action was hardly in the nature of a favor.

Agonizing questions flooded his mind. Was Henry trying to tell him something? That he should resign? That he had come as far as he ever would at Ford? Then maybe he was just plain lucky. The president's chair at Ford, to judge by the short tenures of the men who had occupied it, was a hot one. Henry was living proof that the closer one got to the king's throne the more vulnerable one became to his fancies and foibles.

Iacocca would not remember 1969 as a particularly happy year, even though his Maverick had already run up six-month sales that rivaled those of the record-holding Mustang. One of his most valuable lieutenants, Gar Laux, had been relieved of his duties as vice-president for sales, and he would be sorely missed.

Henry kept himself too busy during the last months of 1969 and the early months of 1970 to see much of Iacocca. In April of 1970 he took Cristina with him to the Soviet Union for a nine-day business trip. Vodka mixed well with Henry's gregarious personality, and he returned home with Soviet approval to build a huge truck-manufacturing plant.

Henry's ebullience at this master stroke of business was short-lived—President Richard Nixon killed it. He sent his secretary of defense, Melvin Laird, to Detroit to chastize Henry. At a press conference he embarrassed the chairman of the board of the Ford Motor Company for having the audacity even to consider such a deal without clearing it with the government, while "the Soviet Union is sending trucks by the shipload to North Vietnam."

Somehow, during the trip to Russia, Henry had also had a change of mind. And, no doubt forgetting that Iacocca had been preaching the same sermon for some time, Henry began sounding off about the harm to the American economy from the onslaught of imports, especially those from Japan.

He now bemoaned the fact that Japanese imports were coming into the United States too freely, while American cars sent to Japan were subjected to so many restrictions and taxed so heavily that the Japanese could not afford them. "We are certainly being discriminated against by the Japanese," he told reporters.

Another problem, government intervention in the automobile business—politely categorized as "regulation"—was escalating. Nixon had appointed scrappy, abrasive John Volpe as secretary of transportation, and he was setting deadlines for meeting emission standards that were unrealistic if production costs were to be held in check. And Volpe's insistence that all cars had to be equipped with air bags before 197? would shoot car prices up even further.

Those rising costs would play havoc with Iacocca's plans for the years ahead. For one thing his hopes for Pinto as a car affordable by people with modest incomes—he had expected to give it a sticker price of about $2,000—would be dashed, and September 11, 1970, announcement day for Pinto and Comet, was closing in.

The fun in the fight for success was being diminished by outside forces, and Lee began to wonder if the prize was worth the battle. He was still bitter over Henry's reluctance to give him the presidency, and he did not like the hassle of making long-range plans with two other individuals. Management by trio was inefficient, ineffective, and confusing. Both Stevenson and Hampson followed Henry, not Iacocca, in their thinking, and little progress was being made in meeting the public's growing demand for smaller, higher-gas-mileage cars.

Lee was tiring of Henry's repeated refusal to consider approval of research toward the more fuel-efficient front-wheel-drive concept. Henry had spoken out against the unfair advantage given Japanese imports through government-mandated inequities, but when Lee and Hal Sperlick argued for a change in policy, his response was negative.

Import sales had skyrocketed during the previous five years. From 1965 through 1967 their sales increases had averaged 100,000 and more over each previous year, and in 1968 the increase was 200,000 above that of 1967. In 1969, for the first time, foreign car sales had topped the million mark.

Henry's answer was an even larger Mustang for introduction in the fall of 1970. The new pony car was to be almost eight inches longer, six inches wider, and about 600 pounds heavier than Lee's original Mustang. Burning inside at this desecration, Lee wondered whether the time had come to leave Ford.

Public utterances by Henry Ford gave the fire building inside Iacocca no chance to burn out.

Henry, it seemed, used every opportunity to fuel further doubts about Lee's tenure with the company. The chairman's interviews with the press could be perceived as messages to Iacocca, reminders not to hold his breath waiting for better things.

Out of the blue Henry had begun giving attention to the prospects of his son, Edsel II, as the Ford heir apparent. "I think he would like to come into the company someday," Henry was quoted by one reporter.

For those who knew young Edsel as a mild-mannered, sincere youth, that "someday" seemed far in the future. No more brilliant a student than his father, Edsel was just finishing prep school prior to enrollment at the none-too-demanding Babson Institute. A certain charisma and the Ford name had been his primary assets in education, according to his counselors. After Babson it was expected that young Edsel might sign on as a sales trainee at Ford. Insiders at the Glass House considered Henry's references to his son's future as little more than a subtle harassment of Lee Iacocca.

In such an atmosphere it would be natural for Iacocca to consider a change. And, if he did decide to leave Ford, plenty of positions were certainly available for a man of his reputation and stature, and not only in the industry he so passionately loved.

As the 1970 clock ticked toward September, Iacocca was busy preparing for the introduction of his Pinto. Conceived as the first truly small car by an American manufacturer, it was so new in concept it would take exceptional stimulation to earn enthusiasm from the Ford dealer body.

Bill Winn, at Iacocca's direction, was once again to develop the most spectacular show ever put together for the automobile industry's introduction of a car to its dealers. The locale selected for the dealer meeting was the Las Vegas Convention Center, where Winn's group built a theater to accommodate nearly 2,000 Ford dealers and their wives.

The entire floor of the convention center's auditorium was restructured to provide seating in tiers beginning at the balcony and sloping down to the main arena floor. A giant theater was created, including an elliptical stage with a motion picture screen 128 feet wide that enabled simultaneous use of three projectors to produce a panoramic effect.

The first American subcompact, Pinto, was scheduled to be the climax of the show. First, however, would be the showing of the new four-door Maverick that Iacocca had added to the original line, brought out only as a two-door compact less than a year earlier.

A two-door Maverick was driven on stage and "magically" converted into a four-door before the dealers' eyes. Winn had the Dearborn Steel Tubing Company create a Maverick prototype with two doors on the passenger side and one door on the driver's side. This one-door driver's side would face the audience at the start of the presentation.

To the accompaniment of specially orchestrated live music the driver's side of the Maverick was dismantled by actors posing as technicians. When the door and side panels were removed, a billowing puff of smoke concealed the car. Under the cloak of smoke the car was revolved to appear, once the billows cleared away, as a four-door automobile transformed on the spot.

The piece de resistance from outer space was the introduction of the all-new and perky little Pinto. With the arena in darkness dealers suddenly saw whirling lights similar to those on police cars lighting up the ceiling of the convention center dome. The lights were attached to a simulated flying saucer, a canopied half-spaceship with its rounded, finished side facing the arena floor.

Building this "spaceship" and raising it to the top of the dome had been a chore for Bill Winn and his people. It was about twenty-four feet in length and had considerable depth. It was huge and heavy, with canisters of carbon dioxide as well as the whirling lights fixed at the bottom. Winn's men had actually restructured the dome to accommodate the weight.

A large cast danced on stage to music from the orchestra as the spiraling lights illuminated the "flying saucer" for the first time. Then spotlights from the saucer were directed toward center stage. Suddenly carbon dioxide exploded from the tanks under the spaceship to create a fog bank for the launch. The spaceship, engulfed in carbon dioxide, landed on the stage, then immediately lifted off again to the roar of another blast of carbon dioxide.

The music, with outer-space tonality, built to a

crescendo as the saucer soared back toward the ceiling and the carbon dioxide fog dissipated to reveal a bright-yellow Pinto. The difficult maneuvering had been so well executed it produced the desired illusion of a Pinto brought down on a spaceship. It actually had been driven on stage while the carbon dioxide fog was at its heaviest.

The Ford dealers had come to Las Vegas more in anticipation of a good time than in expectation of a new car with obvious potential for good sales and profits. As the curtain came down on the show finale, they went wild, giving Iacocca a rousing tribute for providing them with what they felt would be their best seller since the Mustang.

In fact the Pinto proved to be exactly that. Even though only one quarter of the year remained after the public introduction on September 11, the year 1970 proved to be Ford Division's best in sales since Mustang's second year.

Iacocca noted the heavy traffic into dealerships throughout the country for weeks after the introduction and the burgeoning sales of Pinto with a feeling of self-satisfaction. With deep regret he had become serious about leaving the Ford Motor Company. During the months leading to Pinto's introduction prospects for an improved working atmosphere had become bleaker, and the tug of war between Iacocca and the other members of the troika-presidency, Stevenson and Hampson, was wearing him down. Pinto was making it possible for him to say his goodbyes on a high note.

"Lee definitely intended to leave Ford and work for another company," said Bill Fugazy, Iacocca's close friend. "He had some fine offers—one that was particularly good and interested him."

Fugazy did not identify either the company or its location. "I went around with him looking for houses for him to relocate," he added, "but I suggested that he first show the offer to Henry Ford."

Iacocca did reveal his prospective job to Henry Ford II, and a series of discussions ensued. Surprisingly, Henry acted as if determined to keep him at Ford. Lee, no doubt remembering the Knudsen situation, insisted on a contract with long-range terms. Henry resisted but finally gave in.

Lee's first moves after agreeing to the terms set for his presidency of the Ford Motor Company were to tell his wife and to call his father in Allentown. Nick and Antoinette Iacocca caught the first plane out to help their son celebrate.

Henry Ford II called a press conference for the morning of December 10, 1970. With Lee Iacocca at his right, and with Nick Iacocca seated in the back of the room and smiling broadly, he introduced the new president of the Ford Motor Company. He told the media representatives present that he needed a strong president because "Ford operations in Europe are expanding, and I've got to devote more of my time to that."

Turning to Iacocca he expanded further. "I've reached the point where I need some help," he said, "but now Lee's here, and I won't have to worry about

236

it."

It was done. At the age of forty-six Lido Anthony Iacocca, who had predicted he would be vice-president of Ford before he was thirty-five and missed by less than a year, had finally made it to the presidency of the company he had loved since his boyhood.

Now his office would be located right next to Henry's, in the northeast corner of the Glass House. Now, with salary and bonuses, he would be earning some $600,000 a year or more for some time to come.

"That was one helluva Christmas present," Iacocca told reporters.

CHAPTER 9

Lee Iacocca had climbed as far up the Ford mountain as he had a right to expect. The name in the blue oval atop the Glass House all but precluded the final step up the ladder to chairman of the board whatever his personal expectations might have been. It seemed improbable, however, that the man Gar Laux describes as "forever running" could stand still.

As Lee Iacocca took his new office, he realized that the coming decade of the seventies would be a difficult one. Profits would not be easy to come by as the federal government increased pressures for costly safety and pollution standards. Keeping pace with the regulations and the increasing production and labor costs were bound to erode the company's earnings. Now the burden was his, a weight certain to be increased thanks to Henry's vacillating judgments.

His first important job for 1971 may have seemed contradictory to his rarely heeded plea for small, easy-on-the-gas automobiles, but Iacocca had never discounted the public's desire for full-size luxury cars. A full half-century had passed since the first Lincoln was produced by Henry's father, Edsel. Over and above pleasing Henry, Lee enjoyed his part in bringing out the golden-anniversary Lincoln Continental.

The Continental Mark III, which had made its debut two years earlier, had given Lincoln a viable competitor for Cadillac Eldorado. Lee was now determined that the Lincoln Continental would make the same inroads on Cadillac's most luxurious limousine, the DeVille.

Under Iacocca's watchful eye the new Lincoln emerged, to be positioned in advertising as a refined luxury car of tasteful simplicity with a rich interior, driver and passenger comfort conveniences that made riding in it as restful as sitting in one's living room. Its engine was the most powerful available to the public, a 460-cubic-inch V-8 that developed 365 horsepower at 4,600 revolutions per minute. With an overall length of 225 inches and a total curb weight for the four-door of 5,072 pounds, ads proclaimed, it offered a smooth, quiet ride unparalleled in the American industry.

The moneyed aficionados who demanded the new and prestigious in their motor cars reacted as Iacocca had expected. The golden-anniversary Lincoln Continentals, four-door limousine and two-door town car, made inroads on Cadillac's DeVille in about the same proportions as Continental Mark III had on Cadillac Eldorado. Together the Continental and Mark tripled

Lincoln sales by the end of 1973.

Ford and Mercury car sales also swung upward due to a highly charged national economy. With profits reaching record figures, Henry kept himself busy building a reputation as a civic-minded citizen dedicated to restoring Detroit's inner city.

Detroit needed a renaissance, he told the city's business community, and he was going to spearhead a downtown development called the Renaissance Center. Along the Detroit River waterfront a cluster of high-rise buildings, a seventy-story hotel flanked by four office towers, was to be built. The Ford commitment for the start of the project was $6 million.

Ford had no plants or properties to speak of within Detroit's city limits, but the city was the headquarters of its rival automotive giant. General Motors, therefore, could not be left out and matched Henry's investment. In one month Henry had more than two-thirds of the money needed to get the project under way. Not a resident of the city—he lived in Grosse Pointe—Henry Ford II was nonetheless the Lion of the Motor City and was hailed as its potential savior.

With Henry so preoccupied, Lee Iacocca had nearly a free hand in moving the Ford Motor Company ahead. Late in 1970 Matt McLaughlin, head of Lincoln-Mercury Division, had returned from a trip to Ford's subsidiary in Cologne, Germany, and reported that there was an automobile built by Ford of Germany that Lee should look at.

At his first opportunity Iacocca flew to Cologne. The car, the Capri, was a natural to combat Japanese and European imports on their own turf.

Lee made the necessary arrangements to import the Capri and assigned the merchandising of the car to Lincoln-Mercury Division. The jazzy little import, promoted in advertising as "the sexy European car," added to Iacocca's laurels, helping to lift Mercury car sales by some 75,000 in 1971 and enabling Mercury to rack up its three best consecutive years.

Ford Motor Company's annual report to stockholders for 1970, a handsome brochure with a bright-yellow Pinto on the cover, carried the signatures of both Henry Ford II and Lee A. Iacocca. Its figures were a glowing testimonial to Iacocca's management. The company's combined sales for the year were a record $15 billion.

The next year's report, which included glamourous shots of Capri as well as Pinto on the cover, provided even better news for stockholders: "1971 was a year of record sales and near-record earnings . . ." it read, again over the dual signatures. Net income was reported as 27 percent more than that of the previous year.

In 1972, even though Ford's new-car registrations in the U.S. went up an additional 186,000 and stockholders were told it was "the most successful year in your company's history," all was not wine and roses. That same year the Ford Motor Company was subjected to the most humiliating embarrassment in its sixty-nine-year existence.

Congress had instituted Environmental Protection Agency requirements for tests to ensure that 1973-

model engines met air-pollution standards before they were approved for installation. Evidently some Ford technicians had found engines failing the tests, so they refined the prototype engines to meet the standards before filing their reports.

When this was discovered and splashed in newspaper headlines across the nation, Henry and Iacocca were livid. Both claimed not to have known about the infractions. Henry himself took the blame, thinking that perhaps the many speeches he had made criticizing the government's "stupid" standards led his workers to take the chance.

"I still don't like the law," Henry told a press conference, "and I think it ought to be changed. But you have to play by the rules. You don't cheat."

The government assessed a $7-million fine against the Ford Motor Company and permitted correction of the faulty reports rather than totally withhold approval, an act that would have barred Ford cars from the market. Though the fine ate into company profits, 1972 was still a very good year for Ford.

Throughout most of the tumult over the emissions fiasco Lee Iacocca kept himself busy with a labor of love. Since 1967 the company had received hundreds of letters bemoaning the change in Mustang. Those letters finally brought about a change of mind by Henry, and now Mustang was already in the process of being rebuilt on a shorter wheelbase, planned for introduction in September of 1973 as a 1974 model. It was to be called Mustang II.

Iacocca had worked closely with Ben Bidwell, who

had succeeded John Naughton as head of Ford Division, in determining what kind of small car the new Mustang should be. Their early inclinations were to produce it as a compact, the size of Maverick, five inches shorter than the original Mustang.

When the Capri, a subcompact, was introduced so successfully, Iacocca changed his mind. Germany could supply only a limited number of Capris per year, and if the young who flocked to buy it were so intrigued by its size, perhaps Mustang II should be sized as a subcompact as well. Surveys also bore out Iacocca's decision. Subcompact sales in 1970 far exceeded compact purchases.

Iacocca then made another decision. Circumstances in the seventies were much different from those of the mid-sixties, when the first Mustang had made its bow. The car buyers of the seventies had become more sophisticated. Looks alone no longer would sell them. A letter received from a customer in Greenville, South Carolina, triggered Iacocca's thinking.

"I would like to suggest several things that I feel would increase the overall appeal of the new Mustang," said the letter. "The car should offer enough luxury such as AM/FM stereo, custom interior with cut-pile carpeting, complete instrumentation."

Definitely, Iacocca decided, the car had to have shock value in its appointments. As with the first Mustang, it had to look more expensive than its sticker price. A check on the small cars that were selling the best strengthened his belief. Expensive

Capris were selling as fast as dealers could get them. The more expensive models of Japanese imports such as the Datsun 240-Z and Toyota Celica were also outselling their cheaper counterparts.

Iacocca placed responsibility for making Mustang II a sporty subcompact in the image of the best-sellers on the shoulders of Hal Sperlick, his vice president for product planning, who had played a major role in the development of the original Mustang.

Sperlick turned to one of the most famous automobiles design studios in the world, the fifty-year-old Ghia studio at Turin, Italy, which had created bodies for Alfa Romeo, Porsche, Maserati, and Rolls Royce. It had also produced the most expensive Volkswagen, the Kharmann-Ghia.

Some weeks before Iacocca was promoted to president of Ford, he and Sperlick had flown to Italy to discuss their plans for Mustang II with Alejandro deTomaso, head of Ghia. They commissioned deTomaso to build a Ghia-styled, operable Mustang II with a European fastback look. Less than two months later, with Iacocca now president, the prototype arrived in Dearborn.

Ford's executives, used to the two- or three-year lapse between design and complete prototype, were amazed at the speedy production of the handsomely styled Mustang II, painted in a striking red and black, with a sloping rear that swept gracefully down from roof-line to bumper. Iacocca and others, including Sperlick, drove the Ghia model.

In late March deTomaso sent another model to Ford's Dearborn headquarters, this one in the traditional notchback styling that featured a squared rear window vertical to the rear deck. This second model brought on heavy debate among the designers, stylists, and planners. Should the new Mustang II be a fastback or a notchback? Both were attractive. The question was which would appeal more to the American public.

Following the procedure used in building the first Mustang, Iacocca put the various design studios to work making clay models of the 1974 Mustang as they perceived it based on the deTomaso cars. Within three months the four design groups had four clay models ready. Oddly, only one of the four had chosen to build a notchback, a model that offered much of the flair that distinguished the first Mustang. Of the three fastbacks submitted one stood out for its sportiness and overall features.

Iacocca would not make a final choice without getting some measure of public reaction. He had the fastback and notchback sent to San Diego for some buyer impressions of the two. There the preference was overwhelming in favor of the fastback.

Still not fully satisfied, Iacocca had another survey conducted at Anaheim, California. The car buyers there also made the fastback their odds-on choice. The fastback went into production with some minor styling changes.

The front end was modified to give it a wider grille, the top of which was even with the top of the headlamps. Iacocca also decided that side scoops, a distinctive feature of the first Mustang, should also be included in the new version.

Another decision was made to redesign the Mustang emblem, the galloping pony that graced the center of the grille. Many Mustang buyers had complained that the original emblem did not have the excitement generated by the Mustangs of the old West and that the Mustang's legs were sculpted with an awkward gallop. A new, more faithful reproduction of a galloping Mustang was made for the new Mustang II.

Iacocca is like a proud father when it comes to one of his automobiles, fretting over it until its birth is finally achieved. So it was no surprise when he suddenly decided that one more survey of customer preference for fastback or notchback would be worthwhile. For a third study of buyer reaction to the cars he shipped two Mustangs, one fastback and one notchback, to San Francisco.

From the start he had been intrigued with the notchback designed by deTomaso and could not get it out of his mind. He could put his worry to rest if San Franciscans, a different breed of buyers, agreed with those in San Diego and Anaheim.

They were different without question. The San Francisco judgment was a near 100 percent in favor of the spectacular notchback with lines so smoothly blended that it created the illusion of motion while standing.

The survey results did not bring about a total shift

to the notchback. Iacocca felt certain that markets existed for both. Mustang II would be produced with a 50-percent mix of each. Once this decision was made, production for the first year was increased from 250,000 units to 300,000, with each body style available in two models.

The fastback, with its third door at the rear, would be offered as a four-passenger car with folding rear seats to provide storage space and as a performance-type sports car. The notchback would have two four-passenger models, one of which would offer special luxury features and be known as the Mustang Ghia, perhaps the most elegant subcompact available anywhere.

Iacocca's greatest concern as Mustang II took shape was its riding characteristics. He was determined that his new pony car be everything the public expected, and a smooth ride was essential. Small American cars, especially those powered by four-cylinder engines, had front-end suspensions incapable of absorbing the ups and downs of front wheels as they met bumps and dips in the road. He put his engineers to work on the problems.

In the midst of his worries over the riding comfort for the Mustang Lee sustained the most crushing blow of his life. The father whom he loved and revered, and who had suffered for some years with leukemia, suddenly died. Lee returned to Allentown immediately to console his mother and help arrange for Nick's funeral.

Following Nick's interment the spacious home he

had built for Antoinette in Midway Manor was filled with friends and relatives of the Iacocca family as well as many of Lee's own friends and coworkers. Henry Ford himself had come from Grosse Pointe to pay his respects.

It was a strange Henry who was there, according to Antoinette Iacocca. He stood quietly during the after-burial gathering, the only man among the many mourners without a drink. Lee, according to his mother, came up to Henry.

"Henry," Lee said—and it may have been the only time Iacocca ever addressed his chairman as other than Mr. Ford—"if my father could see you standing here without a drink in your hand, he would turn over in his grave."

Lee felt the death of his father deeply and remained reserved and largely unapproachable for months after he returned to Dearborn. It was to be expected. Nick's part in Lee's life was more that of a beloved brother and friend than father.

Lee immersed himself in work. His engineers had solved his worries over the riding qualities of Mustang II by adopting a concept used for some expensive European cars. Called a "subframe," it added the equivalent of a second miniframe, isolated from the body of the car. The front-suspension system worked off this subframe, not off the body itself, and took up the shocks occasioned by bumps and ruts, thus minimizing their impact on driver and passenger.

On December 8, 1972, Iacocca test drove the Mustang II. He was satisfied. The car had a solid feel as well as a smoothness and quietness as it traveled over rough areas, an uncommon quality in a subcompact.

Mustang II was introduced to the public on September 21, 1973. For three weeks its sales spiraled upward. Then on Friday, October 19, the roof started to fall in on the American economy when Libya shut off all oil shipments to the United States because of American support for Israel in the Yom Kippur war.

The Libyan action began a domino effect as Saudi Arabia followed suit the next day, and on Sunday Kuwait and the emirates of Abu Dhabi and Qatar made the oil embargo complete. Gasoline pumps dried up. Long lines formed as service stations doled out what was becoming a precious fuel.

Although the automobile industry was hard hit, it had enjoyed nine months of escalating sales. Ford Motor Company had its best year ever, topping even 1972 by over 100,000 units sold. It was Lee Iacocca's third straight year of record-setting sales as president of the company.

The oil embargo made Lee Iacocca a prophet to be reckoned with. He, along with Hal Sperlick, had been preaching the need for small, more fuel-efficient cars for some years. Now big Detroit cars were being dubbed gas-guzzlers, and the average American shied away.

The cars selling best were Volkswagens, Toyotas, Hondas, and Datsuns. Overall it was, if only for a time, an all-out import market. Foreign-made cars, which already had dented American sales more heavily year by year, beat the great sales year of 1972 by

249

about 200,000.

The only American dealership selling in at least fair numbers were those with foreign-made models. Among these were Lincoln-Mercury dealers with the European Capri, Buick with the German Opel, and Dodge with the Japanese Colt. Like the other foreign-made cars they offered twenty or more miles to a gallon.

It was not a happy new year for American car manufacturers as 1973 slipped into 1974; a year of disaster for the automobile market. General Motors dropped almost 1.5 million registrations. Ford fell back 500,000, Chrysler more than 300,000.

In self-defense the carmakers of America began to adopt the small-is-better philosophy. In this Iacocca already had built an edge for Ford. He had two beautifully styled, easy-on-the-gas cars ready in 1974, one for Ford Division and one for Lincoln-Mercury. Both were brought out on September 27, 1974, as 1975 models.

For Ford Division he had the Granada, a luxury-oriented small car with a Rolls Royce look in the front end. In fact it was merchandised as being as quiet as a Rolls, and television commercials showed decibel meters measuring the noise level in each. Built on the same chassis, but with a more expensive range of interior appointments, was the Mercury Monarch, with its "Mercedes" appeal.

Even in the depressed market of 1974 Ford Granada racked up more than 150,000 sales in its first six months. The more expensive Mercury Monarch totaled 50,000 for the same period. Small was where the action was, and other makers began to fall in line with down-sized models. Even Cadillac got into the act with a car they named Seville, but at $14,000.

Along with Granada and Monarch a third new car was presented to the public on September 27, 1974. Not small in the manner of Monarch, but not large, the Ford Elite was on the "smaller" side, with fair gas mileage. Iacocca had done his homework well in a year when America faced up to the fact that bigger was not the better way to car sales.

While Iacocca was showing his mettle on the automobile front, his boss was obviously having some trouble in the marital area. Henry being Henry, his difficulties with Cristina came with him to the Glass House. As 1975 got well under way the chairman of the Ford Motor Company reverted to his inexplicable harassment of his president.

CHAPTER 10

One morning early in 1975 the telephone rang in the office of Leo-Arthur Kelmenson, president of Kenyon & Eckhardt. He had no chance to complete his hello before the gravelly voice of Henry Ford II cut him off.

"Kelmenson, keep that son-of-a-bitch Winn the f— out of my company!"

The K & E president was shocked. Only a day or so earlier Kenyon & Eckhardt had added the Bill Winn promotion house as a subsidiary, and Winn had just completed staffing his organization.

Henry did not give a reason, and before Kelmenson could react, Henry had slammed his phone back into its cradle. Startled and appalled by the brief explosion, Kelmenson replaced his own phone, bewildered.

He wondered if Henry was drunk. The one-sided conversation had been too brief to get a line on Henry's condition, but something certainly had happened to the Ford chairman. One thing was certain! Whatever caused Henry's action was hardly due to displeasure with Bill Winn or his work.

Winn, a quiet-demeanored, kindly man, scrupulously honest, went about his work efficiently without making waves. He had proved himself an asset to the Ford Motor Company in producing shows that stimulated Ford and Lincoln-Mercury dealers to sales never before achieved. Whatever had evoked Henry's anger, his phone call was a cruel and harsh attack on a good man.

Most perplexing was the fact that Henry Ford had taken this indirect means of getting rid of Winn. One would expect the macho, second-best-to-nobody Henry to take his beef directly to Iacocca or to Winn himself. Passing the buck in this way, Henry reemphasized weakness in his character. His intention could have been nothing more than a secondhand demeaning of Iacocca.

Kelmenson could do nothing but call Iacocca and tell him they would have to get along without Winn in the future, even though the cost to Winn would be considerable. To defy Henry would mean the loss of Kenyon & Eckhardt's most valuable account.

Henry never did mention his axing of Bill Winn as a Ford Motor Company supplier to Iacocca, yet he must have realized the shabbiness of his action. However, three years passed before he recanted his dismissal of Winn, and even then it was not done directly.

Doug McClure had taken over the marketing position at Ford. Aware of Winn's contributions to the company, he asked Henry's brother, William Clay Ford, to intercede on Winn's behalf. Bill Ford succeeded in softening Henry, but again it was not Henry who delivered the news. McClure himself talked to Kelmenson and Iacocca. Bill Winn was restored to a persona grata status at Ford.

Lee, naturally, was grieved at the injustice done his friend, but, like Kelmenson, he could do nothing about it at the time. With so much work ahead he buried his anger in efforts to minimize the company's losses in the depressed economy of the mid-seventies.

As the oil embargo passed into history, it left aftereffects that, combined with the stringent government standards for control of emissions, had a crippling effect on the industry. Gasoline prices maintained an upward spiral that helped bring about double-digit inflation. Rising car prices added to the problem.

Gerald Ford of Michigan had taken over the country's highest office after Richard Nixon's resignation over the Watergate scandal. Ford, determined to lower gasoline consumption and help halt the rising inflation, succeeded in setting a nationwide speed limit on automobiles to conserve gasoline use. People began to drive less and to buy fewer cars. Then, as unsold cars piled up, the automakers laid off workers by the thousands, further damaging an already sick economy.

By the first of March, 1975, nearly 135,000 General Motors workers and over 120,000 at Ford and

Chrysler were on the streets without jobs. This was just the tip of the iceberg; throughout the country other industries dependent on the automobile business also cut their work forces.

However unfavorable the market was, scrapping existing plans would mean added losses. On March 21 Lee Iacocca brought out his newest small car, a Lincoln-Mercury Division counterpart of the Ford Pinto, the Mercury Bobcat. As might be expected, its sales were not spectacular, but they did help Mercury show an increase over the previous year, while Ford Division fell back a quarter-million units. Bobcat provided one more small, fuel-conserving automobile for Lee Iacocca's stable.

Other than in meetings or an occasional pass-by in the corridors, there had been little personal contact between Iacocca and Henry Ford since Henry's rash and unreasonable expulsion of Bill Winn. Iacocca, for one, preferred it that way. Now, however, the need to protect one of his most capable and loyal protégés made it necessary to see the chairman of the board.

Iacocca had sensed for some time that Henry was disenchanted with Hal Sperlick, who had backed Lee in his battles to downsize Ford cars. Having Sperlick away from Henry's daily view would be safer, and besides, in Lee's opinion his good right hand deserved a promotion.

Iacocca resolved to put Sperlick in charge of Ford's extensive overseas operations with headquarters in London, the one area of Ford operations that had shown a substantial profit in 1974 and was well on its way to help save 1975. Lee would need Henry Ford's approval for the appointment.

Lee sought out his boss and made a good case for Sperlick, but Henry would have none of it. Then, without Iacocca's knowledge, Ford named Philip Caldwell, a quiet, uncontroversial man loyal to Henry to fill the post. Iacocca bit his lip.

Customarily the chairman, president, and other high officers of Ford joined a new overseas head in London on the occasion of his taking over his new duties. Since the wives and families of those concerned were usually invited, Lee arrived in London with Mary, Kathy, and Lia.

One evening four couples, including the Iacoccas, were at dinner at the Caldwells' London home. While the elders dined together Iacocca's two daughters ate in the library. After dinner the ladies left the men to their cigars and brandy. Mary Iacocca went into the library to see how the children were.

Sometime later, as Mary stood in the library, Henry entered and from behind put his arms around her and nuzzled her neck.

"Mary, have I ever told you," Henry whispered in her ear, "what your husband has done for us? He has done more to help the Ford Motor Company than anybody ever."

Mary Iacocca was dumbfounded. Here was the chairman of the Ford Motor Company, a man who was often denigrating her husband, telling her what a great man Lee was. Henry had had more than a little to drink, as she could tell from his breath.

In recounting the incident years later Mary Iacocca said: "My mother told me when I was quite young that the truth always comes out when a man has had too much to drink." But she could not understand why, if Henry were indeed telling the truth while drunk, he had been treating Lee as he had.

Lee had walked into the library while Henry still had his arms around Mary and suggested that it was time to go.

"I'm talking to Mary," Henry said to Lee over his shoulder, "and when I'm finished, you can go."

When the Iacoccas were settled in their limousine, eleven-year-old Lia blurted out: "Daddy! Did you see Mommy with Mr. Ford? If you saw him keep kissing her on the neck, you'd divorce Mommy!"

The two faces of Henry Ford were always difficult to fathom, according to Mary Iacocca. Sober or not, when he was with other Ford people his innuendos often cut Lee down, as they would hear later from friends. But with the Iacoccas at any social or business gathering, after a few drinks he would describe Lee as the savior of the Ford Motor Company.

"One time Henry was in Texas," Mary recounted, "and our phone rang at three o'clock in the morning. The phone was beside my bed so I grabbed it. 'Is Lee there?' Henry asked. I said, 'Who is this?' He said, 'Henry.' I knew very well who Henry was, but I said, 'Henry who?' Then he continued talking to me, telling me he was going to write me a letter to let me know what Lee had done for the company and what a great man he was. I never did get the letter."

As 1975 moved toward its close, it became obvious that Henry Ford's inner agitation over his home life was taking its toll. He was as irascible in his Glass House suite as in his Grosse Pointe mansion. His marriage to Cristina had been damaged by the Kathy DuRoss affair to such an extent that a formal announcement of separation became inevitable.

It was first made public by a columnist in the *New York Daily News* and confirmed the same afternoon by Henry's lawyer. Ford himself was away on an overseas trip with Kathy DuRoss at the time, and the Glass House buzzed with anticipation of what might happen once Henry returned.

Henry did not keep people guessing for long after his return to Dearborn. He barged into Iacocca's office one morning. "Get rid of Sperlick!" he told Lee. "I don't want him around here."

It is reported that without another word he charged out the door, leaving Iacocca stupefied, not only by the demand that Lee fire one of his most capable aides, but also by the inexplicable speed with which he came in and went out.

For Iacocca it was both a shock and a bitter pill, and he lacked the heart to relay such devastating news to someone with so much talent, ability, and professionalism, and whom he had admired so much. He called in Bill Bourke, one of Henry's partisans, and had him tell Sperlick. The outspoken Sperlick took his expertise in the development of small cars and joined the Chrysler Corporation.

If it had not occurred to him earlier, Iacocca now

had little doubt that Henry Ford was out to get him and was using every trick possible to pressure him into resigning. If so, Henry underestimated Iacocca's strongmindedness. He had lived by his father's dictum never to quit, and to do so under such circumstances would play into Henry's hands.

Grim-faced and resolute, Iacocca went about his responsibilities and had a down-sized and comparatively inexpensive luxury-type car ready for release in the fall of 1976, the 1977 Ford LTD II. And three others were on the drawing boards for 1977 introduction, one—the Lincoln Versailles as competition for Cadillac Seville—to be shown to the public in April.

An upward turn in the economy was reversing the sales slump of the previous year. Especially heartening to Iacocca was the Mercury and Lincoln sales figures, which matched their best years ever. But the potential increase in Ford profits seemed to have no effect on Henry's determination to get Iacocca to leave.

Henry initiated an investigation into Iacocca's personal and business life and had the respected law firm that handled Ford Motor Company matters conduct the probe.

Iacocca was furious when he became aware of Henry's order, but kept quiet, confident it would prove to be a wild goosechase.

Henry had his investigators request a review of the J. Walter Thompson advertising agency books. According to a former executive of the agency, JWT refused permission, and as a result Henry took away their budget for small-car promotion and gave it to Grey Advertising, only to give it back to JWT a year or so later, after the books were checked and revealed nothing helpful.

Bill Fugazy's office in New York was bugged and broken into. Henry was convinced that because Fugazy got so much business from Iacocca and other Ford executives he was funneling part of his profits back to men he dealt with.

The investigators dug up nothing, a boner on Henry's part that cost Ford Motor Company more than $1.5 million. That nonbusiness expenditure soon would come back to haunt Henry in a lawsuit brought against him by his nephew, Benson Ford II.

The American automobile industry was buzzing over Henry Ford's incomprehensible doings. As chairman of the board of Ford Motor Company and a man in control of enough stock to wield dictatorial powers, it was inconceivable that he would resort to such tactics. A strong man, as he was reputed to be, would have just fired Lee Iacocca without need for a reason. He certainly had done it to others often enough in the past.

Iacocca became so angered at Henry's tactics that he discussed his problems on several occasions with individual members of the board of directors. Most of them were strongly in Lee's corner. The most supportive was Henry's own brother, William Clay Ford.

The directors with whom Lee talked suggested patience. They knew Henry's vacillating and vindictive nature and listened politely to his unsubstantiated charges. As one director said: "Henry would come on with a blazing cannon, but he'd leave with a peashooter."

Henry obviously was willing to try anything that might outrage Iacocca enough to make him quit when he came up with another blow below the belt. Having failed to discover any skulduggery in Lee's business dealings with Bill Fugazy, Henry did what many around the Glass House had predicted he would do. He demanded that Iacocca dissolve Fugazy's agreement with the Ford Motor Company.

Bill Fugazy, who operated a limousine service in the New York City area, had proved himself as friendly and loyal to Ford as to Iacocca. Thirteen years earlier Fugazy had made Lincoln Continentals the backbone of his own fleet.

"I had expected it for some time," Fugazy said. "Henry always used the back door when he came down on somebody stronger than he was."

The situation became so ludicrous, according to one minor executive still at Ford, that a few men were making book on who would crack first, Henry or Lee. The payoff was made when Henry was struck down with angina and hospitalized for almost two weeks.

Henry's sudden attack of angina pectoris did not result from the tension between him and Iacocca, though that may have contributed. Henry for years had suffered from a heart condition. His high living and heavy drinking didn't help—nor did the scandal leading to his separation from Cristina, the stormy months preceding the breakup of their marriage, the problems that had surfaced in his running the vast Ford complex, as well as the hitches in his pet community-service project.

One such problem inside the company concerned the number of Pintos and Bobcats whose gasoline tanks had burst into flames after rear-end collisions. While the problem was kept secret within the Glass House for some time, deaths resulting from a number of the collisions brought it into the open.

Henry's extracurricular activities also played a part in his problems. He enjoyed the front-page newspaper stories and television interviews that heralded him as the savior of Detroit, but he had been called to task for diverting company funds into the project, which, on paper at least, was his personal baby.

Henry had also used the vast buying power of the Ford Motor Company to influence suppliers to help bail out the Renaissance project when more financing was needed to complete its construction. Many of the companies who did business with Ford complained to the press—with names withheld, of course. Henry's image was thus further tarnished.

Whichever of his worries, singly or in combination, caused the heart attack, it must have made Henry think more seriously about the future of his company. If something happened to him, it might well mean the end of family control.

His brother Benson also had a heart problem and was seldom seen around the Glass House. His other brother, William Clay, was more interested in his Detroit Lions professional football team than in automobiles, and while Bill still attended board meetings and maintained a cursory interest in company affairs, he had made it clear in an interview with the automotive writer for the *Detroit News* that he would not want to actually run the Ford Motor Company. He would accept the chairmanship, he told the reporter, if it meant "simply serving as chairman, chairing the company and shareholders' meetings."

Henry also had to face the possibility that the post would not be offered to his brother. William was such a staunch supporter of Iacocca's that, having made it clear he would not run the company, operations would definitely be in Iacocca's hands. That was something Henry could not abide, especially since he realized also that his son Edsel was too young and inexperienced to have much of a chance with the board.

In mid-May of 1977 Henry watered down Iacocca's authority by naming Philip Caldwell vice-chairman of the board, thus placing his own man, and one who had been reporting to Lee, between himself and his president. Henry then restored the troika, creating a triumvirate to operate the company under the broad title of "Office of the Chief Executive." It would consist of himself, Caldwell, and Iacocca.

If Henry expected this new slap to drive Iacocca into a resignation, he was again mistaken. Lee was still determined to stay on, at least for another two years, when he would be fifty-five and qualify for his pension.

The maneuver that dropped him a rung down the

ladder was a cheap shot in Iacocca's eyes as well as in those of other executives within Ford. Nor did the media treat Henry kindly for this move.

The next day Iacocca brought out the new Lincoln Versailles. To the automotive writers he presented his usual genial public self, telling them that his new small luxury car would give Cadillac's Seville a run for its money. He uttered no word of recrimination, only enthusiasm for a new product.

Iacocca, however, pulled no punches with Henry. He let him know that the troika had not worked before and would not work now. He called it a three-headed monster that would not be able to make the decisions necessary to keep Ford afloat in the govern-ment-controlled atmosphere of the times. Henry shrugged him off. He was the boss, and the decision had been made.

Iacocca had expected nothing else, and as always he went back to his work. Already in production and scheduled to be released in the fall were two cars of special significance for him. Though they would be presented under his aegis as president of Ford, they were two of the last three for which his staunch supporter, Hal Sperlick, was responsible.

One was the Ford Fairmont, the other the Mercury Zephyr. Introduced on October 7, 1977, they were small yet roomy enough to be ideal family cars. The kind of automobiles Iacocca and Sperlick had been fighting for, their styling was fresh, and they offered good mileage. Sperlick's third offering would be the Ford Fiesta, the first front-wheel-drive offered by

Ford in America.

Fairmont and Zephyr were as warmly accepted as Iacocca hoped, helping Ford Division to enjoy its best sales year since Mustang II's bow in 1973. But even more heartening were the 1977 record-setting numbers for Lincoln-Mercury Division. And sales for both Lincoln and Mercury attained an even higher return in the early months of 1978.

Ford Division, however, was not quite so fortunate. Sales decreased slightly from the previous year, beginning a worrisome downward slide that would last into the eighties. The culprit was Pinto, whose sales plummeted because of its gas-tank fires and the resultant bad publicity.

Henry could have used the Pinto problem as an excuse to get rid of Iacocca, but no doubt he realized he also had to shoulder some of the responsibility. He held the purse strings, and a few dollars more per car would have provided a different and safer gas tank. Instead of getting rid of Iacocca altogether early in June, 1978, Henry dropped him another notch down the ladder.

Henry named William Clay Ford as chairman of the executive committee while still maintaining the troika setup. In effect this dropped Iacocca another step in the pecking order, making him fourth to Henry, William Clay, and Philip Caldwell.

As if to make Lee Iacocca more aware of the hopelessness of his future at Ford, Henry also announced to the press that he would give up his post as chief executive officer of the company at the 1980 annual stockholders' meeting and retire as chairman of the board no later than 1982. Under this new line of authority William Clay Ford would succeed him as chairman of the board in 1982, and Philip Caldwell would take over as chief executive officer.

This further undercutting of Iacocca's position did not alter Lee's determination to stick it out. Working under Caldwell would not be his cup of tea, but he felt that things would change for the better once Bill Ford became top man. Nor did Lee permit this latest setback to lessen his pleasure in anticipating the graduation of his eighteen-year-old daughter, Kathy, from the highly regarded Kingswood School.

It is a Kingswood tradition during graduation week festivities that the parents of one of the graduates host an after-midnight party called "Afterglow" following the senior prom. The hosts in 1978 were the Robert McGregors, whose daughter Molly was a classmate of Kathy Iacocca's. (Ironically, Bob McGregor was then head of the Detroit office of a San Francisco-based advertising agency that worked for Chrysler Corporation.)

The McGregor home grounds were not spacious enough to accommodate the huge tent usually erected to house the Kingswood seniors and their dates and parents. Even though Mary Iacocca was ill at the time, she and Lee volunteered the broad expanse outside their home on Edgemere Court.

Lee Iacocca was the proud father rather than the beleaguered president of the Ford Motor Company throughout the early-morning hours of the Afterglow party. He entertained the fathers inside and helped serve the young guests mountains of food outside. At 5:30 that morning he was laughing and joking at the kitchen sink as he washed dishes with the help of Bob McGregor.

Lee spent the few weeks following quietly and uneventfully at his Glass House desk. Henry was away most of the time, and Lee was occupied with plans for the fall television spectacular commemorating the seventy-fifth anniversary of the founding of the Ford Motor Company. There were many conferences with Leo-Arthur Kelmenson and other Kenyon & Eckhardt people charged with supervising production of the star-studded two-hour program to be titled "A Salute to American Imagination."

Wednesday, July 12, Lee was aware of the presence of Henry Ford in the suite next to his, but they had no contact throughout the day. Lee left for home about six-thirty, unaware that Henry had called an emergency meeting of the board of directors for that evening. Usually Lee took part in such meetings, but this session with the board was to be highly unusual.

That evening loud, angry voices echoed from the boardroom in the penthouse above the twelfth floor of the Glass House. Henry, as chairman, demanded that the board approve his firing of Lee Anthony Iacocca. Most of the board members argued against such a move. Henry's brother, William Clay, and George Bennett—representing a Boston investment house that held a great many Ford loans—were most vehement in their arguments against Henry's proposal.

The debate continued for over an hour with neither the board nor Henry giving ground. Finally Henry gave the directors an ultimatum.

"It's either him or me!" he shouted.

The board gave in.

Later that evening Lee Iacocca recradled the phone after his conversation with Keith Crain and turned to his wife. "It may be all over tomorrow," he said.

The following afternoon he again hung up a telephone, this time in his Glass House suite after hearing his secretary's words: "Mr. Ford wants to see you in his office."

His face grim, Iacocca walked the few feet down the corridor to the suite in the southeast corner and entered. Ford's secretary glanced at him for a moment, then looked away as she told him to go right in.

(The following scene in Mr. Ford's office is a recreation based on knowledge privy to various individuals close to both Ford and Iacocca. To some degree it is a fictionalized overview of the meeting.)

Lee turned the knob and walked into the plush surroundings of Henry's inner sanctum. Henry was seated behind his desk. In the background, making no effort to hide his feelings, stood teary-eyed William Clay Ford. Obviously Henry's younger brother had been making a last-ditch effort on Iacocca's behalf.

As Lee closed the door, Bill Ford's choked voice entreated in low tones, "Don't do it, Henry."

Iacocca had barely taken a step inside the office when Henry, ignoring his brother, barked: "You're fired."

Iacocca froze momentarily but recovered quickly and continued toward Henry's desk. He took a chair, determined not to leave without making Henry squirm a little. Lee, with deliberation, took a cigar from his pocket and lit it.

"Why are you doing this, Mr. Ford?" he asked finally.

When Henry merely glared, Iacocca took a puff on his cigar.

William Ford's voice came from the back of the room. "Henry, you've got to give him an answer."

Henry, looking at Iacocca, said: "I just don't like you!"

Henry Ford II denied this account months later in an interview with Barbara Walters on ABC television.

"Did you fire him just because you didn't like him?" Walters asked Henry on camera.

"Well, that's been said," Henry answered, "but that isn't true. He said to me, as I recall, 'why are you doing this? Don't you like me?' and as far as I can remember, I didn't answer the question."

The morning after the confrontation in Henry's office, the usual bland excuses for a sudden, and requested, resignation were fed to the press at a news conference. Reporters, wise in the ways of business, did not believe that a friendly parting of the ways had come about.

One newspaper columnist, Nicholas Von Hoffman wrote: ". . . the firing of Iacocca has the look of an act of spite, by a petulantly selfish rich kid." Newspapers across the country covered the event under big headlines. Radio and television reports made it their lead story. Walter Cronkite, the dean of television newsmen, relating the axing of Lee Iacocca to such sensational books about the automobile business as *Wheels* and *The Betsy*, told the public on his CBS news broadcast, "It sounds like something from one of those enormous novels about the automobile industry."

The automobile industry itself was stunned, even though Henry had shown himself to be a fractious individual who had not hesitated in the past to dump Ford presidents on what were perceived to be impulses. But Lee Iacocca had outserved them all. In his thirty-fourth year with the company, almost eight as president, and with his tremendous record of achievement, if any man should have felt secure, it was Lee Iacocca.

As for Lee himself, one of his closest friends says that on his way home from the Glass House that Thursday afternoon his reaction had been one of relief. "Thank God that bullshit is over," he had said to himself.

For Henry Ford II it must have been a different matter. He had some concerns about his action, and perhaps a touch of conscience. Whatever his thoughts, it seems he may have drunk a little more than usual that night.

Sometime around three o'clock the next morning he called the residence of Walter Murphy, the Ford vice-president for public relations and an Iacocca ally. Murphy, who had spent almost as many years with the Ford Motor Company as Iacocca, was awakened from a deep sleep. He picked up the receiver and was given hardly a chance to speak.

"Walter," said the blurred but unmistakable voice of the Ford chairman, "do you like Iacocca?"

Murphy, though still not fully awake, answered without hesitation. "Why, yes, Mr. Ford," he said. "I do like and respect Mr. Iacocca." "Then you're fired!" was the responding blast, following by the slam of the phone.

If Henry had followed through immediately on Murphy's dismissal, Walter would have been deprived of the pension for which he would be eligible in April, 1979. Ford, however, showed some compassion in this instance, allowing Murphy to remain at work until the first of December, after which he would be put on leave until his pension became active.

Iacocca did not receive such consideration. His separation from the Ford Motor Company was set for mid-October, three months after the fateful confrontation. Then, as if to remind the former president of Ford that he was persona non grata around the Glass House, he was assigned a desk in a cubicle at the Ford parts facility on Detroit's Telegraph Road.

It was a needless further abasement of a man who had loved the Ford Motor Company and had worked hard to make it a success. The new office not only embittered Iacocca all the more, but also had other Ford executives muttering imprecations about their chairman. As one Ford vice-president put it: "If this kind of thing could happen to as big a man as Iacocca, what security did any of us have?"

One somewhat embarrassing aspect to Henry's ridding himself of Iacocca resulted from its timing. Lee had been preparing for the introduction of his newest Mustang, the 1979 downsized pony car. Press kits promoting the Mustang subcompact had already been sent to automotive writers. Featured in them was a picture of Iacocca beside his newest car and smiling proudly. Henry sent Bill Bourke scurrying to retrieve the brochures featuring Iacocca.

Closing the books on Lee Iacocca was not as simple for Henry as in the case of Walter Murphy. Iacocca's contract and his stock options gave him great leverage toward a substantial settlement with the company. To handle the details Lee engaged the services of one of the country's great attorneys, Edward Bennett Williams of Washington, D.C.

Williams did a masterful job for Iacocca. When the haggling ended, he had a separation agreement that called for Ford to pay Lee Iacocca one million dollars per year until the end of 1980. The sole proviso was that Lee not work for any automobile company in competition with the Ford Motor Company.

This restriction meant little to Iacocca in the early weeks after the firing ordeal. He was tired of the rat race, and a long rest was beautiful to contemplate. He could spend more time with his wife, whose condition, while fairly stable, had not improved appreciably. He could give more attention to his daughters. And he had no worries about money. Even without the severance settlement, Iacocca was already well off.

Once the ax had fallen, Lee's most distressful moments were those spent trying to understand the fickleness of onetime friends. Men he had worked with closely, vice-presidents and others he had appointed to responsible positions, many J. Walter Thompson advertising executives he had worked with—fearful of recrimination from Henry Ford— abandoned him, afraid to be seen with him publicly for fear of losing their jobs.

At dinner one night with Leo-Arthur Kelmenson, Lee saw Max Fisher, a wealthy Detroit real estate developer, local entrepreneur, and bosom friend of Henry Ford in the same restaurant.

Kelmenson, still involved with the Ford Motor Company as president of its Lincoln-Mercury agency, joked about Fisher's presence with Iacocca. "Now," he said, "we can expect Max to run to Henry and tell him Leo was having dinner with Lee."

"Don't you care?" Lee asked.

"I don't give a damn," Kelmenson answered.

Expanding on the incident, Kelmenson later said, "Many of us valued our friendship with Iacocca more than we valued any reprisals by Henry Ford."

Henry Ford II had always been irritated by Iacocca's socializing with people he did business with, some of whom were among Lee's closest friends. "Mr. Ford used to criticize Lee for having too many friends in the business," says Kelmenson. "Lee's response to Ford was, 'When you work twenty hours a day, when do you have time to develop friends who are not in the business?' "

Kelmenson was one of the first friends with whom Iacocca talked at length after the firing. The following weekend the Iacocca family were guests at the Kelmenson home on Long Island. After dinner on Saturday Iacocca and Kelmenson sat on the deck facing the sea talking about Lee's future plans.

Iacocca told Kelmenson that he was going to do nothing for a while. He was going to take time to think. After so long on an emotional roller coaster, he needed to clear his mind. Yet, as the conversation progressed—mostly reflections on what had happened and how—one thing became clear to Kelmenson. The life of the idle rich was not for Lee Iacocca. One way or another he had to keep moving.

"I was, of course, a very prejudiced listener," Kelmenson said. "Because I felt that of all the things that Henry Ford had ever done, firing Lee was no doubt the most ill advised."

They sat looking out at the Atlantic for hours, with "Lee fantasizing about the future of the automobile industry," Kelmenson added. "Lee felt that there had to be a whole new concept in the manufacturing, sales, and distribution of automobiles. He was gone from Ford, but he was still living and breathing the business."

Back home in Bloomfield Hills Iacocca could not help but begin to sense a void. He missed the early-morning drives to Dearborn and the challenges that faced him each day. He had never cared much for golf, so his days would not be filled in the way of so many of his retired contemporaries. And the daytime hours were the ones most difficult to fill. Evenings friends could visit or be visited. He spent many hours reminiscing and pondering the future with Bill Winn.

One evening in early October Iacocca received a phone call from J. Richardson Dilworth, a director of Chrysler Corporation and investment counselor to the Rockefellers of New York. Chrysler, Dilworth told Lee, was on the verge of bankruptcy. Would he consider bringing it back to life?

Lee was well aware of Chrysler's mounting difficulties, as was everyone involved with the automobile industry. It was a stew pot of seething toil and trouble to which an ordinary man would not give a second thought. Iacocca, no doubt itching to get back in harness, told Dilworth that he would like to think about it.

Over the next week or two he discussed the situation with his closest friends, Winn and Kelmenson. The more they talked, the more surely Chrysler seemed an impossible situation. Did he dare jeopardize his hard-earned reputation as an automobile marketing genius by taking on an almost certain failure?

There was, he told his wife one evening, an overriding factor that could not be ignored. To let Chrysler go down the drain without doing everything possible to save it would add hundreds of thousands of workers to the unemployment rolls. It would also have a devastating effect on the city of Detroit, already in dire straits, as well as the state of Michigan and the nation as a whole.

When John Riccardo, Chrysler's chairman of the board, called Iacocca at Dilworth's suggestion, Lee agreed to discuss the matter. He talked to Riccardo, to other members of the Chrysler board, to Winn and to Kelmenson, even though Kelmenson was still involved with the Ford Motor Company as president of its Lincoln-Mercury and corporate advertising agency. Their personal friendship obviated any accusation of unethical conduct.

Should he or shouldn't he? The decision pulled Iacocca emotionally this way and that. For one thing, not enough time had passed since his release from Henry Ford's whirlpool of controversy for him to savor and enjoy a little peace of mind.

Then, too, there was his pride. Should he take a chance on an impossible job when other fine offers outside the automobile industry were being handed to him? His ego also had its say. He was confident that if anybody could do it, he could, and what great satisfaction there would be in putting a few more gray hairs into the head of Henry Ford II. It was already an open secret that the Ford Motor Company itself was in trouble.

And there was his settlement with Ford. If he took on the presidency at Chrysler, he was not only inheriting a can of worms deemed unsalvageable by many of the best economic brains in the country, he would also be forfeiting more than $2 million guaranteed by Ford.

In the end all the negatives were overridden by two factors. One, he was an automobile man pure and simple. He could be happy in no other business. Even more important was the catastrophic effect on the American economy if hundreds of thousands of workers who depended on Chrysler lost their jobs in one fell swoop.

On November 2, 1978, John Riccardo introduced Lee Iacocca as the new president and chief operating office of the deficit-ridden Chrysler Corporation.

CHAPTER II

Chrysler Corporation had not always been the frail and feeble third among the big three of the automobile industry. In 1936 Chrysler had catapulted past Ford into second place and held on through 1949, thanks to the engineering genius of its founder, Walter Chrysler, the first Henry Ford's floundering management, and the tottering empire Ford left his grandson.

Unlike William Durant and the first Henry Ford, who established the other two automotive giants, Walter P. Chrysler was not only a farsighted engineering wizard, but also a tough, no-nonsense, innovative marketer of automobiles. In this he was much like Lee Iacocca.

Walter Percy Chrysler was born April 2, 1875, in Wamego, a small town in east-central Kansas. He was the son of an engineer for a Union Pacific passenger train, who moved his family 500 miles west to Ellis,

278

Kansas, when Walter was about five years old. Young Walter's greatest pleasure was riding in the steam engine's cab with his father, an enjoyment that planted the seed for his love of engineering.

While still in high school he worked in the Union Pacific railroad shops, beginning as an engine cleaner. He didn't hesitate when he was offered a job as a machinist apprentice. He advanced to machinist when an opportunity arose in Wellington, a somewhat larger town in southern Kansas.

At the age of twenty-six he returned to Ellis to marry Della Forker, his high school sweetheart. It was now 1901, and with all the interest in internal combustion engines throughout the country Walter Chrysler went with the tide. On a visit to the Chicago Auto Show he fell in love with a $5,000 Locomobile.

Though he had only $700, the enterprising Chrysler bought the car, borrowing the needed $4,300 from a banking friend. He disassembled the car's engine, examined its components and their function carefully, then put it back together again. He became an automobile enthusiast on the spot, deciding that if automobile engines were designed and built with the same precision as a steam locomotive engine, the four-wheel vehicle indeed would supplant the horse and buggy.

As a stepping-stone to entering the still fledgling automobile industry, Chrysler took a job as plant manager for the Providence, Rhode Island, subsidiary of the American Locomotive Works. The plant was building replicas of the French Berliet, chain-driven, four-cylinder machines with twenty-four and forty horsepower that were sold under the name Alco. With Chrysler in charge of the plant, the Alco was given a shaft drive in 1907. In 1909 the most famous Alco was produced, a sixty-horsepower six that won the Vanderbilt Cup race in both 1909 and 1910. The Alco passed from the scene in 1913, but by then Walter Chrysler had gone on to better things.

While at the Alco plant Chrysler had met James J. Storrow, a director of the American Locomotive Works who was also the chairman of the General Motors Finance Committee and president of a Boston banking house. Storrow had been brought in to General Motors to help salvage the company, which had been brought to the brink of bankruptcy by William Durant.

Chrysler accepted Storrow's offer of a job as assistant to Charles Nash, who headed the Buick facility of GM in Flint, Michigan. Chrysler started at Buick in 1912, when fewer than fifty Buicks per day were being built, a pitiful figure compared to the thousand and more produced daily by Ford. He brought to Buick a dedication for engineering precision and the moving assembly line initiated by Ford.

Within four years Walter Chrysler made Buick the most profitable division in General Motors and became its president and general manager. In 1916 Bill Durant regained control of General Motors and again started the giant on a downward slide by getting into unprofitable ventures such as the making of farm machinery and tractors. Chrysler fought Durant on these acquisitions in vain. Down the GM drain went $30 million. Chrysler, with a flamboyant personality, pride, a hot temper, and an equally hot vocabulary, gave Durant a blistering lecture and resigned.

Immediately Walter Chrysler was offered $1 million to save Willys-Overland, a car-manufacturing company that had suffered during the economic slowdown after World War I. Chrysler could not turn it down when he found that the Chicago banker who had lent him the money to buy his Locomobile was one of the men asking for help. Though it seemed an impossible task going in, Walter Chrysler restored Willys-Overland to profitability.

Even before he had finished his work at Willys-Overland, the same banking group asked Chrysler to take on the Maxwell, a popular car that was not selling as well as it once had because its axles often broke. Something needed to be done with the huge inventory of unsold Maxwells. Chrysler simply redesigned the axles, and Maxwell's reputation was saved, and the stockpiled cars were sold. After less than two years under Chrysler, Maxwell showed a profit of more than $2.5 million. The following year its profit level was $4 million.

Almost from the day Walter Chrysler purchased his Locomobile in Chicago, his dream had been to one day have an automobile-manufacturing company bearing his own name. He wanted to design automobiles that would, first and foremost, be examples of engineering excellence. The time was now ripe.

Chrysler had brought with him to Maxwell three

brilliant young engineers who had helped him at Willys-Overland. They were Fred M. Zeder, Owen R. Skelton, and Carl Breer. Together the four of them began work on a new six-cylinder automobile featuring the high-compression type of engine developed during the war. Zeder produced a six-cylinder with a high-compression cylinder head that offered seventy-miles-per-hour performance.

The "Chrysler Six," as it was to be called, was also fitted with four-wheel hydraulic brakes, something unique and new to the American market, as well as aluminum pistons, shock absorbers, and oil filters that could be replaced. Chrysler had a prototype of his car ready for exhibit at the New York Auto Show in January, 1924, but auto-show officials denied Chrysler exhibit space because his car was not yet in production. Undaunted, he leased the lobby of the Commodore Hotel, where many newsmen were staying. The Chrysler Six, priced at $1,565, was so well received that a banking syndicate offered Walter a $5-million loan to start production. With so much power and styling at so low a price, Chrysler's car gave buyers the feeling of driving a far more expensive car. In twelve months 32,000 were sold, setting an industry record of $50 million in sales within one year.

In 1925 Walter P. Chrysler bought out Maxwell and discontinued its name, forming the Chrysler Corporation with its headquarters in Highland Park, Michigan, a suburb of Detroit. When profits neared $50 million in 1927, Chrysler expanded and modernized his factory facilities.

By 1928 the complete Chrysler line consisted of the seventy-horsepower Chrysler Six, the four-cylinder Chrysler 58, and a luxury model, the Imperial Six, priced at about $3,100. Walter was also planning to introduce a new, lower-priced model, the DeSoto.

In establishing his Chrysler Corporation Walter Chrysler surrounded himself with capable men. One was B. E. Hutchinson, who had been his treasurer at Maxwell. Hutchinson's first name was Bernice, which he detested, and so he insisted on being referred to by his initials. Another of Chrysler's team, one who had been with him at General Motors, was Kaufman T. Keller, who also disowned his first name and became known solely as K. T. Keller. Keller was placed in charge of manufacturing by Chrysler.

Hutchinson, tight-fisted when it came to expenditures, pointed out that DeSoto could not be produced with cost-efficiency because the company, lacking facilities for forging iron and steel and making castings, had to buy many components. Until Chrysler Corporation could increase factory capacity, it would never be able to adequately compete with Ford, much less General Motors.

It would cost $75 million to bring facilities to efficient size, Hutchinson told Chrysler, and that would mean such a drain on cash reserves that DeSoto could not be produced at the low price hoped for. Chrysler feared that a delay in expansion would destroy any chance to move ahead in the industry. He decided that the only answer was a merger with another automobile maker.

A company-saving opportunity surfaced in 1928. The Dodge Brothers Company was for sale. After John and Horace had died in 1920 the company had been operated by their widows. Their management didn't work out and Dodge was then taken over by the prestigious New York investment firm of Dillon, Read. In May 1928, Clarence Dillon offered the Dodge name and facilities to Walter Chrysler.

The merging of Dodge into Chrysler Corporation was Walter Chrysler's greatest single achievement, even though the Dodge line still consisted of only its original four-cylinder model available as either a sedan or truck. The greatest asset in the Dodge acquisition was the company's huge facility in Hamtramck, another Detroit suburb not far from the Chrysler headquarters. It was one of the world's largest and most efficiently organized automobile factories, covering fifty-eight acres and employing a workforce of 2,000. The moment the deal was consummated Chrysler appointed K.T. Keller as the Dodge production chief. Keller wasted no time. As he took control of Dodge on July 30, 1928, he had huge signs reading "Chrysler Corporation—Dodge Division" strung across all entrance gates.

Walter Chrysler, earlier in the month of July, went into head-to-head competition with Henry Ford's Model A, the car brought out just eight months earlier as the successor to the Model T. Chrysler's new car, named Plymouth, was a six-cylinder, as against the Model A's four. It was rakishly styled in comparison with the Ford and was priced at $670.

"Chrysler has gone into the low-priced field with throttle wide open," was *Time*'s reaction to Plymouth. Nonetheless it took about a year for the car to catch on, and then only after Chrysler demonstrated the reliability and performance of his six-cylinder engines to the world by entering two Plymouths in a race at LeMans. Neither won—an English Bentley finished first and an American Stutz second—but the two Plymouths did make remarkable showings, coming in third and fourth.

The acquisition of Dodge for about $70 million in Chrysler stock and the assumption of a Dodge debt that ran about $56 million made Chrysler Corporation the third largest automaker, behind General Motors and Ford. The added facilities also made it possible for Chrysler to break into a new segment of the market with the DeSoto, an automobile that represented the very latest in engineering.

Styled to resemble the Chrysler, its 21.6-horsepower engine was a side-valve six mounted on rubber insulators to reduce vibration. It was also equipped with full force-feed lubrication, four-wheel hydraulic brakes, a ribbon-styled chrome radiator, and rear-mounted spare tire. DeSoto's 90,000 first year sales made 1929 a banner year for Walter Chrysler.

Chrysler and Dodge cars were as great successes in England as in the United States, with European car makers quickly copying the narrow-shell "ribbon" type radiators that distinguished Chrysler cars. For 1931 Chrysler brought out two new straight eights and a new styling look reminiscent of the long, low

Cord. One of the new eights was the 125-horsepower Imperial with a four-speed, silent third-gear transmission.

Experimentation and research were important to Walter Chrysler, but when the economy became seriously depressed after the Crash of '29, he considered closing the research department. He changed his mind when Harold Hicks, a research engineer who had come to Chrysler from Ford, described some recent experiments.

Hicks had become intrigued with automobile body streamlining. He had discovered that when the body of a car was altered to provide a smoother airflow, the fuel consumption dropped and maximum engine speed increased.

"If that's what research can do," Chrysler told Hicks, "we will always have research." For the rest of Walter Chrysler's life he believed strongly in the value of research. And it led to many innovations that helped Chrysler supplant Ford as America's number-two automaker.

Among these innovations were "Floating Power," (which was achieved through the use of cushioned engine mounting), automatic clutches, syncromesh transmissions, and automatic overdrive.

Research was also responsible for one of Chrysler's greatest and most farsighted technical successes— which also proved its worst commercial failure—the controversial "Airflow" design concept discovered in wind-tunnel tests. Chrysler researchers experimented with various makes and found that the cars were aerodynamically more efficient going backward.

This discovery led to the Chrysler Airflow model, designed with a fully streamlined body and sloping front and rear ends, a styling that proved too extreme for the car buyers of the day. Even though the Chrysler Airflow joined Ford's Edsel as one of the great sales flops in automobile history, it did not halt Chrysler research. In 1937 an independent front suspension was developed, followed two years later by steering-column gear shift and fluid drive.

While Edsel put a crimp in Ford's challenge to General Motors, the Airflow's effect on Chrysler was negligible. It maintained its second-place share of the American market until 1950, when Ford again shot past Chrysler. By that time Walter Chrysler had passed from the scene, having died on August 18, 1940, of a cerebral hemorrhage.

The prolonged illness that led to Chrysler's death had impelled him to turn the company presidency over to K.T. Keller in July of 1935, while Chrysler held onto the post of board chairman. Keller had done such a magnificent job in coordinating Chrysler and Dodge production that the business world had expected the company to maintain the hard won progress begun by Walter Chrysler.

Unfortunately Keller lacked the vision, patience, creativity, and tenacity of Chrysler. The corporation's downward slide, which culminated in the disastrous nosedive Lee Iacocca would be called upon to end a near half-century later, began during Keller's twenty-one-year control of the company.

World War II helped camouflage many of the Keller inefficiencies. In early 1942, Chrysler, in common with all American automakers, shut down civilian car production in favor of war matériel. K.T. Keller proved himself an organization genius in supervising Chrysler's part in the war effort.

Chrysler Corporation had been designing, engineering, and producing military vehicles since 1934, building armored cars capable of mobility and maneuverability under the most demanding conditions and over the most rugged terrain. In 1941 it was awarded a multitude of military contracts, including production of tanks in its newly built Detroit Tank Arsenal.

By 1942 Chrysler produced 2,486 twenty-nine-ton General Grant M-3 tanks and 2,388 of the famous thirty-two-ton Sherman tanks. Before the end of 1945 Chrysler's production of tanks in various designs and for a variety of uses reached 25,000. In addition Dodge Division's newly built plant near Chicago turned out an amazing 18,413 Wright Cyclone 2,200-horsepower engines designed for the B-29 Superfortress.

Chrysler's war involvement under K.T. Keller was mind-boggling. It included production of 18,000 engines for the B-29s, 438,000 army trucks in various sizes, 60,000 Bofors antiaircraft guns, more than 3 billion rounds of small-arms ammunition, almost 3 million 20-mm shells, 101,000 incendiary bombs, and 1,500 searchlight reflectors, which were ultimately replaced by 2,000 radar antennae units and mounts

Also included in this partial list were 100 miles of submarine nets, 20,000 land mine detectors, and 1,000 rail carloads of precision machinery for the gaseous-diffusion plant at the government's atomic bomb project at Oak Ridge, Tennessee.

President Harry S. Truman awarded Keller the Medal of Merit for his war work, then appointed him head of the United States guided-missile program, an area in which Chrysler Corporation also played a prominent role.

The return to car production at Chrysler, as at all manufacturing companies, was a slow process. No new cars were on drawing broads, and time permitted only minor changes in the cars offered the public.

Ford and General Motors went to work planning new cars. Chrysler, under Keller, remained content to continue slightly changed models long after its competition brought out new models. After the production drought during the war Americans were eager to trade in their old models. With cars selling as fast as they reached dealer showrooms, Keller was in no hurry to make changes. Three sales-record-breaking years provided K.T.'s justification. In 1947 Chrysler profits were about $63 million, 1948 topped $89 million, and 1949 brought the company over $132 million.

K.T. Keller, the industry said, had a hat fetish. He was so seldom seen without a fedora covering his squarish-shaped head that the joke around Detroit was that he slept with his hat on. This hat obsession carried over into his car-design philosophy. Every car

Chrysler built, he vowed, would have a roof high
enough to permit a man with a hat to sit up straight
in his seat.

"We build cars to sit in, not piss over," was his
rejoinder when asked why Chrysler did not follow the
industry trend to lower cars.

In the postwar years Chrysler's share of the American car market, which reached a high of 25.7 percent, gradually slipped to under 18 percent in 1950.
During the same period Ford, with new V-8s sporting
longer and lower silhouettes, shot up from its low of
18 percent to 24 percent in 1950.

Keller's most serious blunder was his challenge to
the United Auto Workers in 1949 and his refusal to
accept the terms related to pension funding already
agreed to by Ford and General Motors. The result
was a 100-day strike beginning in January, 1950, that
cost Chrysler Corporation over $1 billion in lost
production. And in the end he was forced to accept a
pension plan approximately the same as the one he
had rejected.

Keller retired as president of Chrysler that same
year, with Lester L. "Tex" Colbert taking over. K.T.
however, remained as chairman of the board and
retained as firm a control over the company as he had
as president.

Colbert had moved up to the corporate presidency
after serving as president of Dodge Division for four
years, after which he was elected a vice-president and
director of Chrysler Corporation. While at Dodge he
had been concerned by the lack of styling that re-

sulted from Fred Zeder's obstinacy and B.E. Hutchinson's tight grip on finances. As he took over the corporation presidency on November 3, 1950, he quickly discovered that making any policy decision called for a battle with Keller and Hutchinson.

Colbert fought for $900 million to modernize Chrysler's antiquated plants. Determined to show Keller the far-ranging weaknesses in the corporation, he hired McKinsey and Company, one of the nation's most respected consulting firms to do an in-depth study of Chrysler operations. When the study was completed, he had all the ammunition he needed.

The McKinsey report criticized the design and engineering policies of Keller and Zeder and emphasized the need for cars that were competitive in performance and appearance. It also underlined the vital need of Chrysler Corporation for international expansion.

Colbert's plans were given a boost in 1953 when B.E. Hutchinson retired. Then, by hiring away from Studebaker a forward-thinking designer named Virgil Exner, he negated the Zeder influence on styling.

Keller retired in 1956, and Colbert assumed the role of chairman as well as president. In midyear Exner revealed a new "Fleet Sweep" styling that incorporated rear-end fins. The 1957 models were attractive enough to boost sales.

The U.S. government had maintained the Keller-started military involvement with Chrysler Corporation by bringing the company into America's missile and space activity. Begun in 1952 with only twenty-

six engineers, it was by 1956 the most profitable
segment of the corporation. It produced the Redstone
and Jupiter missile systems that would later act as
vehicles in the many "firsts" achieved by the American space program. Chrysler Space Division later
engineered and built the Saturn, one of which sent up
the first Apollo manned flight.

Chrysler's space and defense contracts helped keep
the company afloat with Tex Colbert at the helm,
although a succession of tragedies in 1956 hurt the
corporation considerably. Three of the company's
most important officers died within six months: Carl
Snyder, vice-president for manufacturing, in a plane
crash; George Troost, vice-president for finance, after
brain surgery; and Cecil Thomas, vice-president for
international affairs, to gangrene. Colbert had a difficult time filling their posts, but one replacement,
Lynn Townsend, who took over finance, would play a
major role in Chrysler's future troubles.

However he tried, Colbert was unable to halt the
Chrysler slide. He enjoyed a short period of success in
1957, when his fin-designed cars produced a profit of
more than $125 million, but the euphoria was short-
lived. The cars had been produced without sufficient
testing in order to make their introduction date, and
the result was a torrent of complaints.

The cherished reputation of a company dependable
for engineering excellence was blemished. Chrysler
sales dropped so low in 1958 that the year showed a
loss of about $130 million. In market share the
company dropped to 14 percent, while Ford pulled

way to over 26 percent.

On April 28, 1960, Colbert, now desperate, named William C. Newberg as president. But Newberg had stock in companies that supplied Chrysler, and he became a target at the 1960 stockholder's meeting. Charged with conflict of interest, he was deposed within two months of his appointment.

Colbert, thoroughly disoriented by the turn of events, voluntarily gave up both the chairmanship and the presidency he had reassumed after Newberg's firing. To fill his time until he reached retirement age he took the post of chairman of Chrysler of Canada. Lynn Townsend was named executive vice-president to run Chrysler, pending the appointment of a new president.

Townsend, at heart a finance man with a sharp knife to cut costs, wanted the presidency, but his vain, contemptuous nature and acid tongue made him unacceptable to the Chrysler board. The job was offered to executives at Ford and at General Motors, including Semon "Bunky" Knudsen. None took it.

In the end Lynn Alfred Townsend was elected president, an action that was to haunt Chrysler Corporation through fifteen increasingly distressful years. One of Townsend's first orders was the firing of about 7,000 office workers to effect a $50-million-per-year cut in budget.

Townsend's greatest mistake, not evident at the time, was his scattered efforts to increase the Chrysler International division begun by Tex Colbert. In 1964 he expanded English facilities with a takeover of the

Rootes Group of Great Britain, makers of the Sun
beam, Hillman, Humber, and Singer cars. After
total investment of $47 million, Chrysler United
Kingdom Limited evolved as a wholly owned subsidi
ary of the Chrysler Corporation.

Townsend also acquired the French Simca facili
ties, which had a previous association with Ford an
Fiat of Italy. Before he was finished Chrysler Corpo
ration had dealings in six continents. By 1965 foreig
countries accounted for more than one-third of a
Chrysler sales and one-fifth of all Chrysler vehicle
built, but each of Townsend's acquisitions abroa
further weakened Chrysler's financial picture a
home, a deterioration not immediately felt. Chrysler
continuing and exceedingly profitable ties with th
United States government as the prime defense con
tractor for combat tanks and space projects helpe
conceal Chrysler's crumbling position in the industry

In 1967 Townsend moved up to chairman of th
board, and Virgil Boyd, who had come from Amer
can Motors to shore up Chrysler's dealer body, wa
named president.

Townsend brought Chrysler into the muscle ca
market in 1968 with the Plymouth Road Runne
described by a national car-buff magazine as "th
ultimate put-on" when it was first announced. It wa
nonetheless, a no-nonsense, high-performance ca
aimed at the sporty-minded eighteen-to-twenty-two
year-old male, designed to please him with soli
performance and good looks. Road Runner's fir
year sales of 45,000 units produced record-makin

profits of over $300 million.

These 1968 profits, however, proved to be one-time only. Chrysler slid back into its losing ways as Townsend brought out new full-size cars including Imperial, Plymouth Fury, and Dodge Polara, none of which satisfied the public's preference for smaller cars.

Townsend's principal reaction as sales again plummeted was to cut the Chrysler workforce, adding more than 11,000 to the unemployment rolls in a year of slumping economy. He also replaced Virgil Boyd with John J. Riccardo, like himself a former finance-oriented accountant. Townsend believed that with a cost-slasher at his side he could bring Chrysler quickly back to profitability. It was a vain hope.

Riccardo recognized the trend to smaller cars, but the corporation was too deeply in debt and unable to secure the funds necessary to tool up for so radical a change. He did the next best thing, consummating an arrangement with Mitsubishi, a Japanese automaker, to sell its small imports through the Chrysler dealer network. Meanwhile Chrysler would slowly bring out intermediate-sized cars of its own.

By the time this line of cars was ready, the market did an about-face, and larger cars were again in demand. It seemed like a pendulum with Chrysler the loser at each swing. In the summer of 1973 Chrysler was ready to bring out new full-sized cars, but the Arab petroleum exporting countries announced an oil embargo, which sent American car buyers scurrying for small cars. Chrysler lost $52 million in 1974 and had its greatest loss ever in 1975, over $259 million.

The company's future was made even more insecure by the governmental regulations setting mileage and pollution standards for the industry. Chrysler simply did not have the money to comply. At this point Lynn Townsend left the sinking ship totally in John Riccardo's control by retiring.

Operating cash was Chrysler's most vital need, and Riccardo sold off everything Chrysler owned not directly connected to production of cars for the United States and Canada and fulfillment of its defense obligations. Actually the company's Defense Division was the only profit-producer.

The end of the oil embargo brought Chrysler a new but brief lease on life. The car buyers of America swung back to larger cars, and Riccardo could show a near $423-million profit for 1976. While 1977 also showed in the black, the figure dropped to just over $163 million. But 1978, with the company already committed to spending huge sums for plant modernization and for production costs for a new line of cars, had to be projected as a year heavily in the red.

Hal Sperlick, whom Henry Ford kicked out of the Ford Motor Company for arguing the cause of small, fuel-efficient, front-wheel-drive cars, had won his battle at Chrysler. Given a free hand he was primarily responsible for the introduction of Plymouth Horizon and Dodge Omni the year before. They proved to be the kind of cars he had insisted would give imports a battle. But they were not enough.

Dissension at the highest level of Chrysler Corporation did its part in diminishing any possible upturn in company hopes. The naming of John Riccardo as Chrysler chairman and chief executive officer had not been a unanimous action of the board. Many had preferred Eugene Cafiero, an executive vice-president who had been moved up to the presidency when Riccardo succeeded Lynn Townsend as chairman.

Cafiero was continually at odds with Riccardo's hit-and-miss plans for the company's recovery and his doomsday attitude toward possible success. Riccardo had come to Chrysler from an accounting firm and thus was a penny-pincher—a "bean-counter," as a finance-oriented individual is referred to in business. Cafiero had been an automobile man from the start, a Chrysler mover and shaker since 1953, a product-based engineer.

Riccardo kept busy trying to drum up money to bail out Chrysler. In doing so he failed to maintain control of production and product quality. The more he looked for financial help, the more financial help became needed to offset delays in manufacture of products and getting them to market. Riccardo tried one banking and investment firm after another in search of $7.5 billion to put Chrysler on its feet. He was turned down by all.

In desperation he turned to the federal government. As a prelude to his assault on Washington, he collared senators from states in which Chrysler plants were located, twisting their arms for backing on the premise that a Chrysler failure meant economic problems for their constituencies.

Then, too, Riccardo believed he had an ace in the hole in W. Michael Blumenthal, former head of Detroit's Bendix Corporation, who had been appointed secretary of the treasury by President Carter. Blumenthal, having problems of his own within the Carter cabinet, agreed to help, figuring that it would give him added stature in Carter's eyes. Carter was going to need all the votes possible to win renomination, much less reelection, and a good deed for America's laborers would not hurt.

Another stalwart in Riccardo's camp was Douglas Fraser, head of the powerful United Auto Workers. Fraser's prime interest was keeping his union members at work in a revitalized Chrysler Corporation.

Any hope that Blumenthal might be of help faded when President Carter replaced him with G. William Miller, chairman of the Federal Reserve Board. While still with the Federal Reserve Board Miller had expressed himself as against government help to bail Chrysler out of its difficulties, and had actually mentioned bankruptcy as a way out. To place what seemed the final nail in the coffin Miller, soon after he took office as secretary of the treasury, made it clear he was unalterably opposed to help for Chrysler Corporation.

Even when it should not have been, John Riccardo's luck was all bad. In early February of 1978 the new XM-1 combat tank produced by Chrysler was ready for release to the United States government. Heralded as the world's greatest combat weapon, the

XM-1 was reputed to be bigger, more formidable, and better than anything the Soviets had or could come up with in the foreseeable future.

Extensive and colorful ceremonies were planned for the transfer of the tank of the government-owned, Chrysler-operated plant in Lima, Ohio. An assistant secretary of the Army was on hand, along with a number of generals, the widow of General Creighton Abrams (after whom the tank would be named), and representatives of the press, radio, and television.

When the presentation ceremonies were concluded, the public, press, and dignitaries present were treated to a demonstration of the fifty-nine-ton behemoth. It got under way without trouble as hundreds watched in awe. But suddenly it stopped and could not be moved. Its gears had been locked in reverse. Red-faced Chrysler officials ordered it returned to the plant for further work.

As if that embarrassment was not enough, the fates delivered another cruel blow to Chrysler prestige a few months later. The corporation was bringing out its two new cars for 1979, the Chrysler New Yorker and the Dodge St. Regis. William Milliken, Michigan's governor, and Coleman Young, Detroit's mayor, were to drive the first of each off the assembly line.

Governor Milliken was first with the New Yorker. He settled himself in the plush velour seat behind the steering wheel and, with a smile toward the cameras as hundreds applauded and bulbs flashed, he turned the ignition switch. Nothing happened. Sheepishly, he tried again. The engine still did not roar to life.

The car had been equipped with a dead battery.

John Riccardo must certainly have felt himself accursed. It was the last straw. As he turned away to head back to his office in Highland Park, he may have been sending up prayers of thanks that Lee Iacocca had been fired by Henry Ford II a month or so earlier.

CHAPTER 12

Traders at the New York Stock Exchange paid Lee Iacocca a high compliment when he accepted the Chrysler challenge. Showing confidence in his ability to bring the ailing corporation back to life, they sent Chrysler stock up one point per share.

Reactions were more reserved in America's business community in general and the automobile industry in particular. Many hard-nosed businessmen found it inconceivable that any man would give up $1 million a year to take on the thankless job of reviving a company already in its death throes. And within the automobile industry responses ran from sheer amazement at General Motors to trepidation at Ford and American Motors.

GM was far too big to fear substantial inroads, however successful Iacocca might be at Chrysler. At Ford, already in a downward slide, overt bluster was tinged with covert concern based on firsthand knowledge of Iacocca's ability.

"Don't use my name, but we weren't really worried," one Ford executive reminisced in early 1981. "Only God can make a tree, and Lee Iacocca isn't God."

Another man with even more reason to desire anonymity had a more realistic view. "We're still in trouble, and if it wasn't for our international operation, we might be worse off than Chrysler," he said. "We're so vulnerable that if Iacocca performs the miracle he's capable of—well, number three is just a step down from number two."

How much of a miracle it would take not even Iacocca fully realized until he met for the first time with the full compliment of Chrysler Corporation officers about a week after his acceptance. The meeting began on a peculiar note.

Without realizing it, Iacocca initiated the first of many changes he would make at Chrysler the moment he sat at the conference table with Riccardo and all other high-level officers. He lit one of his big cigars, unaware of the startled sensibilities all around.

Smoking during company meetings had been a strictly enforced John Riccardo no-no for a long time. And trigger-tempered Riccardo had more than once exploded at an officer who lit up a smoke in a moment of forgetfulness. This time Riccardo bit his lip.

"Well, I guess rules have to change sometime," he sheepishly commented as he brought the meeting to order.

As Riccardo proceeded to outline all the problems that led to the company's untenable situation, Iacocca sat puffing on his cigar, dumbfounded. He had studied the company's background and had been briefed by Riccardo, but what he was hearing was a startling litany of blunders and mismanagement.

Chrysler had a huge backlog of unsold cars that should never have been built, automobiles produced only to make the books look good, to justify the bonuses paid to executives. These cars represented far more than production hours and dollars, they also accounted for millions of dollars for storage space.

Parked on open lots throughout the Detroit area, spilling across the river into Canada, standing there through rain, snow, blistering heat, and bitter cold, they were indicative of further waste running into the hundreds of thousands of dollars for damaged paint surfaces, broken windshields and windows, and slashed tires.

The ridiculous inventory build-up concept dated back to Lynn Townsend's days. Chrysler's cash drain was further increased by recalls of its 1978 models, all because of hurry-up production that resulted in poor quality.

As he went on, Riccardo noted that the quarter just ended showed a loss approaching $160 million. Iacocca was astonished. The same quarter just two years before had brought Chrysler a $155-million profit. So great a reverse in a two-year period was incredible. The answer lay in gross inefficiency. If ever a company cried for sweeping changes, it was

Chrysler Corporation.

It was unbelievable that the third-largest automobile manufacturer in America, a company as old as Iacocca himself, fifty-six, and doing business on six continents, could be in such bottomless trouble. A thorough housecleaning at top levels was called for.

Fortunately, there was one executive around whom Iacocca could build, Hal Sperlick, his coworker on Mustang, who had joined Chrysler in 1977 after Henry Ford II demanded that he be fired. Sperlick, like Iacocca, was sensitive to the automobile market. He had seen the growing need for smaller cars and for the efficiency that front-wheel drive brought to driving. He had fought for progress at Ford, but despite the backing of Iacocca, had lost.

He was Iacocca's kind of executive, one Lee described as "having a fire in his belly," a tense, impatient man who drove himself and others equally hard. With Sperlick as his chief of product planning and development, Iacocca could proceed to fill out his executive staff with men equally dedicated and equally competent.

Because Sperlick had been able to further his conviction that small, front-wheel-drive cars were the wave of the future, Chrysler was two years ahead of General Motors and three years ahead of Ford in bringing this more space- and fuel-efficient kind of automobile to the American market. It gave Lee Iacocca his one plus for the future.

To improve quality of car construction as quickly as possible Iacocca persuaded Hans Matthias, who had spent twenty-six years at Ford as chief engineer and head of car manufacture, to come to Chrysler. He was to work with Richard Vining on production and quality control. Matthias was an expert in fit and finish of body components, an area that had cost Chrysler dearly in warranty claims.

To handle purchasing and cost control Iacocca brought Paul Bergmoser out of retirement. Bergmoser had thirty years of experience at Ford. Gerald Greenwald was induced to resign his post as president of Ford's subsidiary in Venezuela and come aboard as controller. Gar Laux, another one-time Ford vice-president, was brought out of retirement to take on the Chrysler vice-presidency for sales.

"My friends in Houston couldn't understand why I'd give up the easy life and come to Chrysler," Laux said. "But I figure that if Lee could do what he was doing to save 150,000 people their jobs, who was I to say no? Lee's a rare man, and it's a privilege to work for him anytime."

Laux, a huge, friendly bear of a man, was also a specialist in dealer relations, and one of Chrysler Corporation's most vital needs was a boost in dealer morale. Inventories at most dealerships were at record highs. Dealer orders to the factory had been badly handled. Many were delivered late, some without equipment a customer had ordered, others with equipment not asked for, thus changing the original price quoted to the buyer.

Something needed doing, and Iacocca did it. He called a meeting of the Chrysler Dealer Council, a committee of dealers who spoke for the entire dealer body. He asked them for a list of their complaints, any possible area where the corporation's activities had brought them hardship.

Two weeks after his get-together with this council Iacocca invited every Chrysler-Plymouth and Dodge dealer in the country to meet with him in a week-long grievance session in Las Vegas. He addressed the group in the opening session, holding nothing back. In his usual crisp and dramatic fashion he laid out the grim picture of the corporation's condition, its failures, and its faults in placing the dealers in an untenable position, and he made it clear that it would not be an overnight return to solvency.

"Let me start off with that old Chinese proverb," he said to the assembled dealers, "that says even a thousand-mile journey begins with a single step. I honestly believe that this meeting with you is that first step and the most important one . . ."

One by one he went through the lengthy list of complaints provided him by the Dealer Council and pointed out what he would do to rectify each situation. He showed slides of the 1980 car lineup to be introduced that fall and explained in detail the features of each that would make them marketable and start Chrysler on the road back. He outlined an incentive plan to help the dealers dispose of their heavy inventories.

It was an inspirational let's-go-get-'em speech that Lee Iacocca delivered with wit and persuasiveness in an attempt to rouse a cynical group. He stood at the podium like a football coach in the locker room exhorting his players at half time to overcome a 40-0 deficit. Sports enthusiast that he is, he injected a football parallel into his talk.

"One night at dinner," he said, "I asked Vince Lombardi, the great coach of the Green Bay Packers, who was a friend of mine, why he always seemed able to produce a winner."

Iacocca then went on to expand on Lombardi's three-point formula for winning in sports, business, or life. First, the need for talent. Second, discipline. And "the third priceless ingredient to win," Iacocca pointed out, quoting Lombardi, "is you have to care for each other. For the entire team to win, every time a man makes a move, he has to consider the effect on the rest of the guys on the field."

He compared Chrysler's position to being in the fourth quarter of a do-or-die Super Bowl: "In the fourth quarter, when you are bone-tired, the only thing that keeps you going is your feeling for the other guy. Miss your block, and your buddy gets decked."

Chrysler has talent, Iacocca emphasized, and it was getting the needed discipline slowly but surely. "But now," he said, "we need to care about each other and help each other."

Automotive dealers are normally blasé and skeptical, unmoved by rhetoric and paying allegiance only to the profits, but as one Midwestern Dodge dealer said, "He had us mesmerized. We were hypnotized, and when he got to the last part of his talk, we were all ready to go out and slay the dragon."

"Everybody's looking at us," Iacocca told the dealers as he neared the conclusion of his speech, "and they are betting on us. Betting that we are going to win, and that we're going to bring Chrysler Corporation back to where it belongs in this business."

"We have a fountain of goodwill going for us. Coleman Young, the mayor of Detroit, called me. He wants us to win for the future of Detroit."

"Doug Fraser, the head of the UAW called me. He wants us to win because 150,000 jobs are at stake."

"Hell, even Tom Murphy and Pete Estes called me. They want us to win because they think it will be good for General Motors and the whole industry."

Lee Iacocca is a master of dealer relations, an expertise honed in his early days with Ford in the Philadelphia District. He knew, however, that he alone could not maintain the vital person-to-person relationships that would keep enthusiasm at a high level in each of the thousands of Chrysler-Plymouth and Dodge showrooms throughout the country. He needed an organization like the one at Lincoln-Mercury. There, under the overall supervision of David Gillespie, chairman of the board of Kenyon & Eckhardt, and the day-to-day management of John Hickey, he had the finest, most aggressive dealership activity in the industry.

Even before he accepted the Chrysler presidency, Iacocca felt certain that he would need help from people he had worked with before. And on March 1, 1980, Chrysler Corporation called a news conference at New York's Waldorf-Astoria Hotel. The site, the timing, and the purpose were a puzzle to the ever-speculating press.

Was Chrysler Corporation announcing bankruptcy, as so many American economists were predicting it would ultimately do? Had it finally achieved an agreement with another automobile company to merge? Perhaps Lee Iacocca had changed his mind and wanted out of an untenable situation—and who would blame him if he did?

The questions and the wonderment had a startling effect on the business community. The New York Stock Exchange, in a rare move, delayed trading in Chrysler stock until after the purpose of the news conference was made clear.

It was not John Riccardo, Chrysler chairman, who opened the meeting, but Lee Iacocca, its president. In itself this raised eyebrows. Iacocca did not keep his audience in the dark. He came straight to the point.

"I am pleased to announce," he told the crowded room, "that we are appointing Kenyon & Eckhardt as Chrysler's single advertising agency, effective just as soon as is practicable."

The journalists were surprised. Kenyon & Eckhardt had served as the prime Ford agency for thirty-four years. It had been a long, friendly, and safe relationship, despite the foibles of Henry Ford II. Why would they give up so large and profitable an account, one they had little fear of losing, to take on a question mark, the struggling, near-death Chrysler Corporation? It defied understanding until later facts emerged.

Kenyon & Eckhardt was granted a five-year contract with Chrysler Corporation, a first for the advertising industry. Agency firings and resignations are customarily on a ninety-day basis. An even more unusual aspect of the relationship would be K & E's direct involvement with Chrysler's future product planning and marketing. The agency was to serve as a permanent member of corporate committees responsible for those vital functions. In effect an unusual partnership had been created between Chrysler and its advertising agency.

Meanwhile, John Riccardo, still Chrysler chairman but not directly involved in the agency switchover, was busy in Washington, still trying to get government help. Riccardo's chances for success had dwindled appreciably when G. William Miller took over as secretary of the treasury in Jimmy Carter's cabinet. Miller quickly made his opposition to the loan plan clear. He had also recommended to Carter that any loan amount should be scaled down from a billion or more to only $750 million.

Riccardo faced another stumbling block when Senator Proxmire of Wisconsin succeeded Long of Louisiana as chairman of the Senate Banking Committee. Long had supported Chrysler aid. Proxmire was dogmatically opposed, although he had earlier helped American Motors, which employed more people in his state than any other private corporation.

Before Labor Day, 1979, Riccardo and Chrysler were in an even more tenuous position. With Congress in its summer recess weeks would pass before anything was resolved. Banks clamped down on new loans to Chrysler, and to save cash reserves Chrysler began a series of layoffs. Further diminishing the hopes for Chrysler's future, Mitsubishi of Japan, builders of some of Chrysler's bestselling cars, threatened to stop shipments if cash was not forthcoming. A rumor that Mitsubishi would welcome a termination of its agreement to supply Chrysler with fuel-efficient small cars added to the pall hanging over Iacocca.

To boost sagging morale, as well as to conserve cash for operating expenses, Iacocca announced that he would reduce his salary to $1 a year and that pay cuts averaging 5 percent would apply to management personnel. Riccardo also became a $1-per-year man. If and when the company rebounded, the salaries would be reevaluated in proportion to the increased value of Chrysler stock.

One bright spot in the dreary picture was the continued support of a man who had no ties to the automobile business. It was Edward J. Piszek, a Polish-American patriot who was president of the Philadelphia-based Mrs. Paul's Kitchens. Piszek, who had built a fortune from a $250 start as a creator and seller of fish cakes, started investing in Chrysler stock about the time Iacocca joined the company. He kept buying through the worst of times, his faith in Chrysler's survival unshaken, and now he was the major Chrysler stockholder with one million shares.

Did Piszek buy his stock in Chrysler because he knew Lee Iacocca personally? "No, I did not know him," Piszek said. "I just felt from my observations, and what I had read, that Mr. Iacocca was an unusually gifted natural leader and an accomplished business person. By his very nature I felt he could handle anything he put his mind to."

Piszek did meet Lee Iacocca later during filming of a series of motion pictures he sponsored, produced by James Michener, author of *Hawaii* and a bookshelf of other bestsellers. Michener's series, based on American life and living, featured Iacocca in one of five devoted to American transportation.

"Mr. Iacocca was what I expected, a dynamic man," Piszek recalls. "And I've met him many times since, several times in Washington and several times in Detroit, and he has impressed me more each time. He's a thinker and a doer, but he needs some luck. If the economy settles down and interest rates level off, he won't be able to build enough cars to meet the demand."

In late summer of 1979 Iacocca needed a carload of good luck. Enough cars sat on lots and in dealer showrooms to satisfy the greatest demand, but operating capital to run the company and move those cars was in short supply. John Riccardo's efforts in Washington seemed stalemated, and the worries and pressures took their toll on him. Earlier in the year Riccardo had to cancel a trip to the White House because of hospitalization due to a heart problem.

By September 18, 1979, Riccardo could take no more. He retired, leaving the financial problems and the chairmanship of the company to Iacocca. The added role was a lot for one man to carry, but Iacocca welcomed it. He was now in full charge of Chrysler, finally able to run the corporation without hindrance.

His first move was to name Paul Bergmoser president. With the experienced Bergmoser at the helm, Lee could turn to the fight in Washington for the loan guarantees that would bring Chrysler back to life.

On his trips to the nation's capital John Riccardo had hammered hard that the government regulations, including unrealistic emissions and mileage standards, were responsible for Chrysler's dilemma, and since the government was the cause, it should help in the cure. The concept enraged many legislators, who hardened their stand against helping.

Iacocca's diplomacy in Washington softened the stand of some senators and congressmen, although hardliners such as Proxmire in the Senate and Kelly in the House became even more adamant. Florida's Kelly was later convicted of bribery as a result of the Abscam scandal. Even a congressman from Michigan, David Stockman, openly decried any help for Chrysler. The lead article in a Sunday edition of the *Washington Post*, written by Stockman, was headed: "Let Chrysler Go Bankrupt."

Legislators from states in which Chrysler plants were located, spearheaded by Congressman Blanchard and Senators Reigle and Levin of Michigan, lined up against the Proxmires, Kellys, and Stockmans. Iacocca also had another battler in his corner. It was Douglas Fraser, head of the powerful United Auto Workers, with a stake equal to Chrysler's in the outcome. For Fraser the jobs of nearly 150,000 union members were on the line.

There was, however, a negative side to Fraser's support. He and his union were at odds with the Carter administration, which held life-and-death power over any final loan guarantee approval. Fraser was known to support Senator Edward Kennedy of Massachusetts against Jimmy Carter's 1980 bid for reelection.

As an offset Fraser and Vice-President Walter Mondale were close friends. Mondale, held in high esteem by President Carter, might appeal to Carter's humanitarian instincts on the basis of the plight of laid-off workers and the effect on the nation's economy should Chrysler fail.

Time was critical. Carter was leaning toward help for Chrysler, but he was moving inch by inch, far too slowly to make possible the granting of funds in time to save the company.

His advisers, the domestic experts in charge of finding alternate means to a loan guarantee, if there was one, were taking their time. Somehow the Carter administration had to openly endorse help for Chrysler.

To push matters along Mondale scheduled a breakfast meeting at his home in Washington, inviting both Fraser and Secretary of the Treasury Miller. Miller, who remained dubious about the loan guarantees and continued to hem and haw as time passed, could accelerate action if he could be convinced of the urgency.

Miller circled the issues between sips of coffee. The genial yet tough-talking Fraser impatiently portrayed the dire consequences to the American economy of a Chrysler failure, and the need for quick action.

Miller warned Fraser against haste, emphasizing the need for proper timing in getting Congress to accept any recommendation made by the president. "The pear must be ripe," he said at one point. "If you bite too early, you will become ill."

It was a bit much for the realistic, down-to-earth head of the United Auto Workers. He answered Miller with an icy edge: "The pear, Mr. Miller," he said, "is already rotten. The fruit flies are all over it. Now, when in the hell are you going to bite?"

At a subsequent meeting of Carter's staff the chief adviser on domestic policy, Stuart E. Eisenstat, called the bickering to a halt.

"The nation's tenth largest industrial corporation is not going to go bankrupt during the Carter administration," he announced, ending the discussion with a fist slammed hard against the meeting table.

Within days President Carter sent a message asking Congress to pass a loan-guarantee bill that would provide $1.5 billion in relief for the Chrysler Corporation. It was considerably more than the company had asked for but also included a number of stringent requirements. Chrysler's future now rested with the Senate and the House of Representatives.

To bring about the President's approval Douglas Fraser meanwhile had yielded vital concessions from his United Auto Workers. He had had to make wage

315

concessions from his union that would represent operating savings for Chrysler. Without them Congress was hardly likely to approve Carter's request.

The existing Chrysler contract with the union had expired in September, 1979, but Chrysler workers had not walked out. Fighting with his membership for cuts in the pay scale would be agonizing for Fraser. But he was a realist, a new breed of union leader, and knew that it was give a lot or have thousands of his men jobless.

On October 25 he brought new hope to Chrysler with a contract that offered concessions totaling about $400 million, part of which represented deferred payments to the Chrysler workers' pension fund. As part of the agreement it was understood that Fraser would become a member of the Chrysler board of directors, an unprecedented event in the history of American business.

The 256-member Chrysler Council of the United Auto Workers approved Fraser's recommendation on October 31 with little argument. Chrysler workers, with faith in their leaders, decided that saving their jobs was worth the cut in wages and benefits and later voted for the Fraser concession package.

This expression of confidence on the part of Chrysler employees led the House of Representatives to pass the loan-guarantee bill. The House measure provided Chrysler with $1.5 billion in loan assistance if the corporation could raise an equal amount from other sources, such as suppliers and state and local governments where Chrysler did business. The amount saved through the concessions by the union would be part of the company's $1.5 billion.

The Senate proved a tougher nut to crack. Many senators insisted that the Chrysler work force should sacrifice at least $1 billion rather than the $400 million set down in the House bill. After much argument the Senate accepted the $400-million union contribution, and a bill that satisfied both House and Senate was passed on December 21. It was signed into law by President Carter on January 7, 1980.

While Congress was debating the Chrysler rescue, an emotionally drained Lee Iacocca analyzed Chrysler's position. He saw an immediate need for an intense campaign that would bolster worker morale as well as public confidence in Chrysler. A loan guarantee even in the billions would be money down the drain if Chrysler did not build good cars and sell them.

The quality of the cars was important to Iacocca. He was greatly concerned that Chrysler workers might have become careless or uncaring. That at least some employees took pride in their work despite the precarious position of the company was made clear to Iacocca by what Chrysler executives call the "Case of the Iacocca Cake."

Lillian Zirwas, a maintenance clerk at Chrysler's Lynch Road plant in Detroit, had written an article that was published in the *Axle News*, the plant newspaper. In it Mrs. Zirwas bemoaned the shoddy work being done by some of her fellow employees and boldly told them to shape up or the company would certainly fail.

As might be expected, Mrs. Zirwas was given a rough time for a while by some of her coworkers. The criticism didn't phase her since as many applauded her action. Then one day Mrs. Zirwas was told that she should report the next morning at Lee Iacocca's office. The chairman wanted to thank her personally.

Lillian Zirwas felt she could not go to so important a meeting emptyhanded, so she baked a cake, a special cake based on a personal recipe that included a can of beer and chocolate icing.

Iacocca accepted the cake graciously and thanked her for her devotion to Chrysler Corporation. Mrs. Zirwas told him that she would name the cake after him if he saved Chrysler.

Iacocca took the cake home. The next morning he described it around his office as "the best goddamn cake I ever ate." Soon after Mary Iacocca wrote Mrs. Zirwas, asking for the recipe.

Not long after her meeting with Iacocca Mrs. Zirwas baked the same cake for the wedding of a friend's daughter. A guest at the wedding was so excited about the cake's unusual flavor that he told his sister he wanted the same cake served at his own wedding.

The sister approached Mrs. Zirwas, promising to buy a Chrysler car if Mrs. Zirwas would provide the cake for her brother's wedding reception. Lillian Zirwas baked a three-tier version of the Iacocca cake, and the sister purchased a new Plymouth.

Employee morale was only one of Lee Iacocca's many worries. He was equally concerned with the public's possible reticence in purchasing Chrysler cars, its fear of being left out in the cold for service and parts if the company failed. It was a justifiable fear, one that was becoming more difficult to counteract because of the news stories that continually emphasized Chrysler's difficulties.

A "Chrysler should be let to die" campaign by the prestigious *Wall Street Journal* was echoed throughout the country. Even in Detroit the media highlighted Chrysler's problems rather than items that gave hope for its survival.

In mid-December, 1979, Iacocca called on Kenyon & Eckhardt to devise a morale-boosting program that would raise the spirits of Chrysler employees as well as public confidence in the corporation's future. The Bill Winn Group spent the entire weekend devising and rejecting concepts that might instill belief in Chrysler's ability to weather the storm.

"We went round and round with some pretty highfalutin ideas," Bill Winn recalled, "but in the end it was a simple and, luckily, effective declaration that came out of the hopper."

"We Can Do It!" was the battle cry decided upon as the basic theme for an all-out campaign. "Consider It Done!" was the backup phrase to give the program a positive emphasis.

Banners bearing each statement were displayed throughout Chrysler Corporation plants and dealerships in North America. Showrooms, parts and service departments, and used-car lots reflected Chrysler's belief in itself for employees and customers to see.

The dedication of Lillian Zirwas spread throughout Chrysler factories. No worker dared to be careless or to goldbrick on the job without earning the wrath of fellow employees. An upgrading of Chrysler quality became noticeable in almost every facet of production. This was especially heartening to Iacocca, since the K-cars, which he hoped would cause Chrysler sales to soar, were being readied for 1980 introduction.

"We Can Do It" was only part of Iacocca's initial confidence building campaign. He also searched for other means.

From the beginning it had been agreed that the basic name of the company could not be changed. The name Chrysler, remindful of the automotive genius of Walter P. Chrysler, the company's founder, was worth millions.

In the end, as with the "We Can Do It" slogan, simplicity won out. Chrysler Corporation the company would remain, but it would be the *New* Chrysler Corporation, a name that would not only remind the American public that new management was at the helm, but also that this new guardianship was dedicated to restoring the company to its glory days under its founder.

Iacocca, Kelmenson, and John Morrissey, K & E chairman, then considered means of getting the new identity across to the general public and decided on full-page newspaper and magazine advertisements.

Unlike typical ads selling a product, these would be

in the form of letters to the public from Lee Iacocca, as chairman of the New Chrysler Corporation. Carefully prepared by K & E and meticulously screened by Iacocca himself, the ads were designed also to serve as a subtle lobbying aimed at Congress and the Carter administration. Since the loan guarantees were still being held up, the ads might well put gentle pressure on the legislators and the President.

Reaction to these Iacocca letter-ads was so favorable that Kenyon & Eckhardt executives decided that the same personal approach should be used in the electronic media. They were convinced that to get maximum mileage from the campaign the chairman had to be seen and heard on television and radio.

Iacocca balked at this approach. High-echelon executives of major corporations seldom acted as barkers, selling their own products. Lee also feared that such ads might add to public perception of Chrysler desperation and imminent failure. Besides, he told Kelmenson and Morrissey, he didn't have the time. He was too busy getting the company in shape and fighting for the loan guarantees in trip after trip to Washington.

It was not an easy sell, but K & E had taken a survey that included showing pictures of Iacocca. A remarkably high 40 percent of the people identified Iacocca. Over three-fourths called him by name. Others said he was "boss man at Chrysler" or used similar terms. Some said he was the man who was trying to save Chrysler. Others called him the man who built Mustang and was fired by Henry Ford.

The K & E executives told Iacocca that this was proof that he had become a national figure. His appearance and voice could help immeasurably in convincing American car buyers that he was dedicated to winning Chrysler's struggle for survival. People like former baseball player Joe Garagiola and actor Ricardo Montalban might sell cars well, but Lee Iacocca himself could best sell the future of the New Chrysler Corporation. No one else would have his credibility or would better present the company's plans and potential.

Iacocca finally agreed, and the broadcast announcements were prepared with Lee himself carefully weighing every word. Some television commercials began with him in a chair behind his desk. In others he was seen sitting on the edge of the desk or walking through one of the Chrysler plants.

In every one, as well as in radio spots, he came across as a confident man, comfortable in his role, talking forcefully and straight from the shoulder.

"When we first conceived the idea of using Mr. Iacocca," Ron DeLuca said, "the fundamental consideration was that the public needed to know that Chrysler had a leader, had somebody who could speak in a different way on behalf of Chrysler and its products. There isn't a better spokesman. We couldn't have gone out and hired anybody to do as Lee did in isolating Chrysler's problems and what it's doing to face up to those problems. We just put him in front of the cameras and let him talk."

The dynamic qualities that inspired hard-nosed

dealers were not lost on the man in the street. He empathized when he heard Iacocca say: "If you buy any car without considering Chrysler, that'll be too bad—for both of us," and when Iacocca said: "I'm not asking you to buy one of our cars. I'm asking you to compare," many did just that.

As the year 1979 wound down, Lee Iacocca's face was more familiar than that of any businessman to the television viewers of America. His appearances before Congress began it. The commercials did the rest.

The campaign apparently also had an effect within Chrysler plants. A cheerful eagerness supplanted spiritless indifference. Absenteeism, which had been running exceedingly high, was more than halved. Nonetheless, each of Iacocca's days had its frustrations. The New Chrysler Corporation was no better off than the old when it came to money for operating expenses. A cash flow from the loan guarantees could not begin too soon.

Equally frustrating—perhaps even more so—were the thousands of new 1979 cars sitting in open lots, some 80,000 unordered automobiles. Remnants of the old system of building automobiles before receiving orders from dealers, they drained about $2 million each week in costs for interest and maintenance.

With the 1980 models already introduced, moving these quickly was essential. To do so called for a dramatic, hard-sell campaign that combined immediacy, low prices, and an exciting environment, one that would stimulate dealers to all-out participation.

Iacocca approved a K & E concept that called for tent sales conducted in a carnival atmosphere. But rather than commit to a nationwide clearance all at once it was decided to test the idea in a single market. If the plan bombed, losses would be minimal.

The Minneapolis-St. Paul metropolitan area was chosen for the test sale. A huge tent was set up on the extensive parking lot of Metropolitan Stadium, the playing field of the Minnesota Twins and the Vikings.

All Chrysler-Plymouth and Dodge dealers in the area were invited to participate. Most took advantage of the opportunity and sent salesmen to close car and truck purchases for their own dealerships. A special trailer was set up on the grounds to provide on-the-spot financing.

For three days prior to the opening of the twenty-four hour "Let's Make a Deal" event, the air-waves of the Minneapolis-St. Paul area were saturated with teaser commercial announcements.

This test sale proved a huge success, with thousands swarming over the stadium parking lot and examining automobiles in a carnival atmosphere complete with rousing music and circus-type barkers. Hundreds of cars were disposed of in that single day. It told Iacocca enough to approve extending the concept nationwide.

Tents were set up in appropriate areas in almost every major American city. Special announcements for television and radio were recorded by Joe Garagiola inviting listeners from coast-to-coast to "Let's Make a Deal."

In the end 55,000 of the 1979 models were sold along with hundreds more from dealer stock. This blitz type of marketing proved such a smash hit that soon both General Motors and Ford produced their own versions of the tent sale.

As Iacocca was telling America in his personal commercials, Chrysler was certainly "doing business like Detroit's never done it before." Indeed it was.

CHAPTER 13

At times Lee Iacocca looked back with some fondness on the comparatively serene days at Ford. Now he seemed to be on an unending treadmill.

A typical week had him in Washington on Monday, perhaps into Tuesday, pushing for action on the loan guarantees. Then it would be back to his desk in Highland Park, seeing to company business. Another day would be spent in New York for lengthy strategy conferences with Kenyon & Eckhardt executives and taping his commercials. Late in the week he might be back in Washington.

He had few breaks in his merry-go-round routine. One was a sudden, agonizing trip to Boca Raton, Florida, where his wife had gone for relief from Michigan's cold. When Iacocca received word that Mary had suffered a heart seizure and had been rushed to the hospital, he dropped everything, remaining with her until she was out of danger.

Another interruption in his weekly round, one of the few for sheer relaxation, resulted in a near-crippling accident. During one of his sessions in New York he took off with his friend Bill Fugazy to visit Lake Placid during the 1980 Olympics.

For more than a year he had had few opportunities to enjoy watching sports events. After one of the early wins by the United States Olympic hockey team, he stepped on the ice as he and Fugazy were getting ready to leave the arena. Iacocca's feet went out from under him on the slippery surface, and he bruised a hip.

He laughed it off as retribution for having taken time off. And when the Americans dramatically upset the Soviet team, he considered the hurt worthwhile.

Still walking with a limp, Iacocca returned to his desk. The "Let's Make a Deal" promotion had sold an appreciable number of the 1979 overstock. The confidence- and morale-boosting campaigns had done reasonably well, but there was still much to be done to encourage the belief that Chrysler products were of good quality.

Soon after Lee had joined Chrysler, he had initiated a quality-control program by hiring Hans Matthias to oversee manufacturing procedures for the 1980 products, the new models of the Chrysler New Yorker and Dodge St. Regis as well as the all-new Chrysler Cordoba and Dodge Mirada. Double and triple quality checks had been set up for major systems such as engine, electrical, emissions, and air conditioning, as well as for protection against wind noise and water leaks, and for the fit and finish of doors and bodies. Matthias established permanent task forces to study defects in sheet metal and paint jobs, to eliminate squeaks and rattles, and to devise corrections for other problems that denote a poorly built automobile.

To top off his quality crusade Iacocca also had not only installed the industry's most advanced computer testing system, but had stolen a march on General Motors and Ford, by being the first to install an automatic welding system. Called the Robotgate by Chrysler engineers, this new means of assembling body components helped ensure construction of solid, rattle-and-leak-proof bodies.

With all the innovative equipment and control checks in place, Iacocca now could take a chance and introduce the buyer-guarantee he and K & E had been working on since autumn.

On January 24, 1980, an advertising push announced the "Chrysler Guarantees" program, which included rare buyer protections that Chrysler's competition considered potentially ruinous.

One phase of these guarantees offered a thirty-day or 1,000-mile money-back guarantee if the buyer did not like the car. Another offered $50 to anyone who took a test drive in a Chrysler Corporation vehicle— car or truck—and then purchased either the Chrysler or a competitor's make.

"We're not foolish. We're just confident," Iacocca told the American public in his televised messages.

Ford and GM didn't think Iacocca was foolish.

They thought he was crazy. The $50 giveaway was bad enough, but money back in thirty days? The returns were certain to kill Chrysler Corporation.

Iacocca, however, had the last laugh. He had projected a possible return of 1 percent of the cars sold. Less than .2 percent were actually returned.

"Really, some of that .2 percent didn't literally return their cars for a refund," John Morrissey reported. "There was one buyer, for example, who brought back his Omni because it was too small for his family. He merely traded for a larger car."

Thanks to the unheard-of "guarantees" Chrysler was selling cars, but lack of cash still continued to be Iacocca's great concern. Though $1.5 billion waited, not one cent could be touched until that figure was matched by Chrysler, and little more than the $400 million represented by union concessions was already on the table.

Of the $250 million expected to be committed by the states in which Chrysler did business, only $150 million had been tentatively approved. This was the amount offered by Chrysler's home state, Michigan, where Governor Milliken was in favor of the plan. The seven other states involved were moving slowly due to logistic and legal problems. Legislative approval was necessary, and their legislatures were in recess.

The week ending February 1 brought some cause for celebration. Chrysler stock, which had become the biggest loser in corporate history had taken a healthy rise during that week's trading on Wall Street.

Chrysler's common shares, which had reached a low of $5.50 in late November, had jumped 25 percent during the week to close at $10.75 per share. Preferred stock, which no longer paid dividends, closed $12.87, up $2.50.

The following week a beaming Lee Iacocca addressed the annual convention of the National Automobile Dealers Association in New Orleans. He was now confident that Chrysler would raise the money needed to qualify for the federally guaranteed loans, and he was brimming with ideas to revive the depressed automobile market.

In his succinct, pointed style he told the thousands of dealers representative of all car lines that the government should enact a ten-cent-per-gallon tax on gasoline as a stimulant for the economy. This, he said, would add up to $10 billion, which could be funneled back to the public with a $1,500 credit for purchase of an American-made car.

"This would stimulate the market for new domestic cars, probably to the tune of a million units," he claimed. "It would create jobs. It would conserve fuel by making people more prudent in buying gas." And, suggesting that the Congress might have to pass laws controlling foreign import sales, he added that a program such as his "would be a clear signal to foreign manufacturers that we can make things tougher for them" if some balance wasn't made in the Japanese tax structure that makes American cars too expensive for Japanese buyers, yet gives Japanese cars a competitive edge in America.

As for Chrysler Corporation's future prospects, Iacocca reported that on Monday following the meeting in New Orleans he would be in Washington to meet with the Loan Guarantee Board. He would be notifying the board that $125 million in concessions had been made through a wage freeze on Chrysler white-collar workers and that another $100 million was available through a loan from Europe's largest auto manufacturer, Peugeot-Citroën, pending approval by Chrysler's banks and the government.

Later the same week Iacocca received even more hopeful news when sales figures for the first ten days of February were released. It was the kind of win-while-still-losing good news that only an automobile man could appreciate. In comparison with the same ten-day period in 1979 Chrysler Corporation had lost 11 percent. But GM's drop was 14.9 percent, Volkswagen of America dropped 23.7 percent and Ford Motor Company a whopping 42.8 percent.

There was still a long way to go, of course, and money remained in short supply, but Lee Iacocca could be forgiven for gloating over those figures and wondering what Henry Ford was thinking. The report was even more gratifying because they did not include any sales from a new incentive announced before their release.

To help dispose of the more than 100,000 Chrysler 1979 models still in dealer stocks, Iacocca initiated a rebate program. Buyers were offered from $200 to $700 back, depending on the vehicle, on the purchase of any car or truck, domestic or import, included in the program. The rebate could be used by the buyer as cash or applied to the down payment or purchase price.

This new rebate program to clear 1979 stocks was to continue at least through March 20. Coordinated with the revolutionary Chrysler guarantees on 1980 models, it offered great expectations for a surge in overall sales, a two-way effort that Iacocca hoped would not only reduce inventories but also increase Chrysler's share of the market.

If Lee Iacocca had been inclined to give it consideration, the time was ideal for a concerted charge against Ford sales. Henry was now in trouble on two fronts. For more than a month the Ford Motor Company had been involved in a damage suit related to the Pinto's susceptibility to fire in a rear-end collision. And media reports were giving lead attention to the sensational aspects of the divorce trial between Henry and Cristina due to begin on February 19.

Rumors were afloat that Henry's sale of a huge block of Ford stock was to provide her with an out-of-court settlement of about $5 million. Cristina, however, was believed to be asking for twice that amount.

Iacocca, however, had worries of his own and was too busy to give much thought to the woes of his former boss. There was an immediate need for cash, and the remaining commitments necessary to meet the requirements of the loan-guarantee bill were not yet in place. The only hope for quick money was action by the Michigan legislature to approve the

$150 million recommended by Governor William Milliken. If that did not come soon, the company would have to close down, if only temporarily.

Still another urgent concern faced Iacocca. The XM-1 combat tank, which had embarrassed Riccardo the previous year, was now ready for acceptance by the U.S. Army. The defense arm of Chrysler had, they hoped, corrected the defects that aborted the 1979 presentation.

February 28 was the date set for the XM-1 unveiling. A tour of the Lima facility preceded a press conference at which more than 150 journalists and all three major television networks were present. With Lee Iacocca delayed at Highland Park on company business, the news conference was chaired by J. Paul Bergmoser, Chrysler president.

Ready to answer questions of the press, in addition to Bergmoser, were O. G. White, director of Chrysler's Defense Manufacturing Division; P. W. Lett, director of the company's Defense Engineering Division; Dr. Percy Pierre, Assistant Secretary of the Army for Research and Development; and General E. C. Meyer, U.S. Army chief of staff.

Most of the questions were directed to General Meyer, since the press had concern about the reliability of the tank's engine under combat conditions. One question was whether the tank was indeed ready for production.

"The soldiers who have used it are satisfied, and then I'm satisfied," Meyer replied.

When asked whether the XM-1 was better than

anything the Soviets now had or was in the works
Meyer told the newsmen: "This new tank will be
better than anything the Russians have or anything
we know they have on the drawing board." He also
admitted that it was possible the Soviets had a more
sophisticated tank, but American Intelligence was not
aware of it.

General Meyer also reported that the army had
asked that 7,058 XM-1 tanks be built within the next
ten years. He refused to give a price estimate for each
tank, although it was generally believed to be $1.5
million for each. One enterprising newsman asked
whether Chrysler's assets in the tank plant (the plant
is actually owned by the government but operated by
Chrysler) could be mortgaged to provide some of the
cash Chrysler needed. General Meyer's answer was
that it was probably illegal to try and mortgage assets
that were partially or jointly owned by the army.

The rollout ceremony following the press conference was held inside the huge tank plant, where a
large area near the back had been cleared and where
Bill Winn's men had erected a reviewing stand and
bleachers. The platform had been set directly between two doors through which two of the massive
tanks would be driven on cue.

Lee Iacocca, suffering from a cold, arrived in time
for the ceremony. With him on the platform, in
addition to the general and assistant secretary, were
the former astronaut, John Glenn, now senator from
Ohio, and the mayor of Lima, Harry Moyer. The
mayor welcomed the dignitaries and, in his brief talk

reminded Lee Iacocca that Lima was probably the only city in the United States where Chrysler was showing a profit. Iacocca bristled slightly at the ill-timed remark.

Senator Glenn's remarks were more circumspect, congratulating Chrysler and the Army for tanks that were "peacemakers and peacekeepers, which by their very existence would no doubt prevent the need for their ever being used in combat."

As the army band struck a stirring Sousa march, the doors flanking the dais rolled up to reveal an XM-1 combat tank in each doorway. The tanks roared in beside the platform and came to a stop, their 105mm cannons and machine guns pointed at the audience.

Iacocca stepped to center stage to heavy applause. In his opening remarks he apologized for his cold and joked about his slipping on the ice at Lake Placid during the Olympics.

"I want to present the U.S. Army the first two XM-1 production tanks," he concluded. "The quality of their manufacture is outstanding. I am sure that their performance in the field will measure up to the same high standards."

General Meyer accepted the tanks on behalf of the United States Army and then told the assemblage that the XM-1 would then and there be renamed the "Abrams Tank" in honor of General Creighton W. Abrams. A veteran of three wars with army service of forty-two years, Abrams had been commander of the forces in Vietnam from 1967 to 1972 and was named Army Chief of Staff in 1972, two years before his death.

General Abrams, Meyer recounted, was widely known as one of the army's most aggressive and successful armored vehicle commanders, of whom General George S. Patton, Jr., once said: "I'm supposed to be the best tank commander in the army, but I have one peer—Abe Abrams. He's the world champion."

Meyer then escorted General Abrams' widow, Julia Harvey Abrams, to the tank at the left of the platform. Handed a bottle of champagne swathed in red, white, and blue, Mrs. Abrams smashed the bottle over the tank's cannon. She brought a laugh from the crowd as she licked a finger dripping with champagne.

As Mrs. Abrams walked back to her seat, a tank corps enlisted man came forward and attached to the tank a decal imprinted with a bolt of lightning piercing a white cloud to nickname the tank "Thunderbolt," which had been the name of the tank Abrams commanded during the Battle of Bastogne in 1944. And to ensure that Chrysler was not forgotten, a K & E staffer took the liberty of applying a decal reading "Ram Tough," the ad slogan for Dodge trucks.

The ceremonies concluded with a demonstration of some of the tanks' capabilities on a small test track next to the plant. An enlisted man, Sp/4 William Watson, put the 59.9-ton, 387-inch-long (with cannon forward) tank through its paces, speeding around the track at 45 miles an hour, running through a series of waist-high obstacles, and climbing a steep grade.

"It goes like hell," twenty-four-year-old Watson said after the demonstration. "I love this tank. I drove an M60 at only ten miles an hour over rough terrain, and I was all black and blue from bouncing around. You hardly feel it in the XM-1, it just seems to float."

Iacocca returned to his home base with a sigh of relief. A failure by the tank could have crippled his hopes for the money needed to keep Chrysler going.

But there was no peace of mind back in his Highland Park office. The money expected from the state of Michigan had yet to be approved by the legislature as the month of March got underway. Things were at a do-or-die stage. The federal guarantees would slip down the drain without the Michigan loan, which was also needed for even more immediate needs.

On March 6 the Michigan legislature approved the loan for $150 million. The signature of Governor William Milliken was still needed, and the governor was away from the state capital and would not be back before Monday, March 10.

Michigan's governor enjoys the panoply of office and prefers signing important bills with press cameras flashing and TV cameras rolling. But March 10 would be too late to do Chrysler the good it needed. It was imperative that the bill be signed before the banks opened on that Monday.

Milliken was finally located at his home in Traverse City. He agreed to forgo any ceremony and had the

Chrysler-aid bill brought to him from Lansing. He signed the bill without fanfare on Saturday, March 8.

The pressure eased, but only a little and only temporarily. To intensify Iacocca's problems in getting the concessions needed to complete the terms of the federal loan guarantees, the First Security Bank of Utah, one of Chrysler's smaller creditors, began suit in federal court seeking repayment of $1 million owed the bank.

March was not going out like a lamb. During the last week of the month a Belgian bank, Banque Bruxelles Lambert S.A., filed a similar action in New York to force payment of $10 million plus interest that had been due the end of January.

Chrysler had been able to convince most of the 150 world-wide banks to whom it owed over $1 billion to forgo any action until it met the loan-guarantee requirements. If the action by these two small institutions had a domino effect, disaster would ensue.

Iacocca's never-give-up temperament kept him going. There were some bright breaks in the clouds. Household Finance Corporation, America's largest maker of loans to the general public, was seriously considering the purchase of Chrysler Financial Corporation, the company's financial arm, which lends money to dealers and individuals to purchase cars. This sale could bring in almost half a billion dollars.

Then, too, Iacocca's meeting in Ottawa with Herb Gray, Canada's industry minister, on March 24 had offered hope for a multimillion-dollar loan that would keep Chrysler's engine plant in Windsor, Ontario, in operation. A two-hour meeting with Gray had ended with favorable overtones.

The rosy bloom, slight as it was, faded in April as Chrysler sustained a double-barreled blow. On April 11 Household Finance released a statement to the press that it had notified Chrysler "of its determination that an investment in Chrysler Financial Corporation is not appropriate at this time."

Public knowledge of Household Finance's decision came two days after Chrysler reported that its 1980 losses likely would reach $750 million, $100 million more than had been estimated less than three months earlier. At about the same time the company was ordered by the Federal Trade Commission to replace rusted fenders on 200,000 1976 and 1977 Volares and Aspens. The cost to the company would be about $45 million, already figured as part of its estimated year's loss of $750 million.

The Household Finance turndown was the more serious of the two for Iacocca. The funds from the sale were a significant part of the amount needed to qualify for the loan guarantees, and the Loan Guarantee Board had already reported to Congress that Chrysler had commitments for less than one-third of the money needed. Sale of just 51 percent of the financial subsidiary would have offset the $300 million demanded by the board from sale of Chrysler assets.

Expectedly, Iacocca was a bit testy when he addressed the Automotive Service Industry Association convention in Chicago later in the month, telling the

ASIA members that no industry in America had been battered by the government as had the automobile industry, and that Chrysler had sustained the worst beating of all because of its limited capital.

"Our government has added $600 to the price of every car built in this country this year because of regulations that include emissions, safety, and gas mileage," he said, later adding: "It is only a matter of time before American companies will find themselves in the same position as Chrysler, and when it happens, those companies will learn, just as Chrysler did, that the root of the problem is government regulations."

Iacocca further pointed out that Chrysler has had to pay out $160 million every month to comply with federal regulations that had raised the price of American automobiles from $1 to $3 a pound. Because of this, he said, America was losing great shares of its market to imports.

"I worry about this," he added, "because we aren't in a position to compete with them on an equal basis. Government officials say that we, the American automobile industry, are out of touch with the automobile market. We're not out of touch. We're out of money."

As April yielded to May, there was no underestimating the near death of Chrysler Corporation. The company could not survive the month without the loan guarantees.

It was the Canadian government that came to the rescue. An emergency Saturday meeting was called in Toronto on May 10, at which Canada approved $200 million in loan guarantees. This, combined with a separate $10-million guarantee by the province of Ontarios, pushed Chrysler over the top as to "outside" help requirements.

That same day the Loan Guarantee Board approved granting the $1.5 billion authorized by Congress, also voting to appropriate an immediate $500 million. Immediate, in this instance, meant a delay of the weekend and more, thanks to Secretary Miller.

"That entire weekend," one official close to the action said, "the Treasury Department insisted that every piddling paper and detail be specific and in order, so that the interests of the taxpayers were fully protected."

A situation that led to another agonizing delay occurred on Monday night, May 12 in New York. Hurrying to get hundreds of documents signed for the next day's meeting in Washington, Chrysler officials and lawyers were startled when a cleaning woman came in screaming that the skyscraper in which they were working was on fire.

The man signing the papers, Steve Miller, Chrysler's assistant treasurer, and thirty lawyers bolted for the stairs, leaving the documents behind. After scrambling down thirty-three flights, they dashed out into New York's Park Avenue to a hail of falling glass.

An hour later they were able to retrieve the precious documents that held the fate of Chrysler Corporation, but they had to convince the Manhattan firefighters of the urgency before they were allowed back in the building.

Once an elevator was activated for their use, the men were back on the thirty-third floor, stuffing papers into boxes and mail carts, not knowing whether they had everything or not.

Serious at the time, the picture of straitlaced lawyers pushing mail carts down Park Avenue to the offices of another law firm amused many in legal circles.

During the finalization of the loan guarantees the next morning, May 13, 1980, Senator Donald Riegle of Michigan took advantage of the near-tragic consequences the fire could have occasioned.

"The fire shows," he said, "that not even an act of God can stop the Chrysler recovery."

CHAPTER 14

Iacocca could now breathe more freely. It had been a traumatic eight months of waiting, wondering, and fighting, eight months that took their toll. At one point it seemed as though he might have a nervous breakdown.

"I was scared," he has said. "Afraid inside that the whole thing would come down before we had a chance. That the whole thing would collapse, and I would cut out physically."

He had been in Washington on one trip after spending many weeks of reviewing his answers to questions he would be asked at the congressional hearings. Almost immediately on his arrival he was taken into the Surgeon General's office.

"I was sort of seeing double," Iacocca explained. "All the stuff suddenly hit me, and I got fuzzy-brained."

That was over now. The chips were down, and

Chrysler's fate was to a great degree dependent on Iacocca. If the company could overcome the depressed climate in the automobile business and the assault of the import cars, which was increasing monthly, and if the new Chrysler cars would do the job, the agony would have been worthwhile. The near-dead Chrysler Corporation would be resuscitated as a healthy New Chrysler Corporation.

However, if Iacocca's aim was off target, even $1.5 billion in loan guarantees wouldn't put the company back together again. For the immediate present the company badly needed a drop in interest rates to make purchase of a new automobile practical for the average wage-earner.

The company needed sales to provide a cash flow. A huge payroll had to be met each week. Operating expenses and the continuous planning for new products that ate up more millions each month added to the problems.

Iacocca made it clear to the press that if the loan guarantees had not been approved, Chrysler's cash on hand would have been exhausted before the end of May and the company would have indeed ceased operations. Hundreds of thousands of people would have been out of work, and the American economy would have been in straits more desperate than any since the 1930s. That had been made clear by the secretary of the treasury as soon as the long battle had been resolved.

"If we had let Chrysler go bankrupt," G. William Miller had emphasized, "it would have cost the taxpayers three billion dollars over two years in welfare, lost revenue and unemployment." Simple arithmetic said that that was twice the cost of the loan guarantees if they were never repaid by Chrysler.

Thus the government's help made it possible for Iacocca to offer real hope to Chrysler stockholders at the annual meeting on May 30, 1980, despite the previous year's loss of more than $1 billion.

As Douglas Fraser, head of the United Auto Workers, put it: "If you look at Chrysler today and Chrysler of a year ago, you're looking at vastly different companies."

The most startling change, as the meeting in Rockford, Illinois came to a close, was in the makeup of Chrysler's newly elected board of directors. Never before had the board of a corporation been weighted so heavily with former executives of a competing organization.

In addition to Lee Iacocca as chairman, the new directors included the president, Paul Bergmoser, and Gerald Greenwald, Gar Laux, and Hal Sperlick, elected that same day as executive vice-president of finance, sales and marketing, and engineering, respectively. All were one-time Ford Motor Company executives.

This new Chrysler board also reflected a historic first. Nominated to the board by Lee Iacocca, and elected, was Douglas Fraser. Never before in the annals of American business had any union leader penetrated the upper echelons of management in any major corporation.

The Chrysler comeback, Iacocca assured the stockholders, was on its way. A penetrating look at the company's immediate past showed it to be not so much a helpless concern, but one that—through mistakes and mismanagement—had been rendered financially anemic. The loan guarantees would provide a strength-restoring transfusion.

The year 1979, Iacocca made clear, was a year to forget. Chrysler's mind-boggling difficulties that year had come about as a result of a combination of situations beyond anyone's control. Escalating gasoline prices and gasoline shortages, rising inflation, record-high interest rates, and a fear of recession had slowed car sales to a trickle.

Operating expenses, of course, continued despite the drastic drop in car sales. The company was forced to spend some $160 million a month, even though operations had been restructured to cut costs.

Chrysler's multiplying problems had dropped it in 1979 from tenth to seventeenth among America's largest manufacturers. Yet, through its worst times it had managed to meet its high monthly cash payouts. Even though 1979 losses were a staggering $1 billion, the company had good reason to hope for better times. Its worldwide sales in an agonizing year had totaled $12 billion.

Iacocca assured the stockholders that plants were in the works to further reduce costs and increase operating efficiencies. Three plans had already been closed down, and the closing of a fourth, the Detroit facility where Chrysler's full-size cars were assembled, was but a week away. Three others were scheduled for shutdown in the fall. The stockholders were assured that these closings would not cripple the company's manufacturing capabilities. Seventeen factories would still be operating in Michigan, eleven in the metropolitan Detroit area.

Chrysler also had twenty-three plants located in twelve other states. And it still held substantial interests in foreign firms, holding—for one thing—an equity position of about 14 percent in France's Peugeot-Citroën, the largest European automobile company. Of immediate and continuing value and importance to Chrysler was its 15 percent interest in Japan's Mitsubishi Motors. Chrysler, of course, marketed Mitsubishi-manufactured cars in the U.S. and Canada. These included the Dodge and Plymouth pickup trucks, Plymouth Champ, Arrow, and Sapporo passenger cars, and the Dodge Colt and Challenger. Chrysler worldwide sales in 1979 included over 270,000 of these.

Iacocca returned from the stockholders' meeting to put the finishing touches on the new cars he believed would bring Chrysler back to profitability. These were the K-cars, roomy front-wheel-drive automobiles whose engineering was in the hands of Hal Sperlick. Plans called for three body styles, two- and four-door sedans and a station wagon, for both Plymouth and Dodge nameplates.

The "K" designation was originally a code, not expected to be part of the cars' identity. But it had been presented so forcefully to the loan-guarantee committee as Chrysler's salvation, and the media had speculated so widely about them, that America became K-car conscious.

Iacocca, considering the coverage already given the unborn car, decided sometime before it was ready for the market that it would be a mistake not to take advantage of the built-in familiarity. He decided that the letter "K" had to be part of the names given the new cars. In the final determination the Plymouth version came to be called Reliant K and the Dodge Aries K.

Iacocca was not too worried about the K-cars' acceptance, but he was concerned about the state of the economy. If it was no shakier than it had been in the spring, sales of about 500,000 for both Plymouth and Dodge versions seemed right. Marketing expert that he was, Iacocca was sure that the American public was ready for front-wheel-drive compacts like the K's.

If his estimate proved right, and if the economy held up, there was hope. K-car acceptance added to the projected sales of the hot Omni and Horizon subcompacts, other Chrysler-built cars and trucks, and the Mitsubishi imports would get Chrysler moving.

Iacocca also had another automobile in the works for introduction during 1980. A couple of conservatives on his staff believed this car a mistake, for it was a reach-for-the-moon kind of luxury automobile to compete with Cadillac Eldorado and the Continental Mark. It was important to Iacocca that the public see

he New Chrysler Corporation as a full-line producer
of cars.

Iacocca originally called this new personal luxury
car LaScala. The silvery model shown during a private preview for ad agency personnel had a Rolls-
Royce aura in its styling. It seemed to have what was
needed to compete with Cadillac and Lincoln.

When the car was ready for production, the
Lascala name was discarded. In the old Chrysler
Corporation's heyday one of the world's finest luxury
cars was named Imperial, so the new luxury car was
given the advantage of a known and respected name.

Iacocca's Imperial was to be built unlike any other
American luxury car. And it was to be marketed
unlike any other. It would be a complete car, an
automobile that left the showroom equipped with
every accessory normally desired by buyers and paid
for as extra options. Its equipment was to include the
fuel-efficient 318 cubic inch V-8 engine and the most
sophisticated, technologically advanced instrumentation in the industry. And its price, about $20,000,
would be competitive with Cadillac Eldorado and
Continental Mark.

Luxury cars, with their higher use of fuel as well as
high prices, were frowned on by the government. Let
the Europeans build Mercedes, Rolls Royce, and
BMW, but American carmakers, especially a Chrysler in such financial trouble, should forgo them.
Nevertheless, a sizable percentage of Americans want
the prestige of luxury cars, so a market does and will
exist, and the more luxurious and expensive automo-

biles make a higher ratio of profit than the smaller, more mundane models. For Chrysler each Imperial sold—and Iacocca limited production to 25,000 units—would provide profit equivalent to as many as five or more Omnis, Horizons, or K-cars.

All of this planning and execution of plans by Iacocca and his staff was still very much on a speculative basis. Chrysler was still waiting for $500 million of the cash due under the loan-guarantee bill. It would not be forthcoming until about 400 banks involved in the company's refinancing signed off on the concessions included in the loan guarantee. Too many were still reluctant, and just as many were taking their time.

Though it was a suspenseful, nerve-racking, nail-biting wait, there was nothing to do but continue as though the loan guarantee money would be forthcoming soon. Business had to go on as usual. Cars had to be sold.

Gasoline prices had continued to rise, having climbed considerably over the dollar-per-gallon mark. Miles-per-gallon had become the number-one criterion for car purchases by lower- and middle-income Americans. And Chrysler had high-mileage cars.

Plymouth Horizon and Dodge Omni offered thirty plus miles per gallon, more than any other American built automobiles. As for imports, the Mitsubishi cars such as Dodge Colt and Plymouth Arrow gave other imports a good run for their money when it came to mpg.

Here, then, was an obvious and built-in plus to be

emphasized in an advertising blitz. Kenyon & Eckhardt developed a campaign that both waved the flag
and pinpointed the mileage advantages in buying
Chrysler products. A red-white-and-blue motif was
used in advertisements in newspapers and on television. The high-mileage Dodge and Plymouth car
names were projected as "The American Way to Beat
the Pump." Graphics for the ads and commercials
featured situations in which men and women
smashed service station gas pumps with clenched
fists.

Then, just as the month of May neared its end,
Iacocca was faced with a more personal concern. On
Memorial Day his wife entered Massachusetts General Hospital in Boston for a new and still somewhat
experimental treatment for arteriosclerosis, or hard-
ening of the arteries. Lee remained with Mary at the
hospital. She had suffered from this ailment, in addition to her other afflictions, for over three years. The
aorta, the main artery that carries blood from her
heart, was blocked, severely reducing the blood flow
to the legs and producing constant pain.

Until recently the only recourse had been bypass
surgery, a dangerous and difficult procedure. It had
not been recommended for Mrs. Iacocca. Because of
her diabetic condition and heart attacks, the risk was
too great. So she and Lee came to Boston for a
nonsurgical technique called angioplasty.

The treatment, which involved pushing a catheter
through the artery to relieve the blockage, was a
success. One week after Mary's admission to the

hospital, she was able to return home with a much relieved Lee.

Iacocca's most pressing business preoccupation on his return was the quality of his K-cars, the keystone of Chrysler's renaissance. Their new 2.2-liter, four-cylinder engine had to be the best it could be, providing better mileage than might be offered by the four-cylinder engine in GM's X-cars. Iacocca and Chrysler had little to fear from Ford, which was way behind in plans for front-wheel drives.

To ensure top-quality construction for this new engine, Iacocca had ordered modernization of the Trenton, Michigan, engine plant. Its new assembly line now included thirty-four automatic inspection stations as well a computer-controlled "hot" test that automatically examined more than thirty engine functions.

Iacocca was leaving nothing to chance. Since the days of Walter P. Chrysler, engineering had been perceived by the public as the one certain Chrysler plus over its competition. He was determined to build on that decades-long perception with quality cars that were precisely assembled and now, strikingly styled. Styling, for years, had been a Chrysler shortcoming.

A soon-to-be initiated change in the company's labor relations, one exclusive to Chrysler and part of its concessions to the United Auto Workers, was expected to go a long way in improving production quality. In mid-summer almost every Chrysler employee in the United States would become a part owner of the company as over $1.5 million in common stock would be distributed among workers over a four-year period.

Employees who had accepted salary and benefit cuts—virtually everyone in the company—were eligible for these stock shares. Already evident in the plants was an increased dedication among workers, a self-interest in doing a better job to produce better automobiles.

Whatever incentives had produced this turnaround, Chrysler people were already doing their best to refute the belief that if an automobile was built by American labor, it was one of inferior quality. They were exhibiting a sense of pride and self-confidence in the cars they turned out.

These workers were showing a high degree of personal involvement in their work, and a team concept had been instituted to increase motivation and dedication. Groups of a dozen or more called "quality circles" debated ways to do specific jobs more efficiently.

With this attention to detail Chrysler-built cars were coming off the assembly road-ready. Yet, particularly in the case of newly designed automobiles, such as the Imperial and the K-cars, automobiles that had not had the benefit of thousands of miles of actual use, more checks were necessary. These, called "car evaluation and reliability tests," were the final quality checks before a car line was released for sale.

For the new Imperial, a special quality-assurance center had been built adjacent to the plant in Windsor, Ontario, where the car was assembled. Here, after assembly, each individual Imperial—which had already been subjected to countless inspections—was given additional examinations with a warm engine. After an underbody fluid-leak inspection utilizing a high-pressure water spray, the car was checked for front-end alignment and given a tough 5.5-mile road test over a special track that included almost every possible type of terrain. At each inspection step the Imperial received a sign-off if everything was in order. Otherwise it was not approved for shipment.

The evaluation and reliability tests for mass-production models like the K-cars were necessarily different. Single body styles for each car line, Plymouth and Dodge, were given round-the-clock 5,000-mile driving tests at the Chrysler Proving Grounds near Chelsea, Michigan, just west of Detroit.

The 5,000-mile test was planned to be equal to 12,000 miles of actual driving. The extensive proving grounds are laid out with two-lane blacktop roads, with roads that have circular pieces of asphalt set irregularly so that jouncing, jarring rides are simulated, with gravel roads complete with chuckholes and loose stones, with hills of varied grades, with roads that curve, and with a six-lane, high-speed concrete, track about five miles long.

At the conclusion of the test, cars were examined meticulously. Rattles, loose fittings, brakes, transmission, and body condition were points of concern after the grueling run.

Writers for car-buff magazines such as *Motor*

Trend, Road & Track, and *Car and Driver* were the first outsiders to see the already widely heralded K-cars. Iacocca invited about a hundred of the journalists to a ride-and-drive get-together at the proving grounds.

At a luncheon for the assembled writers Iacocca expressed high expectations for public acceptance of the cars. "I predict that a guy investing in a K-car will probably drive it a year and sell it for more than he paid for it."

He also reported that he believed Chrysler could sell at least a million cars in 1981, with perhaps 500,000 being front-wheel drives from the K-car, Omni, and Horizon lines. It could be done, he assured the crowd, if only the nation's economy would show an upturn.

"If that doesn't happen," he added, "we're bankrupt. We're wiped out. And Ford will probably be wiped out and be in the same position we are in today, struggling, loaning, borrowing, selling off assets. And GM will be badly wounded. No question about it."

There was much more that Iacocca could have said, but he put it off for another time. He had seen the trend fifteen years earlier while at Ford and had tried, with Hal Sperlick's backup, to do something about it. He had found himself hamstrung at the time.

In order to improve Chrysler's cash position, and to concentrate on the automobile business, in June Iacocca decided to separate Chrysler's Defense Division from the parent corporation. Defense was the most profitable division in the company. Setting it up as a separate corporation would save it in the event that the corporation itself was forced into bankruptcy. Not that Iacocca thought failure was imminent, but he thought it better to be cautious.

In a speech at San Diego Iacocca acknowledged being "in the import capital of the world." In the state of California imports were taking almost 50 percent for the car market, as against twenty-seven percent nationwide. Another point he made was that American carmakers had abdicated the American market to the imports.

Iacocca went on to say that the priority of the moment was to "anticipate and meet the needs of the today's fast-changing automobile market."Consumer attitudes had shifted. Where the buyer's previous experience with a car make was first consideration in deciding on a new-car purchase, it had slipped to sixteenth in importance. Exterior styling had dropped from second to ninth. Value for the money, which had been eighth in importance, was now number one, and quality of workmanship had leaped from sixteenth to second as one of the primary new-market values. The K-cars, which would be introduced in the fall, would put Chrysler "in an absolutely ideal position."

That introduction represents, he went on, "our first major step in meeting the Japanese challenge. When added to the models we already produce, Reliant and Aries will give Chrysler the capacity to produce nearly one million front-wheel-drive small cars a year starting this fall. That puts us in a position to take on the imports, head to head."

Iacocca called solving the explosion of the Japanese imports as the first of two major problems to be faced in the following two years. The second was that the total number of new-car sales in the U.S. was declining. One solution for this problem was an innovative suggestion he had made to the government and that he emphasized at every opportunity.

This problem, he said "can be resolved through a $1,500 personal-investment tax credit for the purchase of fuel-efficient equipment, new automobiles, when pre-1976 cars are traded in. There are 42 million pre-1976 cars still on the road averaging 12.9 miles per gallon."

New automobiles like the K-cars with average mileage in the twenties could "save up to 450 million gallons of gasoline a year" if they replaced the pre-1976 gas-eaters on the road. The tax credit would make it worthwhile for Americans to trade in their older cars, thus increasing sales of new American-built cars by up to 1.5 million and enabling the automobile industry to call back to work nearly 200,000 laid-off workers.

As the weeks in June ticked off, the agony of waiting for the loan money increased for Iacocca. Many of the 400 banks continued to drag their feet. To add to his worries, in mid-month the Michigan National Corporation, a bank holding company, confiscated $900,000 of Chrysler funds on deposit in its banks as partial payment for outstanding loans. The next day the bank reversed its position and freed the funds. It was none too soon. The $900,000 was for operating expenses, including suppliers' bills, debts that had been deferred the previous week, when for the first time Chrysler failed to pay its suppliers on the date due.

One worry over Michigan National's action was its effect on other banks still uncommitted to the loan guarantees. Reportedly the banks had secretly agreed among themselves that if one bank held out, all would do so. Michigan National's maneuver could have dealt Chrysler a deathblow.

For Iacocca June seemed to be busting out all over with reversals. Another was a missing $8 million Volkswagen had paid for Chrysler's share in its Brazilian subsidiary. VW had made an unfortunate choice in its bank to handle the transfer of funds, the Deutsche Genossenschaftsbank, which held past due notes against Chrysler in approximately that same $8-million amount. The German bank simply seized the money rather than complete the transfer to Chrysler in New York.

More than half of the month had passed, and still some banks continued to hold out against acceptance of concessions that would minimize the amount owed them by Chrysler. The unyielding were only a few among the 400 needed for agreement—two large European banks and a handful of small institutions in the United States—but they were more than enough to force a Chrysler bankruptcy. To forestall disaster the loan guarantee board postponed a meet ing scheduled for June 18 to approve $500 million as a first installment to Chrysler.

Whatever his inner feelings, Lee Iacocca remained outwardly optimistic and unflappable. With the bravado of a man sure he would win, he ordered production of his K-cars to begin two weeks ahead of schedule. This new timetable would permit building 180,000 K-cars by the end of 1980, 30,000 more than originally planned. It also meant that the first K would roll off the assembly line in Detroit on July 29 rather than on August 12.

As if there were no problems and Chrysler was indeed a going concern, he invited 280 of America's largest fleet buyers to a preview of prototypes of his Plymouth and Dodge K-cars. In typical Iacocca oratory he had the car buyers reacting more like people trying to sell him rather than as typically reluctant customers.

"You wouldn't believe the reaction unless you saw it," Fran Hazelroth, Chrysler's director of fleet sales, reported. "He had them—people we wanted to sell to—eating out of his hand. When he finished his talk, they gave him a standing ovation like you never saw."

The fleet buyers did more than that. They bought K-cars on the spot, ordering almost 50,000, with one firm signing up for 5,000 K-wagons without asking the price. "Imagine, all this while the company was still struggling for help," Hazelroth added.

Iacocca's seeming confidence proved justified. On June 20 the last two holdout banks agreed to the terms of the loan-guarantee bill. The final approval was that from the Deutsche bank in Germany that had held onto the $8 million.

The loan guarantee board held its approval meeting a little after eleven on the morning of June 24 and quickly voted the immediate issuance of the first $500 million of Chrysler. Lee Iacocca, in Mexico completing plans for an engine plant to be built in that country, and Gerald Greenwald, executive vice-president for finance, were the first Chrysler recipients of the news.

The following day a jubilant Iacocca was on hand in New York to receive a check for the $500 million as well as to chair a news conference in the Waldorf-Astoria Hotel. He projected a picture of the never-say-die optimist as he answered reporters' questions, sidestepping everything negative.

"I am no longer talking about how things are going with the banks," he said. "The financial episode is over."

He tabbed as heroes the hundreds of individuals inside and outside Chrysler who had worked so hard to make the day possible, calling them the saviors of hundreds of thousands jobs in American industry. He told reporters that it was time that industry in the United States worked closely with labor and the government to solve its problems.

"We already have a tripartite group running Chrysler," he pointed out, "one in place to further the reindustrialization of America."

With that reference to Douglas Fraser's position as a member of Chrysler's board of directors and the government's part in helping Chrysler, he brought the news conference to a close and left to film a television commercial with Frank Sinatra.

A month or so earlier Sinatra had had dinner with Bill Fine, a friend of his, when Iacocca appeared on a television interview. After watching the TV screen for a moment, Sinatra, who did not know Iacocca at the time, turned to Fine. "You know," Sinatra told his friend, "I really want to help that guy."

Fine set things in motion. He phoned Leo-Arthur Kelmenson at Kenyon & Eckhardt. Kelmenson phoned Iacocca. Iacocca called Kelmenson back and told him: "Get this in the works."

Iacocca met with Frank Sinatra, and the two sons of Italian immigrants hit it off from the start. Iacocca could not commit Chrysler to Sinatra's normal fee, but America's best-known singer did not care. He agreed to promote the New Chrysler Corporation for $1 a year, the same salary being accepted by Iacocca himself. The Chrysler chairman added a new Imperial to the dollar.

The TV commercial filmed that June 25 at the Waldorf, later expanded to newspaper and magazine double-page spreads, showing one "chairman of the board" (Sinatra's nickname) discussing Chrysler's future with another chairman of the board, Iacocca.

Later Sinatra would film and record a full series promoting the new Chrysler Imperial in song with the theme: "It's time for Imperial." With Sinatra's help other stars came aboard, including Gregory Peck, all of whom recognized Chrysler's shaky financial position and made the commercials for the basic union scale.

For Lee Iacocca rays of light were finally penetrating the gloom of his first year and a half at Chrysler. His company had been given a life-restoring transfusion, and he was getting added help from unexpected quarters. Production of his K-cars was in high gear. Yet, as the summer of 1980 moved into its hottest months, he was becoming increasingly irritable at the constant sniping of the media.

Commentators and reporters continued to accentuate the negative of Chrysler's situation in an economic climate that forecast losses of $1 billion or more during the year for both General Motors and Ford. Under such circumstances they thought Chrysler's survival impossible.

In addition Iacocca's launching of the K-cars at a time of recession was severely criticized. The production costs were projected to be a noose for quick strangulation. And Chrysler facilities were described as antiquated relics of a bygone age, despite the millions spent for their modernization.

The *Wall Street Journal*, bible of the business world and read by many of Chrysler's dealers, suppliers, and customers, had been especially negative in editorials and reports. In July Iacocca sent a long letter to the editor "to set straight the very serious false impression about Chrysler."

After its explanatory introduction the letter read: "But the *Wall Street Journal* won't leave it alone. We continue to have served up to us a daily barrage of negative tidbits from the inch-thick report to Congress, pointing out that even though we have the money we need, even though we have a restructured company, even though we have new management, the right product and great quality, lightning *could* strike! The economy *could* get worse! Car sales *could* be even lousier! It's time to lay out some facts."

Iacocca's letter, published in the *Journal*'s July 31 edition, closed with:

"In spite of recession, in spite of the brickbats, in spite of inflation, we are on our way back. The only thing that could possibly stop us is a constant recitation of the possible pitfalls that lie ahead. Well, life is full of pitfalls. The *Journal* can concentrate on nothing else if it wants to. But life is also full of opportunities—and we're making the most of ours.

"Let me make one final suggestion. Get your reporters started working on a story for next summer—the turnaround story on Chrysler Corporation. We'll be there, getting ready to introduce a 1982 line of products that will knock your eyes out."

CHAPTER 15

Sports enthusiast that he is, Lee Iacocca was well aware that "K" is the symbol for strikeout in baseball. But not believing in superstition, he went ahead and used the letter "K" to denote the cars meant to save Chrysler. General Motors had introduced its X-cars, leading off with the Chevrolet Citation, one year earlier, marketing its first front-wheel drives. Nevertheless, thanks to Hal Sperlick's Omni and Horizon, the giant was a tardy second in entering the domestic front-wheel-drive derby.

Omni and Horizon were compacts, and GM had no front-wheel products in that class. The K-cars would put Chrysler toe-to-toe against the GM X-cars in the mid-size front-wheel-drive category. Here the K's had an edge, not only over the X's, but over almost all imported front-wheel drives, whatever their class.

Plymouth Reliant K and Dodge Aries K were more spacious than the GM X-cars, holding six passengers rather than five. The K-car two- and four-door sedans offered trunk space. The hatchback-type X did not. And the K-cars, unlike the X's of GM, offered a station wagon model, which had appreciably more cargo space than any X would provide.

Since "value" was now the public's top criterion for a new-car purchase, Iacocca was sure he had little to fear from X-car competition if the public would only heed his request that they "compare."

While some months would pass before the K-cars would enter the market, Iacocca felt that whetting the public's appetite might hold back a few potential X-car sales. Accordingly, he announced a public showing of the first K-cars off the assembly line. Wednesday, August 6, 1980, was billed as K-day.

Chrysler's Jefferson Avenue plant in Detroit was gaily festooned for the occasion. Red, white, and blue bunting was everywhere. Over one entrance was a huge "We Can Do It!" banner. Another banner read "Consider It Done!" The entrances and the streets were jammed with onlookers, the general public as well as Chrysler workers. Flanking the end of the assembly line inside were Lee Iacocca, other Chrysler executives, and politicians.

Michigan's Governor Milliken and Detroit's Mayor Young were on hand, as they had been two years earlier at John Riccardo's ill-fated introduction of new Chrysler models. Donald Riegle and Carl Levin, the senior and junior senators from Michigan, had come from Washington for the ceremonies. Douglas Fraser was there, too, representing the men and women who were building the K-cars.

Iacocca had reserved for himself the distinction of driving the first car off the line. Far better that he be embarrassed if there were a battery failure or other malfunction. As the car, a cream-colored Plymouth Reliant K two-door came to the end of the assembly line, Iacocca stepped toward it with a broad smile and opened the driver-side door.

"Here we are," he said, "two years and a couple of billion dollars later, and ahead of schedule." With that he entered the driver's seat and turned the ignition switch. As the Reliant's engine came alive with a muffled roar, the crowd, led by the governor and mayor, cheered.

Iacocca put the car in gear and slowly pulled away flashing a V for victory as television cameras recorded the moment. His Plymouth Reliant K was the first in a series of K-cars to drive down Detroit's Jefferson Avenue. Governor Milliken, Mayor Young, Senators Riegle and Levin, and Douglas Fraser followed in Dodge Aries K's and other Reliants.

When they returned to the plant and got out of the cars, there was much joshing all around. Senator Riegle told Iacocca that he was going to drive a K-car to Washington and give a ride to Senator Proxmire of Wisconsin, the major stumbling block in the fight for the loan guarantees. Not to be outdone, Senator Carl Levin claimed he would change the spelling of his first name to have it start with a K rather than a C.

Iacocca had set October, the traditional time for presenting a new car to the public, for the national introduction of his 1981 model cars, but the K-cars were already known from coast to coast. Not only had the designation been heard repeatedly on network news programs during the congressional hearings on the loan guarantees, but a teaser campaign had swept the country as early as July.

It began during the Republican National Convention held in Detroit. Banners reading "K-cars are coming!" were towed by airplanes throughout the Detroit downtown area for the benefit of the hundreds of delegates in general and Ronald Reagan in particular.

"K-cars are coming" teasers then blitzed the national scene in newspapers and on radio and television, while a pertinent campaign was being prepared for the fall introduction. This, Iacocca told his agency, should be one that would do double duty: awaken American car buyers to the benefits of front-wheel drive and, at the same time, launch an assault on imports.

The new slogan, "America is not going to be pushed around any more," told the country two things. One, the K-car with front-wheel drive pulled, not pushed as did rear-drive cars. Two, Chrysler was one American automaker that had no intention of abandoning the small-car field to imports.

Beginning on September 7 the "K-cars are coming" ad campaign was made more specific. Now newspaper ads and radio and television commercials were naming names. "Aries is coming!" and "Reliant is coming!" Where color was possible, the ads and

TV commercials were asplash with red, white, and blue. Messages had patriotic connotations supporting "the American way to beat the pump" and "America is not going to be pushed around any more."

Iacocca's own personal television commercials had the same format. In mid-September, during Chrysler's sponsorship of the movie *Shogun* he appeared on screen to the tune of "Yankee Doodle" and told his huge audience that in early October Chrysler would be offering the American car buyer "the red, white, and blue Yankee Doodle direct-power drive system," a reference to Chrysler's American-designed front-wheel-drive technology.

Surveys had shown that 30 percent of Americans already were aware the K meant a new car from Chrysler. With the preintroduction ads blanketing the print and broadcast worlds, that figure was expected to grow appreciably and send hundreds of thousands of potential buyers into Chrysler-Plymouth and Dodge showrooms.

To give this growing awareness a boost before the first public showing of the K-cars, Iacocca had a special press preview in the nation's capital in mid-September. More than fifty of the country's leading automotive writers showed up at Washington's Shoreham Hotel to inspect and drive Iacocca's great hope.

While *Motor Trend* magazine would later name the Chrysler K as the 1981 "Car of the Year," few of the writers made any definitive assessments of the car concept as such. Typical was an article by Charles Williams in the *Washington Post*, "Iacocca's Cure for

What Ails Us."

Williams drove a Dodge Aries K Special Edition and began his story with some high-powered prose. "It resembles," he wrote, "somewhat an un-Sanforized Cadillac Seville but it corners flat, this boxy, sexy Glencoe Green Metallic 1981 Chrysler K-car, squealing toward the light at the end of the Shoreham parking garage tunnel like a snakebit mongoose circling back to even the score."

The closest he came to an evaluation of the car or its prospects came in two paragraphs near the end of his lengthy article. "If the K-car succeeds," he wrote, "it will be because Chrysler has accurately read the New American car buyer. He is fed up and he is not going to take it anymore, and the price he is willing to pay is a car with a trunk as big as the Ritz and a hood as long as a Steinway grand.

"What he gets in return is 25 miles per gallon city and 41 miles per gallon highway, depending on how you drive, and a car that has everything he is used to except size. It has plush seats and imitation walnut paneling and a pretty peppy response when you mash the accelerator, and it looks not like a Mercedes Benz, as Ford's Granada was alleged to when it came out, but like a real American car."

And, of course, an American automobile is what Iacocca wanted it considered, a Yankee Doodle car. If only it could do for Chrysler what Mustang did for Ford, and do it as quickly, his worries would be over.

As introduction day for the K-cars neared, Iacocca found good reason for bolstered hope. An upturn in the economy seemed imminent, and there were positive indicators for a resurgence in the automobile industry. The inflation rate had declined. Interest rates, which had reached a horrendous 19.8 percent in April, were leveling off at 12 to 13 percent. And fuel costs seemed to have stabilized. In some states gasoline prices had dropped as much as four or five cents per gallon.

Also heartening—and especially gratifying to Iacocca, who had given priority to improving product quality—were the recently released results of a buyer survey conducted by an independent research firm. The survey showed Chrysler to be the 1980 leader in eight out of eleven categories related to quality production.

New-car buyers who were surveyed called Chrysler cars better than those produced by General Motors or Ford in such important areas as quality of workmanship, condition on delivery, paint, fit of body panels, chrome, moldings, and value. In a similar 1979 survey Chrysler had been shut out by GM in all eleven categories.

Iacocca was confident that his 1981 K-cars—and all other Chrysler-Plymouth and Dodge cars and trucks—would also show up the competition. After all, he had invested over $1 billion in 1980 to upgrade plants by installing the most sophisticated electronic equipment available. This, plus the dedication of his workers, would assure even more improved product quality than in 1980.

Iacocca's exhaustive and expensive efforts to up-

grade product quality for 1981 were no longer an in-
company secret. Newspapers and magazines were
giving it wide exposure.

In hailing the impending introduction of Chrysler's
K-cars *Motor Trend*, reported in September, 1980:
"Surely these must be indicators of quality, signs of
times that have come. But more than this, they reveal
that maybe for the first time an American automaker
has calculated the demeanor of the general car-
buying public. With the Aries and Reliant, New
Chrysler will be able to serve us a substantially better
car that will last longer in the face of heavy rock salt
and traditional buyer neglect."

The *Motor Trend* piece hailed the K's: "These are
the cars we need." And, in closing his statements
prior to an in-depth evaluation of the Plymouth
Reliant he test drove, Ro McGonegal, the writer,
noted:

"The only thing that will prevent these cars from
becoming saviors is a chronic worsening of the economic situation. New Chrysler is still under the
avalanche, and they, like the other American car-
builders, will need the next four years just to dig their
way to the surface. Cars that are built and presented
like the Aries/Reliant will assure them a broad power
base from which to start climbing."

This was heady, confidence-building reporting—
just what Iacocca needed as the New Chrysler Corporation's 1981 product line, including the K-cars, was
introduced on October 2. On the same day advertising
picked up steam as a number of celebrities joined

Frank Sinatra in publicizing new Chrysler-built automobiles.

Gregory Peck, Steve McQueen, Angie Dickinson, Sammy Davis Jr., Muhammad Ali, and others gave the K-cars a send-off by telling TV viewers that "America's not going to be pushed around anymore."

Throughout the first two weeks of October Chrysler-Plymouth and Dodge showrooms throughout the United States and Canada were jammed. Sales of K-cars broke Chrysler's records during their first ten days of public sale, then tapered off alarmingly. Iacocca's merchandising instincts told him that he had made one of the few marketing mistakes in his long career. He had permitted the K-cars to be delivered to dealers with too much added-cost equipment, thus putting their prices out of reach of many buyers.

Base prices for the K-cars with standard equipment were in the $5,000 range, which not only broadened their market but also allowed buyers to add special equipment they could afford. Too many of the Reliant K and Aries K models in dealer showrooms were tagged at $8,000 or more.

Purchase of the cars at such prices was made more difficult for the average buyer by a new reversal in the economy. In late fall of 1980 the inflation spiral resumed, and interest rates increased. The fickle economy was again a roadblock to Chrysler's resurgence.

Iacocca could do little about the high-priced K-cars already in showrooms. He did, however, call in groups of dealers for a series of personal meetings to impress on them the need for making price concessions. Better, he reminded them, to sell a car at a lesser profit than not to sell at all. Iacocca had already ordered that a high percentage of future cars be shipped as the lower-priced base models.

The dealers reacted to Iacocca with confidence. More than a few of them had had previous exposure to Iacocca, having come over to Chrysler after operating Ford and Lincoln-Mercury dealerships during his tenure at Ford. In Iacocca's first year at the Chrysler helm more than 100 Ford and General Motors dealers had taken on Chrysler-Plymouth or Dodge dealerships. And their respect seemed justified when Chrysler revealed one of the biggest and most spectacular tie-in campaigns in advertising history. This was the "K-Car Comes to K-Mart" promotion, devised in cooperation with North America's largest over-the-counter retailer, with 1,700 stores in the United States and Canada. The millions who visited K-Mart stores were exposed to Plymouth Reliant K and Dodge Aries K and given incentives to visit local showrooms.

Even with these successes Chrysler remained in serious trouble. It was little consolation that GM was no better off and Ford was in even worse straits. The record ten-day sales at introduction time of 10,000 K-cars had not held up, slipping badly in mid-October. Sales recovered slightly in mid-November, then dipped again.

Sales of other products were even more disheartening. Omni and Horizon, the next-best sellers, rose and fell in almost the same proportion as the K-cars. Other Chrysler-built cars suffered more drastically.

In 1980's closing months trepidation grew on Chrysler's executive row. The steadily souring economy seemed about to kill the new-car market and force Chrysler into the bankruptcy that had been evaded a year earlier.

In the third quarter, the three-month period immediately preceding the new-car introductions, Chrysler Corporation had registered a $490-million loss. Ford went $595 million into the red, and GM ran a $567-million deficit, the largest quarterly loss in its history.

"Now those kind of losses can't be the result of just bad planning or bad management or just plain stupidity," Iacocca told a newspaper Advertising Bureau luncheon on November 13. "Maybe, just maybe we knew what we were talking about last year [when Iacocca had also addressed the group]. Something is wrong. Something was wrong a year ago, it's still wrong today. . . ."

One major culprit was still the uncertain, still exorbitant interest rates, at that time near 17 percent and heading toward 20 percent. "The car and house buyers don't want twenty-percent mortgages or twenty-percent car interest rates. So they're all walking away from the market. . . . A lot of people will wind up with car payments that are bigger than their house payments."

Fate, partially in the form of unconscionably high interest rates, was working against Iacocca's dream of a Chrysler rescue, but, always searching for solutions, he came up with a way to beat the interest blockade. He called a press conference for December 4, 1980, to announce his untried idea.

"When we announced our third-quarter results just one month ago," he told the assembled reporters, "we said that if there was some moderation in interest rates in the weeks ahead, Chrysler Corporation would report a profit for the fourth quarter of 1980."

He went on to point out that at the time the prime rate was at 13 percent and his hopes had been for a drop to at least 12 percent. "Instead," he said, "it went to eighteen-and-a-half percent—seven moves up in four weeks! It is now very clear, to me at least, that if the prime rate had in fact stayed at thirteen percent, Chrysler would have been substantially in the black in the fourth quarter."

Bemoaning "an ill-conceived federal effort to control inflation through monetary policy alone," he reminded the media that the last time the prime rate exceeded 12 percent was in 1865—"one hundred fifteen years ago."

"We can't change the prime rate," he added, "but starting today—and continuing until January 20, when the new administration takes over—Chrysler Corporation will help make up the difference between what the cost of credit for a new car should be and what it actually is."

It was an innovative yet simple plan. Anyone buying a domestic Chrysler car (other than Imperial) with a commercial loan would receive a cash allowance based on the difference between the current interest rate and what was considered a normal 12 percent. For example, a car purchased with the interest rate at 18 percent would earn the buyer a 6 percent allowance, or $420 on a $7,000 car. The rebate would fluctuate with the movement of the prime rate.

"That puts us in the business of helping to stabilize a roller coaster money market that's gone out of control," Iacocca summed up. "But the Lord helps those that help themselves. It is up to us to do what the federal government can't do for itself. . . ."

Iacocca's revolutionary form of rebate helped provide a bright spot in an otherwise dismal business period. Chrysler was the only American carmaker to show a sales increase in December, 1980, over December, 1979. Even though the increase was a meager 2.6 percent it brought smiles; GM had *dropped* 6.2 percent and Ford's loss was a scary 12.6 percent.

The year did not close without another attempt by the *Wall Street Journal* to urge a premature burial for Chrysler. An editorial on December 11 asked that the outgoing Secretary of the Treasury G. William Miller "put Chrysler Corporation out of its misery" by denying extra funds available under the provisions of the loan-guarantee bill.

"What the country needs now," the editorial read, "is someone with the courage to stand up and do what needs to be done with Chrysler. This means saying no to more federal loan guarantees."

Fuming, Iacocca again replied to the *Journal* in a letter the newspaper published on December 26. He told the *Journal* editors they should have titled their editorial "They Shoot Horses, Don't They?" "You have announced," Iacocca wrote, "that because the patient has not yet been restored to full health by the ingestion of half the prescribed medicine, he should be put to death. I am grateful you are not my personal physician." He further said that the editorial was "a mean-spirited broadside against an organization of human beings who are fighting to preserve American jobs."

As if to shove the *Wall Street Journal*'s words down its editorial throat, he subsequently did not wait for the usual time to report Chrysler's December good news. During one ten-day period that month sales had totaled 21,296, including 7,096 K-cars, the best ten-day increase since Iacocca's heralded K-Day introduction. Just as important as the K-car sales was the fact that dodge Omni and Plymouth Horizon buyers numbered 42 percent more than those in the same period of the previous year.

Obviously consumers believed that Chrysler would stay in business. With sales holding up so well in a depressed economy, Iacocca felt a boost in spirits. There was a good chance that the final quarter of 1980 would show a profit. And with his 1981 product line there was an even better chance for a good first quarter.

In addition to the K-cars and the luxury Imperial, new vehicles for 1981 included a new line of light-duty Dodge trucks, built to be better buys than comparable Fords or Chevys. There were also two new sport-utility vehicles, one for each division, a Dodge Ramcharger and a Plymouth Trail Duster, as well as a Dodge Mini-Ram wagon to compete directly against VW's Vanwagon.

What Iacocca had to do was build onto December's sales. He told the press that "1981 belongs to Chrysler, because no American car company is better equipped to meet the new market requirements of the eighties than the New Chrysler Corporation." This confidence helped make Christmas merrier for Chrysler employees.

For Lee Iacocca, however, Christmas was not a joyous holiday. His wife Mary was forced to spend Christmas Day in a suburban Detroit hospital. Earlier in December, on the 14th, she had been admitted to the hospital's cardiac unit. By the 18th she had improved enough to go home, but on the 20th she had suffered a relapse.

Christmas cheer for the Iacocca family was set aside until the day after Christmas, when Mary Iacocca was judged well enough to return home.

CHAPTER 16

Lee Iacocca was now into his third year as head of Chrysler. He could only hope that 1981 would bring the turnaround that had so far eluded him. Holding the company together as well as he had under the worst of circumstances was a minor miracle in itself.

Despite the tenuous position in which Chrysler still found itself, Iacocca had accomplished a great deal. He had brought out cars suited to the altered American lifestyle. He had instituted cost-saving measures while building employee confidence. He was selling more cars than the year before, while both General Motors and Ford were selling fewer.

Yet Iacocca felt as though he was walking into quicksand. On January 20 a new administration was taking over in Washington, and each passing day meant a day less for the Loan Guarantee Board to issue additional funds before Ronald Reagan took office.

At the moment there was no telling what Reagan or his secretary of the treasury designate, Donald Regan, might do. The new President had been heard to say that he saw nothing wrong in a bankruptcy for Chrysler. And his choice for secretary of the treasury was an out-and-out foe of the loan-guarantee philosophy.

"Those who live by the sword," Donald Regan had pontificated, "and you can finish that statement for yourself." The implication was clear.

The month of January was slipping away far too fast to suit Lee Iacocca. Even should the Loan Guarantee Board approve the issuance before the 20th, there was a mandated fifteen-day wait before the actual cash would be available, and there was always the chance that the new secretary of the treasury would undo the work of G. William Miller. Should that happen, the New Chrysler Corporation would be in serious trouble. It would run out of operating funds before the end of January.

Iacocca had talked with Ronald Reagan during the Republican national convention in Detroit in July. At that time Reagan had assured Iacocca of his support, but there was no ironclad guarantee that the new President would not change his mind or that his secretary of the treasury would not take it on himself to reverse the approval of the Carter administration.

That Chrysler sales were on an upswing might not be enough for Donald Reagan, particularly if he took overall industry figures for 1980 into consideration—they were the worst in twenty years. Iacocca could only wait and hope.

Merely holding base without reminding the Carter government, and the Regan group waiting in the wings, of the need for action was not Iacocca's way. One year earlier he had acquainted the Carter administration with his suggested program for easing the problems facing the automobile industry. The time had come, he decided, to make a further move, one that would bring his proposal directly to Congress and to the incoming President and his staff.

Iacocca prepared and mailed under the date of January 12, 1981, a letter to senators and United States representatives. With that letter he included a seven-page "white paper" outlining his three-point program in detail. "It was a good program when it was first proposed," his letter told the members of Congress. "As events have developed, it is even more critical now."

In what he suggested as a "National Automotive Recovery Act" he reiterated the three needs he had preached for three years and which had been given the Carter administration the year before: (1) a two-year agreement with Japan to stop shipping vehicles built on overtime; (2) providing the $1,500 tax credit for anyone buying a new American car when a pre-1976 model was traded in; and (3) a freeze on all environmental and safety regulations for two years.

"Some people," he told congressmen in closing his letter, "are afraid this program unfairly favors the automobile industry, even though it clearly benefits the national economy. To those people, I would suggest that any industry which can promise the restoration of 250,000 jobs and the saving of 300 million gallons of fuel be given the same kind of assistance."

The nature of Congress being what it is, Iacocca had little hope that anything would be done. At least he had made his views known to people who could, if they would, do something about the problems.

The first half of January was a roller coaster of good and bad signals as to the loan guarantee. G. William Miller repeatedly postponed approval, asking for revised plans from Chrysler, the UAW, and Chrysler suppliers. On January 13 the union made further concessions. On the 14th Chrysler gave its lending banks a revised schedule for the repayment of loans.

That same day industry sales for the first two weeks of January showed that Chrysler continued on the upgrade with a 4.7-percent increase over the 1980 period, while Ford, GM, AMC, and even VW sustained substantial losses. Of special interest to Iacocca was the fact that over half of the more than 16,000 Chrysler units sold were K-cars, and 4,000 were Omnis and Horizons. Obviously his faith in front-wheel drive was not misplaced, and Chrysler had an excellent chance to survive.

January 14 was also the day G. William Miller called a meeting of the Loan Guarantee Board to discuss granting the additional $400 million. If the board approved the grant, and if the incoming Reagan administration did not block the issuance of funds, Chrysler would have the money before month's end and continue to operate.

Iacocca was waiting with Douglas Fraser outside the boardroom at four in the afternoon. For three long hours they waited. Not until seven o'clock that evening were they called into the boardroom and told that formal approval, which was dependent upon acceptance of the plan by the union, banks, and suppliers, would be announced the next day. Due to the mandatory fifteen-day delay before issuance of the funds, everything now lay in the hands of the new President and his secretary of the treasury designate, if Iacocca could negotiate the additional concessions from the union and banks.

Iacocca did not have to wait long for an indication of Ronald Reagan's position. In an interview published in *U.S. News & World Report* that same week, Reagan, in referring to Chrysler Corporation, was quoted as saying:

"There is a reason to believe that government mandates have had something to do with troubles in the auto industry. If so, government has two responsibilities. The first is to bail out or help bail out a company that's suffered because of that. The second is to do away with the mandates and the regulations that cause the trouble in the first place."

They were beautiful words to Iacocca. If Reagan could do something about the regulations that had escalated the production costs of an automobile, it would go a long way in bringing not only Chrysler but the entire industry back to profitability.

On January 16, G. William Miller called the Loan

Guarantee Board to order, ready to formalize approval of the $400 million to Chrysler. Suddenly he was forced to close the meeting and postpone action until Monday the 19th. A break had developed in the long Iranian hostage crisis, and Miller was needed to help release some of the Iranian assets held by American banks since the seizure of the hostages in November, 1979. Return of the assets was a condition for the freedom of the illegally detained hostages.

Over the weekend Douglas Fraser worked tirelessly to get new concessions to Chrysler from his membership. Chrysler workers had been asked to take wage and benefit cuts that added up to $9,600 per year for each Chrysler worker as an alternative to no work should Chrysler fail.

It was to be a month long wait before final action. The Reagan administration had taken over, and not until February 27 did Donald Regan, the new secretary of the treasury, call a meeting of the Loan Guarantee Board. Even then he did not approve the issuance of the additional loan guarantees without taking a swipe at Iacocca and Chrysler, charging that the Carter administration had let things slip through and warning that under his chairmanship of the board Chrysler would have a much tougher time getting added money.

The new loan guarantees gave the New Chrysler Corporation another lease on life. Now $300 million more was still available, but in an interview published in a March issue of *Fortune* Iacocca disavowed any possibility of asking for that money. "I would sell my kids before I went back to Washington for that next $300 million," he told the interviewer.

The February issue of *Fortune* had included "Chrysler on the Brink," an article that echoed the *Wall Street Journal*'s disbelief in Chrysler's survival even with the loan guarantees. It was not something that a Lee Iacocca would accept without rebuttal. The published interview resulted.

All of the questions asked by the interviewer, Pamela Sherrid, were provocative. At one point she asked: "Chrysler has shown all its product for this model year. What will happen in the spring, when GM introduces its subcompact J-car and Ford its sporty version of the Escort/Lynx?"

Iacocca's answer was a product blueprint through Chrysler's 1984 model year. "Chrysler can produce 1.2 million front-wheel-drive cars a year, averaging 30 miles a gallon," he said. "Nobody else in Detroit can make that statement, even after the J-cars come in. Ford has no response to our K-car compact until late '83. You may say "You're in for a tough fight. It's dog eat dog.' Well, the business has always been that way."

He then proceeded to lay out Chrysler's product plans. A front-wheel-drive LeBaron and Dodge 400 to be introduced as 1982 models in the fall of 1981, with a LeBaron convertible "that will knock your eyes out" in the spring of '82. Also in spring "a sporty pickup on the Omni-Horizon base that will be the first little truck to get 50 miles per gallon on the highway."

For the 1983 model year Iacocca promised a

"stretched K"—two-door, four-door, and wagon models with wheelbases three inches longer than the current K-cars. As a 1983½ model (the designation usually used for models introduced in the spring) he predicted "a super Mercedes-type coupe" and a sports car, a two-door, front-wheel-drive fastback that would finally bring all Chrysler-Plymouth and Dodge vehicles into the FWD category. Another, for 1984, was what Iacocca described as a "unique new vehicle that is half-van and half-bus."

"We didn't take the millions from the government and buy new drapes for the offices," he reminded the *Fortune* interviewer, "we are spending $160 million a month on future product."

Iacocca's confidence in his company's survival was backed up by Chrysler sales during the first ten days in March. They were up 51.2 percent over the same period the year before, while GM posted only a modest 7 percent gain and Ford sustained a loss of 3.6 percent.

With a look to the future Iacocca now did some executive restructuring. Gar Laux, his vice-chairman, and Paul Bergmoser, president, had both come out of retirement to help him in his early months as Chrysler's head man. They had served him well and deserved a rest. Besides, it was time to infuse the top levels of his New Chrysler Corporation with young blood that would keep the company on course for years.

Iacocca named Gerald Greenwald, forty-five years old and a financial expert, as his new vice-chairman, and Hal Sperlick, fifty-one, as president. Both had been his long-time trusted lieutenants. Both held philosophies of business identical to his and had comparable confidence that Chrysler would become highly profitable in two to three years.

Speculation was rife among members of the press and other automobile executives as to Iacocca's purpose in making the change at that particular time. Was he contemplating retirement in a year or two and preparing his heirs for their future assignments? One thing seemed certain: Whatever Iacocca's personal plans might be, Greenwald and Sperlick would be the two men to carry on at Chrysler once Iacocca decided he had had enough.

At any rate, with two trusted men in position to oversee the corporation's day-to-day operations, Iacocca could now free himself to keep an eye on the broad picture . . . and, perhaps, find it possible to spend more time with his family.

There were many elements of consideration for Iacocca in his look at the future. One was completion of his $75-million conversion of the St. Louis assembly plant to the production of front-wheel-drive cars for 1982 models, the "Super K" or "stretched K" cars for Chrysler LeBaron and Dodge cars three inches longer in wheelbase than the original K's.

Another important matter was increasing the Chrysler-Plymouth and Dodge dealer bodies. While over 100 new dealers had turned to Chrysler within Iacocca's first year, there had since been some attrition. He decided that a dealer-recruitment campaign with large ads in *Automotive News*, the weekly read by almost everyone in the automobile business, was necessary.

Because of the depressed economy and insufficient sales to cover operating costs, many dealerships in America had closed their doors. Not one of the domestic carmakers had been spared, but Chrysler had suffered the least. Iacocca hoped to attract an influx of new dealers with financial backing that would keep them afloat.

Iacocca's next move was aimed at a resumption of marketing Chrysler products in Europe. Chrysler had been out of that market since John Riccardo's sale of European operations to Peugeot-Citroën in 1978. To launch the K-car sales in Western Europe Kenyon & Eckhardt opened an office in Brussels on April 16. An all-out campaign in Holland, northern France, and Belgium would begin in May. Then, as Chrysler established distributor and dealer facilities, the effort would be expanded to include other Western European countries.

Iacocca set in motion the same sales strategy used successfully by the Japanese in the competitive Continental market. They had moved into one country at a time, progressing to another only after success in the first.

Once acceptance of Chrysler products was evident in the first target nations, Iacocca planned to move into Norway, Sweden, and Switzerland, and then, by 1982, into Austria, Germany, Italy, and Spain. Great Britain would have to wait because no right-hand-drive models were yet set for production.

On the home front full-page newspaper advertising was aiming at the Japanese imports. One ad, signed by Iacocca, featured him smiling confidently. The headline, positioned as a message from Iacocca himself, read: "To anyone in America who thinks Japanese cars are better than ours I'll give you fifty dollars to compare ours against theirs or any competitive car. And I'll give it to you no matter whose car you buy. We're not foolish. We're confident."

Meanwhile, sales were picking up, a 24-percent increase over the previous year in the first ten days of April. To get national attention for Chrysler's upswing as well as exposure for its new 1982 products he invited newspaper, magazine, and broadcast reporters to the Styling Dome in Highland Park. They came from across the country, and most wrote glowing reports about Chrysler's rise from the ashes.

Indicative of the majority reaction was the report of John R. White, published in the *Boston Globe*. He wrote, in part: "If you think Chrysler is ready to roll over and play dead, guess again . . . Chrysler is up and about, planning for the get well party. . . . The company is building some pretty attractive stuff with some very attractive mileage numbers. And more is yet to come. . . ."

It was this kind of publicity, 180 degrees opposite to the *Fortune* story of a few months earlier and the *Wall Street Journal*'s two-year pro-bankruptcy campaign, that Iacocca hoped for and Chrysler needed. A month after the *Boston Globe* story *Business Week* pinpointed the value to Chrysler of this about-face in the media.

"Industry analysts say," *Business Week* reported in its issue of June 1, 1981, "much of the spurt in sales is simply the result of Chrysler's financial travails moving off the front page and out of the 6 o'clock news. Without such bad publicity, the company found it easier to market the inherent appeal of its new front-wheel-drive K-cars."

Chrysler sales, in relation to the previous year, continued to improve, but not enough to ensure profitability with the corporation's huge debt. Interest rates, which had resumed their climb, had risen to 19 percent on May 4. At that figure a $6,000 automobile would cost the buyer an additional $1,140 in one year's interest. Such a high level of interest scared off buyers.

Also of no help to Chrysler was the introduction of General Motors' new series of front-wheel drives, their J-cars, on May 21. With the automotive giant's million-dollar advertising blitz there was no telling how many front-wheel-drive Chevrolets, Pontiacs, and Cadillacs would fill American garages instead of Chrysler's Omnis, Horizons, and K-cars. A weakened Chrysler Corporation could not match General Motors in advertising dollars, even though it did enjoy advantages over General Motors and Ford as well. Even before Iacocca took over, Chrysler had established a lead in front-wheel-drive experience thanks to Hal Sperlick's Dodge Omni and Plymouth Horizon. Iacocca's introduction of the K-cars increased public perception of Chrysler's leadership in front-wheel-drive knowhow. Johnny-come-latelys such as the GM J-cars and Ford's Escort and Lynx would be suspect for months.

Another Chrysler advantage lay in the price. Iacocca had promised in April that Chrysler would not raise prices, as GM and Ford had done. GM's increase was 9.4 percent, Ford's 6.5 percent. As a result Chrysler K-cars—with six-passenger roominess as against five for the J's and four-passenger for some Ford front-wheel-drive vehicles—enjoyed a $1,000 price advantage.

Despite the early introduction of the GM J-cars as 1982 models—Chrysler 1982 cars would come in the fall—Chrysler sales for May of 1981 showed a higher increase over May of 1980 than the increases posted by General Motors or Ford. This made Iacocca's forecast of a profitable second quarter, made at the 1981 annual meeting, believable.

The annual shareholders' meeting was held the same day that the May figures were released, June 4. Some 800 stockholders, gathered at Wilmington, Delaware, applauded as Iacocca reported that "we've overhauled the entire operation, improved all of our operations, and lowered our break-even point to nearly half of what it was just one year ago."

It was a pleasant and jovial meeting overall, with Chrysler's continuing problems placed on a back burner. The attending stockholders praised Iacocca, even though their prospects for dividends seemed negligible for years to come. Their smiles and good-natured banter contrasted sharply with the scowls, angry shouts, and bitter denunciations of previous meetings that had brought John Riccardo to the brink of nervous breakdowns.

The shareholders lauded Iacocca's TV commercials. They laughed at his one-liners. Many sought him out once the meeting was adjourned to say they considered his K-cars to be the finest Chryslers ever built.

In late July Iacocca confirmed a second-quarter profit of $11.6 million. This was no great shakes as automotive profits go, but it was enough for a smiling Iacocca to boast of the achievement before a meeting of reporters at the National Press Club in Washington. After nine successive quarters deep in red ink one in the black was something to crow about.

"To do it against all the odds, in spite of double-digit inflation and a twenty-percent prime rate, and in the most depressed market in fifty years, is a little miracle," he said.

It was a moment to bask in the sun, and Iacocca took advantage of the opportunity. With plants shut-down in the current quarter for model changeovers a loss was expected. The fourth quarter, too, would be a question mark.

"If interest rates fall to fifteen percent or less, we'll have a brilliant fourth quarter," he told the reporters. "At twenty percent, it'll be a disaster."

Iacocca was not far wrong. The sales figures for the third quarter, ending September 30, revealed a near-disastrous loss of about $200 million. The prime interest rate had not hit twenty percent but had come perilously close.

The one bright spot in the gloom was Chrysler's performance through the summer and into early fall. Each month showed an increase over the equivalent month of the previous year, while neither GM or Ford could match the struggling Chrysler. September, 1981, sales were 2.33 percent over September, 1980. General Motors' were down 2 percent, and Ford had an infinitesimal increase of .3 percent.

Meanwhile Iacocca had continued the personal public relations campaign that he had begun with his appearance at the National Press Club. He scheduled meetings with dealers, Chrysler suppliers, and bankers. He followed his National Press Club appearance with talks to the Empire Club in Toronto, the National Advertisers in San Francisco, and the Newspaper Publishers in Detroit. He made countless trips to the nation's capital.

In Washington he talked with Ed Meese, President Reagan's right-hand man, with Treasury Secretary Donald Regan, Transportation Secretary Drew Lewis, and the head of the Federal Reserve Board, Paul Volcker, the man most responsible for control of the prime interest rate. He discussed strategies with Senators Riegle and Levin and Congressman Blanchard, all from Michigan, and sought out senators and congressmen from other states in which Chrysler employed thousands of workers.

At every meeting and in every talk he sold the strength of the struggling New Chrysler Corporation and the improved quality of its products as evidence in independent surveys. He pointed out that these surveys showed that car buyers rated Chrysler ahead of both General Motors and Ford in product quality.

Chrysler, he told all he met with, was also ahead of GM and Ford in fuel economy, and left both far behind in front-wheel-drives, with 90 percent of its production for 1982 based on this technology. All these Chrysler pluses were advanced to prove Chrysler's ability to weather the storm if only it would get some help from Washington, help that would also give a shot in the arm to the entire industry and the American economy.

It was not money that Chrysler needed, Iacocca emphasized. Even though more millions were still available in loan guarantees, Chrysler did not plan to tap that source again. What Chrysler and the entire industry needed was realization in Washington that "they better not wait for the effects of supply-side economics to trickle down to the little guy who wants to buy a car or a house."

Expanding on that premise in a report to his executive management committee, Iacocca said: "The administration and Congress have caught hell from the public for interest rates that are the highest since the Civil War. And they're beginning to question monetary policies that divert money away from housing and autos where the jobs are, and into nonproductive areas like corporate acquisitions, short-term money markets, and interest on the national debt."

Again and again in his talks Iacocca reminded his listeners of the substantial advantage enjoyed by the Japanese in marketing their cars in the United States, an advantage initially created by America in helping Japan recover from the war. In America's determination to establish and hold ties to Japan and maintain it as a Far East buffer against Communism, the United States set trade agreements without thought to reciprocity.

Encouraging Japan's industrial growth, America not only helped them build their automobile plants, it also permitted them to ship their Toyotas, Datsuns, and Subarus with export advantages not enjoyed by American carmakers shipping to Japan. Combined with the lower wage scale in Japan, which permitted the production of a Japanese car at $1,000 or more less than an equivalent American car, these factors impaired the American car industry.

Some measure of relief, Iacocca preached, was essential to help the domestic automakers compete on an even basis with the imports. About two million Japanese cars were sold in the United States in 1981, a year in which American carmakers lost about $2 billion in the first nine months.

Iacocca took time off from his ceaseless travels to introduce Chrysler's 1982 product line on October 1. He brought out the 1982 Plymouth Reliant K and Dodge Aries K, as well as Plymouth Horizon and Dodge Omni, all little changed from their 1981 counterparts. Four weeks later he presented Chrysler Corporation's all-new models for 1982, a redesigned

LeBaron Series and a Dodge 400, both of which represented Iacocca's commitment to 90 percent front-wheel-drives for 1982.

The 1982 front-wheel-drive LeBarons were offered in two- and four-door models and a special-edition convertible, the latter a daring move on Iacocca's part. American convertibles had been all but extinct for years. Testing the waters, Iacocca found that young (and youthful-thinking) drivers yearned for a return to open-air motoring. Though he realized it was a limited market, Iacocca built a car that, as he put it, would bring "fun back to driving."

The rakish two-seater LeBaron convertible was on the expensive side, sticker-priced in the neighborhood of $14,000, a cost according to detractors that would make it the equivalent of a Chrysler Edsel. The expense of producing such a luxury might be enough, they said, to drag Chrysler into failure.

Iacocca, however, had not miscalculated the hunger for an upscale open-air car. Not long after its introduction it claimed more than 200 orders, with $200,000 in deposits in the bank. One of the orders carried the name of Brooke Shields, the teenage motion-picture star.

As if to forecast a future phasing out of the Chrysler Cordoba, Iacocca named Ricardo Montalban as broadcast spokesman for the LeBaron Series. "My new car," Montalban told TV viewers, was the realization of "Lee Iacocca's dream to combine luxury with mileage."

The Dodge 400 was Dodge Division's answer to

Chrysler LeBaron, a sporty four-wheel-drive two-door aimed at the younger, less affluent buyer group. Shown on television, it was featured with Kelly Harmon behind the wheel. The beautiful blonde identified the Dodge 400 as "America's personal driving machine."

Advertising strategy for the all-new cars was the subject of a long conference between Iacocca and his marketing staff and his agency. John Morrissey, chairman of Kenyon & Eckhardt Advertising, suggested that the most powerful approach would be Iacocca's own presence in newspaper ads and television commercials. Having done well with earlier efforts, Iacocca was easily persuaded.

Kenyon & Eckhardt proceeded to develop hard-sell, full-page newspaper ads utilizing a quote from Iacocca made to reporters on September 28, 1981, as a lead-in statement beside Iacocca's picture.

The newspaper ad layouts featured glamour shots of the specific cars being advertised along with their suggested retail prices and a bold headline that said: "'82 cars at '81 prices!"—a competitive edge for Chrysler, since General Motors and Ford had announced price increases not long before. The advertisements also proudly proclaimed that buyers would receive "Chrysler Savings Certificates worth $300 to $1,000 on all these cars and trucks," a rebate offering that enabled Iacocca to steal another march on GM and Ford.

Both competitors had been receiving flak from the Federal Trade Commission over their own rebate plans. Their varied money-back offers often required a dealer contribution, which was not allowed by the FTC unless the fact was clearly spelled out. The FTC had discovered that some GM and Ford dealers victimized the customers by raising their sticker prices to compensate for their contributions.

Iacocca's "money-back from Chrysler" plan made it clear that every cent of cash rebated came totally from the New Chrysler Corporation, and that sticker prices would be no higher—and might even be lower, at the dealer's discretion—than listed in the ad.

The same theme was utilized for television and radio promotion of Chrysler's 1982 products. Again, Lee Iacocca was the spokesman. TV saturation reached its peak during the final weeks of 1981 and the first of 1982. Iacocca was seen and heard time and again on college bowl games and in National Football League playoff games.

Sales figures show that the ad compaign's success was limited by the depressed state of the economy. November, 1981, sales for all manufacturers were down from the previous year, with Chrysler showing the lowest loss among the Big Three. For the eleven months to November 30 Chrysler was the only one to show an increase, a modest .8 percent, as GM sustained a 1.6-percent drop and Ford a .5-percent loss.

When the full results for 1981 were announced on January 5, 1982, Chrysler was the only American car manufacturer to show an increase in sales over the previous year, 10.9 percent, while GM reported a 7.5-percent loss and Ford a 6.1-percent decline.

Under the existing economic conditions it was an achievement for Iacocca, a tribute to his business acumen and initiative in a crisis-ridden industry that had suffered its worst sales record in twenty years. The American carmakers indeed had fallen on hard times, dropping from an all-time high in 1973 of more than 11 million sales to little more than 6.2 million in 1981.

Iacocca's tightfisted policies had not only enabled his corporation to pay its bills, but had also produced enough revenue to repay the loans still owed to American banks. In late January Chrysler announced that the final $47 million still owed on the $1.3 billion deferred during the loan-guarantee fight would be paid six weeks before its due date. This early retirement of the debt owed to 150 banks resulted in a saving of over $2 million in interest costs.

Nonetheless the New Chrysler Corporation was hardly out of hot water. The Federal Reserve Board's tight-money policy kept interest rates on the rise, and the 1983 budget submitted to Congress by President Reagan did not promise any help.

As January faded into February, there seemed little hope that the car market would take an upturn. People just couldn't afford to buy even the lowest-priced cars when interest rates could add $2,000 and more to the already inflated initial cost.

The first ten days of February were disastrous for the entire automobile industry, with sales sinking to the lowest levels for that period in twenty years. Chrysler was down 4.5 percent, Ford 14.8 percent, and Volkswagen of America a horrendous 56.5 percent. General Motors, however, had only a minor loss of 0.4 percent.

In February's second ten-day sales period Chrysler suffered the most among the big three, falling 14.2 percent behind the same period the previous year, as both General Motors and Ford posted gains, the former 3.9 percent, the latter 4.6 percent.

Iacocca, while concerned about the economy and interest rates, remained optimistic, promising a turn-around in 1982 with a return to the profit column. His only "if" was that there be no further deterioration in the economy.

In a letter to Chrysler shareholders Iacocca wrote: "Given even a modest upturn in the economy in 1982, we look forward to a year of full recovery."

Cash flow was the primary concern. He still had $300 million available from the original $1.5 billion assured by the Loan Guarantee Board. But Iacocca had been saying for a year and more that he would never go back to Washington for money—the trauma of his first go-around was still fresh in his mind.

To provide sufficient cash to keep operating until the economy made its expected swing upward, the New Chrysler Corporation got out of the defense business, its most profitable asset. On February 20 Iacocca announced that Chrysler's lucrative tank-building subsidiary was being sold to the General Dynamics Corporation for $348.5 million. That should keep Chrysler afloat long enough to weather the current storm. It had to be done, Iacocca told a group of newspeople, as a protective move to provide Chrysler with cash.

"What if," he told the press, "interest rates go back to twenty percent? What if the ten-percent tax cut in July doesn't kick in—that was the subject of our White House luncheon with the President. . . ."

It was Iacocca at his best, winning points with the reporters with hard-hitting rhetoric. "I'm a businessman," he went on. "I've got to have a sheet to windward. What if the industry drops below five million in March and April? Possible? You're damn right if it's twenty-percent interest. So we don't live in any fool's paradise. We have to look ahead at the next three months, and this is the best insurance policy we have. So we need that kind of cash infusion."

Iacocca displayed confidence throughout the news conference. Referring to the Defense Division sale he said: "I really think this was necessary for us, at the threshold of having good products, of having enough cash to do things from a profit-and-loss standpoint, rather than how much cash we need next Friday to survive. So I want to end on the note that we feel healthy, we feel good about it. . . ."

Iacocca had valid reasons to "feel good about it," especially if the "it" was his accomplishment to date, even though Chrysler was by no means totally healthy as yet. Whatever else may lie ahead, he had done a remarkable job.

He had brought a company with terminal illness a long way despite the deepest automotive recession in a half-century. He had restructured Chrysler Corporation through one of the most comprehensive programs in the history of world business.

He had inherited a cancer-ridden company and restored it to a semblance of health. Based on his record in 1981—twelve months of increased sales over the previous year while seemingly healthy GM and Ford lost ground month after month—Iacocca had accomplished the near-impossible.

The government had helped with its $1.2 billion in loan guarantees, but he had put that money to good use. He shut down old, outmoded, costly plants and modernized others with new technologies that rivaled the best in the world.

He led the way among American carmakers in converting to front-wheel drive, and he developed new high-quality products, among them the acclaimed K-cars, and improved the quality of the others.

Lee Iacocca had done what he set out to do in late 1978 when he agreed to try saving Chrysler. Only one factor had prevented a full cure—excessive interest rates.

On March 1, 1982, prospects for Chrysler solvency were given a substantial boost by Michael Driggs, executive director of the Chrysler Loan Guarantee Board in Washington. In a January report to a subcommittee of the House of Representatives Appropriations Committee the Loan Guarantee Board was guarded in commenting on Chrysler's survival. Driggs's report on March 1 cited Chrysler as being "in a better position than it has been since before the beginning of the loan guarantee program."

Chrysler's top management, the Loan Guarantee Board found, had cut costs across the board so thoroughly that its break-even point was reduced drastically. This low break-even figure indicated to the board that Chrysler Corporation might well record a profit for 1982, despite the condition of the economy and the certainty that the first and second quarters would reflect substantial losses.

Operating cash, once counted on a day-to-day basis, had now reached $750 million, including the near $350 million from General Dynamics for the purchase of the Chrysler defense subsidiary. Thanks to that infusion of cash Iacocca was able to report a profit, not the expected loss, for the first quarter of 1982.

The report, made as April came to a close, revealed that Chrysler had enjoyed a quarterly profit for the first time since the January-March quarter of 1977. The profit figure was $149.9 million, almost double the 1977 pre-Iacocca first quarter profit of $75.4 million.

On the face of it, Chrysler also had again bested its Big Two competitors during the quarter, as it had done every quarter in 1981. General Motors had posted $128 million in profit for the quarter. Ford had sustained a $355 million loss.

Chrysler's survival now seemed assured according to business analysts. They were finally echoing what Lee Iacocca had been preaching all along. He had been telling anyone who would listen that his company's cash position was good, that Chrysler was now dealing from strength and would certainly post a profit in calendar year 1982.

Since all this has come to pass, Lee Anthony Iacocca has performed the most amazing feat in American business history.

EPILOGUE

Inevitably there will come a day when Chrysler Corporation will have to do without Lee Iacocca. As a matter of fact early in 1981 one of the men close to him said that Lee Iacocca would probably resign in 1983. The same individual pointed to Iacocca's appointment of Gerald Greenwald and Harold Sperlick to the number-two and number-three posts in the company as evidence of his intention to retire.

Iacocca himself somewhat confirmed it in an interview published in the August 3, 1981, issue of *Newsweek*, and again in late September with Michael Robinson, a reporter for the *Detroit News*. The *Newsweek* story reported that "Iacocca plans to stay until 1983 and then ask the Chrysler directors to turn the company over to Greenwald and Sperlick."

That he would step down at Chrysler in 1983

seemed likely, barring any unforeseen circumstance. But retire? Hardly. A dynamo keeps going until its power is spent. At fifty-nine, his age in 1983, a man with the drive of a Lee Iacocca was hardly ready to sit in a rocking chair, to tend roses, or to chase a golf ball.

Leo-Arthur Kelmenson, president of Kenyon & Eckhardt and one of Iacocca's closest friends, says Lee pondered his future to some degree the evening they sat on the deck of Kelmenson's Long Island home a week after Iacocca was fired by Henry Ford. Kelmenson says that as they looked out over the waters, Lee mentioned a grandiose dream, establishing a world-encompassing automobile company.

"He called it Global Motors," Kelmenson said. "Then he laughed as he realized the initials were GM, the same as General Motors."

"Global Motors"—if that was Iacocca's way to go after retirement from Chrysler—could be a totally new organization, or it might be formed of a merger of selected present-day carmakers, American and foreign. He shelved the idea when he accepted the Chrysler challenge in 1978, but rumors of such a possibility surfaced in 1979.

In June *Automotive News* featured an article that said Volkswagen was buying Chrysler Corporation. It implied that since Volkswagen's chairman, Toni Schmuecker, was a close friend of Lee Iacocca's, such a purchase would be more in the nature of a merger of Volkswagen and Chrysler. When no such thing happened, the rumor died.

In any event, once Iacocca leaves Chrysler, he might resurrect the idea of a Global Motors. While that is no more than speculation, people who know Iacocca best will lay odds that he will not remain idle for long.

At one time in the summer of 1981 a Detroit columnist suggested that Lee Iacocca was seriously considering politics, with the governorship of Michigan in his sights. Iacocca laughed it off, and one of his close friends reported that in no way would Lee Iacocca consider running for governor in Michigan. After Chrysler such a move would be the equivalent of leaping from one erupting volcano into another. The state was in as much financial trouble as Chrysler Corporation when Iacocca took it over.

The United States Senate is not beyond possibility. Neither is the White House. And certainly, in these days of budget crunches, international problems, and humanitarianism, a Lee Iacocca might well fit the bill. As a businessman who cuts costs with efficiency and resolve to keep a dying Chrysler Corporation afloat, as a dynamic, self-made man, he might very well have appeal for the electorate. His lack of political background should not be a drawback. As recently as the Eisenhower presidency a nonpolitical figure was elected. Nonpolitical though he may be on the surface, Iacocca has not hesitated to speak out on political matters, particularly as they affect the economy and the automobile industry.

In 1980 he proposed legislation that would help offset the high interest rates that prevented lower-income buyers from the purchase of a car. He called on the President and Congress to provide a $1,500 tax deduction for Americans who bought a new American-built automobile.

More recently Iacocca has suggested a twenty-five-cent-a-gallon tax on gasoline as a means of raising revenue to help balance the budget. He has offered, as an alternative, a year-long excise tax on such products as oil, liquor, gasoline, cosmetics, and tobacco, while warning against any extension of the excise tax to include living essentials such as housing, medicine, and food.

"I'm all for controlling inflation through a program of fiscal and monetary control," he said during a lengthy New York interview in January 1982. "But it can't be done that fast. It took forty years to create the havoc we have today. It cannot be undone overnight, yet that is precisely what we're trying to do. We're embarked on a policy of instant solutions to long-range problems, and it won't work."

Through necessity Iacocca has made himself the consummate politician, and talks like one. He is the unyielding salesman, decisive and forceful. A Franklin Roosevelt with a brash street-wise and street-talking style that mesmerizes audiences. What he believes, he says directly, yet he employs the philosophic trappings of a man stumping for office.

"What the Japanese do have that is better [than we have]," he says, "is a combined labor and business policy that sets long range goals and provides the means to achieve them. We don't have in this country a national policy that helps solve any basic problems. And if we ever hope to give American ingenuity the chance it needs to restore the strength of this country's basic industries we had better develop such a national policy—and fast!"

In an equally incisive and provocative vein he has pointed out: "We need a management attitude in this country, starting with guys like me, and the wisdom to avoid preaching doctrinaire free enterprise. . . . Adam Smith went out of style decades ago. This is not a *laissez faire* society of 1890. Don't kid yourself. Our world-wide competition learned that lesson a long time ago. They know how to work together to meet a national goal—and it's time we learned how to do that here!"

These are the kinds of statements one would expect from Ted Kennedy, Walter Mondale, or Bob Dole, not from an automobile executive.

Iacocca does not mince words. "The Federal Reserve Board should establish a policy of credit conservation," he says. "They should nudge the banking community into supplying credit at favorable rates to job-creating industries. Tilt money away from investments that don't create jobs or increase production."

It is the sort of talk one might hear from a candidate for public office. "I asked Paul Volcker," Iacocca adds, "how much of the available money supply this week went into creating one job through investment in productivity? I asked that a year ago and still haven't got an answer."

Though Volcker paid no heed to Iacocca, the Reagan administration obviously recognized his multi-faceted abilities. In May 1982 he was named to head a cabinet-level commission charged with the refurbishing of Ellis Island.

It seems that James Watt, former secretary of the interior, who was assigned by President Reagan to search for a man capable of dedicating himself to such a task, decided on Iacocca after seeing him in one of his television commercials.

When advised that the purpose of the new commission was to restore the deteriorating gateway for so many thousands of immigrants into America, Iacocca eagerly accepted. After all, his father had come through Ellis Island twice and his mother once.

Thus, Lee Iacocca is being indoctrinated into the Washington scene in a role other than that of a man fighting for the survival of his company. This new challenge might prove to be just what is needed to whet his appetite.

If an office such as the presidency of the United States is indeed in Lee Iacocca's future plans, a realistic timetable would set it for 1988, or perhaps as late as 1992. Even then he would be five years younger than Ronald Reagan when he became President.

Democrat? Republican? People who know Iacocca intimately say he is ideologically neither or either, with reservations. Liberal-conservative or conservative-liberal, either would suit him well. Thus, he could be wooed by both parties.

In 1980 a motion-picture actor born in Illinois, near the banks of the Mississippi, made it to the White House. What then, would stop a nationally known, highly regarded, successful businessman from near Pennsylvania's Lehigh River from doing the same?

INDEX